THE ULTIMATE CV BOOK

write the perfect CV and get that job

MARTIN YATE

KOGAN
PAGE

D0317883

First published in the United States in 1993 as *Knock 'em Dead* by Adams Media Corporation
First published in Great Britain in 2003 as *The Ultimate CV Book* by Kogan Page Limited

Reprinted in 2003

Kogan Page Limited
120 Pentonville Road
London N1 9JN
United Kingdom

www.kogan-page.co.uk

British Library Cataloguing in Publication Data

A CIP record for this book is available from the British Library

ISBN 0 7494 3875 4

Typeset by Jean Cussons Typesetting, Diss, Norfolk
Printed and bound in Great Britain by Bell & Bain Ltd, Glasgow

Table of Contents

Chapter 11: CVs for Special Situations 233

Appendix: CV Banks 247

Index 249

Introduction

Most of the books on writing CVs haven't changed to accommodate today's dynamic work environment. That is the reason for this book: To help 'now' people get the very best jobs!

Look at the other CV books on the market; they are full of CV examples with dates going back to what seems, to most job seekers, like the Bronze Age. They use job titles that no longer exist and techniques that no longer work – techniques that in many instances can be downright damaging to your job hunt.

This book is unique in two very important ways.

First, you'll get to read real CVs from real people. Each of the CVs in this book is based on a 'genuine article' that worked wonders for its writer. Included are CVs for today's and tomorrow's in-demand jobs, as defined by the US Bureau of Labor Statistics and confirmed by the professionals on the front lines: corporate recruiters and other employment industry professionals across the country. The odds are that you are already working in one of these jobs, or wishing you were.

Also included in the 'real-life' section of this book is a selection of CVs from people with special challenges. These reflect the pressures and needs of a modern, profession-oriented society struggling into the information age. Like the CV that got a £4-an-hour factory worker a £40,000-a-year job; or the one that helped a recovering alcoholic and drug-abuser get back on her feet again. There are winning CVs of people recovering from serious emotional challenges and mental problems, of people re-entering society after jail, starting again after the divorce, and changing careers. And what's more, these examples have proved themselves effective in every corner of the nation; their writers landed both interviews and jobs.

Second, I explain the ins and outs of putting a CV together as painlessly as possible. I'll show you the three best ways to look at your background and present your CV. Then I'll show you all the available options for inclusion. Why certain things should be in your CV and how they should look, and why other things should never appear. Wherever industry experts disagree, I'll give you both sides of the argument, and my reasoned solution to the dispute. That way you can make a prudent decision about your unique background, based on possession of all the facts and the best advice going. In addition, you will see the infinite variety of styles and approaches that can be used within my guidelines to help you create a truly individual CV.

These two unique concepts, the numerous CV examples and the nuts-and-bolts sections about CV production and distribution give you everything needed to create a distinctive, professional CV: one that will get you that job.

The Marks of a Great CV

Who needs a CV? Everyone. Certainly you do, unless you are so well known that your reputation is already common knowledge to all potential employers. If that were the case you probably wouldn't be reading this book in the first place.

Anyone, in any job, can be viewed more favourably than his or her competition – if he or she is better organized and prepared, which is what a good CV demonstrates. It's a staunch friend who only speaks well of you and can gain you entrance into undreamed-of opportunities.

Now, no CV ever gets carefully read unless a manager is trying to solve a problem. That problem may be finding a quicker way to manufacture silicon chips. It may be getting the telephone calls answered, now that the receptionist has left. As disparate as these examples might seem, both are still concerned with problem solving. And invariably, the problem that needs a solution is the same: productivity. The simple question is, 'How on earth are we going to get things done quicker/cheaper/more efficiently without a _____?'

CVs that get acted upon are those that demonstrate the writer's potential as a problem solver.

Your CV must speak loudly and clearly of your value as a potential employee. And the value must be spoken in a few brief seconds, because, in the business world, that's all the attention a CV will get. The CV takes you only the first few paces toward that new job. It gets your foot in the door, and because you can't be there to answer questions, it has to stand on its own.

A CV's emphasis is on what has happened in your business life, what actions you took to make those things happen, and what supportive personal characteristics you brought to the job. It is about how you

contributed to solving a business' problems. It has nothing to do with generalizations or personal opinions.

The CV itself came about as a solution to a problem: How does a manager
avoid interviewing every applicant who applies for a job? Can you imagine
what would happen to a business if everyone who applied for a job was
given even a cursory 10-minute interview? The company would simply
grind to a halt, then topple into bankruptcy. The solution: come up with a
way to get a glimpse of applicants' potentials before having to meet them
face-to-face. The CV appeared and evolved into an important screening and
time-saving tool.

While that solved one problem for the employer, it created another for the
job applicant: 'Considering that my background isn't perfect, how do I write
a CV that shows off my best potential.' The first attempt to answer that question is how the gentle art of CV writing came into being.

In the world of recreational reading, CVs are pretty far down on the list.
They are usually deadly dull and offer little competition to murder
mysteries, tales of international intrigue and love stories.

Nevertheless, CVs are a required part of every manager's daily reading,
and, exactly because they are usually deadly dull, are generally avoided. To
combat this deep-seated avoidance, there is a general rule that will help your
CV get read and acted upon in the quickest possible time: it needs to be short
and long. Short on words, but long on facts and an energy that reflects the
real you.

Good CV writing focuses attention on your strengths and shows you as a
potential powerhouse of an employee. At the same time, it draws attention
away from those areas that lack definition or vigour. You can do this even if
you are changing your entire career direction, or starting your life over for
other reasons, and I'll show you how.

There is a hidden benefit, too, in the CV-writing process: it focuses your
attention and helps you prepare for job interviews. In a very real sense,
putting a CV together is the foundation for succeeding at the job interview.
Preparation for one is preparation for the other.

For example, the interviewer's command to 'tell me about yourself' is one
of those tough interview demands that almost all of us have difficulty
answering satisfactorily. Were you totally satisfied with your response the
last time it came up? I doubt it. You can only answer it well if you have taken
the time to analyse and package all your strengths and weaknesses in an
organized fashion. It is the only way you will ever learn to speak fluidly
about your background and skills in a fashion guaranteed to impress the
interviewer. So, why not kill two birds with one stone – prepare for the interview by preparing a CV that will open all the right doors for you.

Interestingly enough, the majority of interviewers accept the contents of a
CV as fact. Additionally, a good number of interviewers base all their ques-

tions on the CV content: this means that in a very real way you can plan and guide the course of the majority of your interviews by preparing an effective CV.

Those without CVs are forced to reveal their history on a job application form, which does not always allow the perfect representation of skills, and which gives the interviewer no flattering starting point from which to base the interview questions.

In addition to helping you get your foot in the door and easing the course of the interview, your CV will be your last and most powerful advocate. After all the interviewing of all the candidates is done, how do you think the interviewers review and evaluate all the contenders? They go over their notes, application forms and the CVs supplied by the job candidates. You will want to make yours something powerful and positive.

Finally, the preparation of a good CV has the broad, intangible benefit of personal discovery. You may find, as you answer some of the questions in chapter 4, that your experience is deeper than you imagined, that your contributions to previous employers were more important than you thought. You may look on your career direction in a new light. And you may see your value as a solid employee increase. You will gain confidence that will be important not only for a good performance at the interview; but for your attitude toward the rest of your career.

No sane person will tell you that CV writing is fun, but I will show you the tricks of the trade, developed over the years by executive recruiters and professional CV writers, that make the process easier.

What makes this book truly different is that the CV examples in it are based on real CVs from real people, CVs that recently landed them real jobs in 'in-demand' professions. They were all sent to me by employment specialists from around the nation. For example, the health care examples were screened initially by professional health care recruiters, and those in data processing by computer recruiters. These are the pros on the firing line, who knows what works and what doesn't in today's business marketplace.

You will find everything you need to make writing fast, effective and painless. Just follow my instructions, and in a few hours you'll have a knock-out CV and never have to read another word about the damn things as long as you live. With that in mind, do it once and do it right – you'll generate a top-flight CV without knocking yourself out!

So now, for your delight and edification, we'll review the marks of a great CV: what type of CV is right for you, what goes in (and why), and what always stays out (and why), and what might go in depending on your special circumstances. This is followed by countless CV examples and a 'painting-by-numbers' guide that makes writing easy for anyone!

With the changing times and circumstances, there are few rigid rules for every situation. So in those instances where there are exceptions, I'll explain them and your choices. The judgement call will be yours. And when you are finished, you will have one of the very best CVs, one that will be sure to get you that dream job.

2

Three Ways to Sum Yourself Up

> 'Give me a moment of your busy day! Listen to me, I've got something to say!'

That's what your CV must scream – in a suitably professional manner, of course. Not in the manner of the would-be retail clothing executive who had his CV 'hand-delivered' … attached to the hand and arm of a store window mannequin.

As it happened, that was only the first surprise in store for the personnel director who received the delivery: the envelope was hand-decorated in gothic script; the cover letter inside was equally decorative (and illegible); the CV writer had glued the four-page CV to fabric, and stitched the whole mess together like a child's book. The crowning glory, however, was yet to come: all the punctuation marks – commas, colons, full stops, and the like – were small rhinestone settings. Yes, it got noticed, but its success had to depend entirely on the recipient's sense of humour – which in this case was most noticeable for its absence.

Here's the point: trying to do something out of the ordinary with any aspect of your CV is risky business indeed. For every interview door it opens, at least two more may be slammed shut.

The best (and most businesslike) bet is to present a logically displayed, eye-appealing CV that will get *read*. That means grabbing the reader right away – on that first page. And that's one big reason for short, power-packed CVs.

We all have different backgrounds. Some of us have worked for one company only, some of us have worked for 11 companies in as many years. Some of us have changed careers once or twice, some of us have maintained a predictable career path. For some, diversity broadens our potential, and for some concentration deepens it. We each require different vehicles to put our work history in the most exciting light. The goals, though, are constant:

- to show off achievements, attributes and cumulation of expertise to the best advantage;

- to minimize any possible weaknesses.

CV experts acknowledge just three essential styles for presenting your credentials to a potential employer: Chronological, Functional and Combination (Chrono-Functional). Your particular circumstances will determine the right format for you. Just three styles, you say? You will see CV books with up to 15 varieties of CV style. Such volumes are, alas, merely filling up space; in the final analysis, each additional style such books mention is a tiny variation on the above three.

The Chronological Resume

This is the most common and readily accepted form of presentation. It's what most of us think of when we think of CVs – a chronological listing of job titles and responsibilities. It starts with the current or most recent employment, then works backward to your first job (or ten years into the past – whichever comes first).

This format is good for demonstrating your growth in a single profession. It is suitable for anyone with practical work experience who hasn't suffered too many job changes or prolonged periods of employment. It is not suitable if you are just out of school or if you are changing careers. The format would then draw attention to your weaknesses (ie your lack of specific experience in a field) rather than your strengths.

The exact content of every CV naturally varies depending on individual circumstances. A chronological CV usually incorporates six basic components.

- *contact information;*

- *a job objective;*

- *a career objective;*

- *a career summary;*

- *education;*

- *a description of work history.*

Chronological

Jane Swift, 123 Anystreet, Anytown, AT1 0BB. Tel: 020 8123 4567. jane@anyaddress.co.uk

SUMMARY: Ten years of increasing responsibilities in the employment services industry. Concentration in the high-technology markets.

EXPERIENCE: Howard Systems International, Inc.   1995–Present
Management Consulting Firm
Personnel Manager

Responsible for recruiting and managing consulting staff of five. Set up office and organized the recruitment, selection and hiring of consultants. Recruited all levels of MIS staff from financial to manufacturing markets.

Additional responsibilities:

- Coordinated with outside advertising agencies.
- Developed PR with industry periodicals – placement with over 20 magazines and newsletters.
- Developed effective referral programmes – referrals increased 32%.

EXPERIENCE: Technical Aid Corporation   1988–1995
National Consulting Firm. MICRO/TEMPS Division

Division Manager   1993–1995
Area Manager   1990–1993
Branch Manager   1988–1990

As Division Manager, opened additional West of England offices. Staffed and trained all offices with appropriate personnel. Created and implemented all divisional operational policies responsible for P & L. Sales increased to £20 million, from £0 in 1984.

- Achieved and maintained 30% annual growth over 7-year period.
- Maintained sales staff turnover at 14%.

As Area Manager, opened additional offices, hiring staff, setting up office policies, and training sales and recruiting personnel.

Additional responsibilities:

- Supervised offices in two counties.
- Developed business relationships with accounts – 75% of clients were regular customers.
- Client base increased 28% per year.
- Generated over £200,000 worth of free trade-journal publicity.

As Branch Manager, hired to establish the new MICRO/TEMPS operation. Recruited and managed consultants. Hired internal staff. Sold service to clients.

EDUCATION: London University
BA (Hons) Public Relations, 1987.

This last item is the distinguishing characteristic of the chronological CV, because it ties your job responsibilities and achievements to specific employers, job titles and dates.

There are also some optional categories determined by the space available to you and the unique aspect of your background. These will be discussed in chapter 3.

The Functional CV

This format focuses on the professional skills you have developed over the years, rather than on when, where or how you acquired them. It de-emphasizes dates, sometimes to the point of exclusion. By the same token, job titles and employers play a minor part with this type of CV. The attention is always focused on the skill rather than the context or time of its acquisition.

In many ways, the content of the functional CV is similar to the chronological type. Only the approach is different. It is a case of not so much of what you say, but of how you say it.

This functional format is suited to a number of different personal circumstances, specifically those of:

- mature professionals with a storehouse of expertise and jobs;
- entry-level types whose track records do not justify a chronological CV;
- career changers who want to focus on skills rather than credentials;
- people whose careers have been stagnant or in ebb, who want to give focus to the skills that can get a career under way again, rather than on the history in which it was becalmed in the first place;
- military personnel embarking on a civilian career;
- those returning to the workplace after a long absence;
- people closer to retirement than to the onset of their careers.

The functional CV does present a major challenge for the writer. Because it focuses so strongly on skills and ability to contribute in a particular direction, you must have an employment objective clearly in mind. When this is achieved, such a CV can be very effective. Without this focus, however, or if you are looking for a 'job, any job', this format loses its direction and tends to drift without purpose.

Though a functional CV is a bit more free-form than a chronological one, there are certain essentials that make it work. In addition to contact information and a job and/or career objective, these include the elements that follow:

- *A functional summary.* Different skills are needed for different jobs, so the functional summary is where you make the tough decisions to determine what goes in and what stays out. Consider the case of an executive sales secretary bored with her job but challenged by the excitement and money the sales force is enjoying. She will want to emphasize those abilities that lead to success in sales, such as written and verbal communication skills, and time management. On the other hand, she will almost certainly leave out references to her typing and shorthand abilities, because these skills don't contribute to her new goals.

- *Dates.* Strictly speaking, a functional CV needn't give dates. Up until a couple of years ago, you could still sometimes get away with omitting them. That is no longer the case. Today, a CV without dates waves a big red flag at every employer in the land. So, what if your employment history doesn't have all the stability it might? The functional CV is perfect for you, because dates can be de-emphasized by their placement. You put them at the end of the CV, or perhaps on a second page, for example, in a small block type; and you use year dates, omitting the details of day, week and month. The idea is to force the reader's attention to your skills, not your history.

- *Education.* The inclusion of education and other optional categories is determined by the space available to you and the unique aspects of your background (see chapter 3).

Functional

Jane Swift
123 Anystreet
Anytown, AT1 0BB
Tel: 020 8123 4567
jane@anyaddress.co.uk

OBJECTIVE: A position in Employment Services where my management, sales and recruiting talents can be used effectively to improve operations and contribute to company profits.

SUMMARY: Over ten years of Human Resources experience. Extensive responsibility for multiple branch offices and an internal staff of 40+ employees and 250 consultants.

SALES: Sold high-technology consulting services with consistently profitable margins throughout the United Kingdom. Grew sales from £0 to over £20 million a year.

Created training programmes and trained salespeople in six metropolitan markets.

RECRUITING: Developed recruiting sourcing methods for multiple branch offices.

Recruited over 25,000 internal and external consultants in the high-technology professions.

MANAGEMENT: Managed up to 40 people in sales, customer service, recruiting and administration. Turnover maintained below 14% in a 'turnover business'.

FINANCIAL: Prepared quarterly and yearly forecasts. Presented, reviewed and defended these forecasts to the Board of Directors. Responsible for P & L of £20 million sales operation.

PRODUCTION: Responsible for opening multiple offices and accountable for growth and profitability, 100% success and maintained 30% growth over seven-year period in 10 offices.

WORK EXPERIENCE:

1995 to Present   Howard Systems International, London
National Consulting Firm
Personnel Manager

1988–1995   Technical Aid Corporation, London
National Consulting & Search Firm
Division Manager

EDUCATION: BA (Hons) 1987, London University

REFERENCES: Available upon request.

The Combination Chrono-Functional CV

For the upwardly mobile professional with a track record, this is becoming the CV of choice. It has all the flexibility and strength that come from combining both the chronological and functional formats. If you have a performance record, and are on a career track and want to pursue it, then this is the strongest CV tool available. This format, in addition to contact information and a job objective, incorporates a number of identifying factors, outlined below:

- *A career summary.* The combination CV, more often than not, has some kind of career summary. Here you spotlight a professional with a clear sense of self, a past of solid contributions and a clear focus on future career growth. The career summary, as you might expect, will include a power-packed description of skills, achievements and personal traits that fairly scream 'Success!'

- *A description of functional skills.* This is where the combination of styles comes into play. Following the summary, the combination starts out like a functional CV and highlights achievements in different categories relevant to the job/career goals, without any reference to employers.

- *A chronological history.* Then it switches to the chronological approach and names companies, dates, titles, duties and responsibilities. This section can also include further evidence of achievements or special contributions.

- *Education.* Then come the optional categories determined by the space available to you and the *unique* aspects of your background.

Combination

Jane Swift
123 Anystreet
Anytown, AT1 0BB
Tel: 020 8123 4567
jane@anyaddress.co.uk

OBJECTIVE:

Employment Services Management

SUMMARY:	Ten years of increasing responsibilities in the employment services marketplace. Concentration in the high-technology markets.
SALES:	Sold high technology consulting services with consistently profitable margins throughout the United Kingdom. Grew sales from £0 to over £20 million a year.
PRODUCTION:	Responsible for opening multiple offices and accountable for growth and profitability. 100% success and maintained 30% growth over seven-year period in 10 offices.
MANAGEMENT:	Managed up to 40 people in sales, customer services, recruiting and administration. Turnover maintained below 14% in a 'turnover business'. Hired branch managers and sales and recruiting staff throughout the United Kingdom.
FINANCIAL:	Prepared quarterly and yearly forecasts. Presented, reviewed and defended these forecasts to the Board of Directors. Responsible for P & L of £20 million sales operation.
MARKETING:	Performed numerous market studies for multiple branch opening. Resolved feasibility of combining two different sales offices. Study resulted in savings of over £5,000 per month in operating expenses.
EXPERIENCE:	Howard Systems International, Inc. 1995–Present Management Consulting Firm Personnel Manager Responsible for recruiting and managing consulting staff of five. Set up office and organized the recruitment, selection and hiring of consultants. Recruited all levels of MIS staff from financial to manufacturing markets. Additional responsibilities:

- developed PR with industry periodicals – placement with over 20 magazines and newsletters;
- developed effective referral programmes – referrals increased 320%.

Technical Aid Corporation   1988–1995
National Consulting Firm, MICRO/TEMPS Division

Division Manager   1993–1995
Area Manager   1990–1993
Branch Manager   1988–1990

As Division Manager, opened additional West of England offices. Staffed and trained all offices with appropriate personnel. Created and implemented all division operational policies. Responsibilities for P & L. Sales increased to £20 million, from £0 in 1984.

- Achieved and maintained 30% annual growth over seven-year period.
- Maintained sales staff turnover at 14%.

As Area Manager, opened additional offices, hiring staff, setting up office policies, and training sales and recruiting personnel.

Additional responsibilities:

- Supervised offices in two countries.
- Developed business relationships with accounts – 75% of clients were regular customers.
- Client base increased 28% per year.
- Generated over £200,000 worth of free trade journal publicity.

As Branch Manager, hired to establish the new MICRO/TEMPS operation. Recruited and managed consultants. Hired internal staff. Sold service to clients.

EDUCATION: BA (Hons) 1987, London University

One of these styles is perfect for you. Pick one, and in the next chapter we'll begin to fill it in with the CV basics.

The Basic Ingredients

It used to be that there were just a few set rules for writing a great CV. Everything was simple – you did this, you didn't do that. Now, however, many of the jobs for which those rules were made no longer exist – so many of the traditional hard and fast rules no longer apply.

New technologies are creating new professions overnight and, with them, new career opportunities. The content of these new professions and careers is dramatically different from the employment world of a few short years ago. Times and the rules of the game have changed, and these changes require that we adopt a modern and flexible approach to CV writing.

What used to be strictly off-limits in all CVs is now acceptable in many and required in some. (The need for technical jargon to explain skills, for example, comes to mind.) Elements that were once always included, such as the mug shot, are now frowned upon in almost every instance. And so it goes on, creating a fog of confusion for everyone. What are the rules?

Today, writing a CV can be likened to baking a cake. In most instances, the ingredients are essentially the same. What determines the flavour is the order and quantity in which those ingredients are blended. There are certain ingredients that go into almost every CV. There are others that rarely or never go in, and there are those special touches that are added (a pinch of this, a dash of that), depending on your personal tastes and requirements.

Sound complicated? It really isn't. This chapter will explain it all. If a certain ingredient must always go in, you will understand why; the same goes for something that should never appear in your CV. In circumstances where the business world holds conflicting views, these views will be explained so that a reasoned judgement can be made. In these instances you will always get my reasoned opinion, based on my extensive experience and contact in the human resources field.

First, let's look at the ingredients that are part of the mix of every successful CV.

What Must Always Go In

Name

We start with the obvious, but there are other considerations about your name besides remembering to put it on your CV. Give your first and last name only. It isn't necessary to include your middle name(s). My name is Martin John Yate – but my CV says simply Martin Yate, because that is the way I would introduce myself in person. Notice also that it isn't M. J. Yate, because that would force the reader to play Twenty Questions about the meaning of my initials, and the average CV reader isn't looking for light entertainment. Even if you are known by your initials don't put them on your CV. If you use quotation marks or parentheses, those on the receiving end might think it a little strange. Better that it comes out at the interviews when the interviewer asks you what you like to be called: at the very least you'll have some small talk to break the tense interview atmosphere.

It is not required to place Mr, Ms, Miss or Mrs before your name. But what if your first name is Gayle, Carrol, Leslie, or any of the other names that can easily be used for members of either sex? While it isn't strictly necessary, in such instances it is acceptable to put Mr Gayle Jones, or Ms Leslie Jackson. The reasoning is based on human frailty and the ever-present foot-in-mouth syndrome: in contacting you to follow up on your CV, your interviewer is likely to make the mistake of asking to speak to Ms Gayles Jones or Mr Leslie Jackson. Though it is a little mistake that is easily corrected, the possible future employer is immediately put in the awkward position of starting the relationship with an apology. If your name falls into the `gender-less' category, avoid the complication and employ a title.

Finally, for those who are the IInd, IIIrd, Junior or Senior holders of their name: if you always add 'Jr' or 'III' when you sign your name or if that is the way you are addressed to avoid confusion, go ahead and use it. Otherwise, it is extraneous information on the CV, and therefore not needed.

Address

Always give your complete address. Do not abbreviate unless space restrictions make it absolutely mandatory – you want the post office to have every possible advantage when it comes to delivering those offer letters efficiently.

If you do abbreviate – such as with St or Apt – be consistent. The county of your residence, however, may be abbreviated according to post office standards. Always include the correct postcode.

The accepted format for laying out your address looks like this:

John Smith
123 Anystreet
Anytown AT1 0BB

Notice that the city and postcode all go on the same line, with a space between city and postcode.

Telephone Number

Always include your telephone number: few businesses will send you an invitation for an interview in the mail. Including your area code is important even if you have no intention of leaving the area. In this era of decentralization, your CV might end up being screened in another part of the country altogether!

Examples:

020 8123 4567
(020) 8123 4567

The inclusion or exclusion of a work telephone number is a little bit more of a problem.

> *The case for inclusion:* Featuring your daytime contact number allows prospective employers to reach you at a time of their convenience.
>
> *The case for exclusion:* Being pulled out of the Monday meeting every five minutes to take calls from headhunters can ruin your whole day. The funny thing about employers is that they always prefer to lose you at their convenience rather than yours. In addition, keeping the company number off the CV adds to its life expectancy. Who needs another detail that may be obsolete in short order?
>
> *The solution:* Unless your current employer knows of your job search, leave the business number off the CV, but put it in your cover letter. Good cover letters do this with a short sentence that conveys the information and demonstrates you as a responsible employee. For example, something like this can work very well:
>
> 'I prefer not to use my employer's time taking personal calls at work, but with discretion you can reach me at 020 8123 4567 extension 555, to initiate contact.'

E-mail

Your e-mail address has become an integral part of your contact information, as important as your telephone number. In fact, its importance goes beyond that of your phone number. The ability to use a telephone doesn't say anything about your professional skills while an e-mail address implies that you have already adapted to the new technology of the workplace. That's a must for any worthwhile job in the new century. If you have an e-mail address, use it. If you don't, get one – and get with it.

If you are planning on using your e-mail address from work, keep in mind that it increases the odds of your boss learning that you are looking at broader horizons. E-mails leave a trail that an employer can follow, and as many as 35 per cent of managers are believed to track their employees' e-mail. So using your company e-mail address is almost as stupid as listing your immediate supervisor as the principal contact for your job hunt.

Using company e-mail outside regular working hours won't work either – the trail is still there for prying eyes to see. And think about what it tells potential employers about how you're likely to act once you're on their payroll!

Job Objective

This section sometimes appears on CVs as:

Position desired
Job objective
Objective
Employment objective

All are acceptable. Regardless of the heading, the job objective has traditionally meant one or two sentences about the kind of job you want and what you can contribute to the company in return for such a job. You will recall from chapter 2 that the use of a job objective in your CV will depend in part on the style of CV you employ to present your qualifications. Remember that the functional CV in particular almost demands one.

That notwithstanding, feelings run strong about whether or not to include a job objective in the CV, so let's review the cases for and against, then reach a considered conclusion.

> *The case for inclusion:* Without a job objective, a CV can have no focus, no sense of direction. And if you don't know where you are going; you can't write a CV, because the body copy has nothing to support. The CV revolves around your objective like the earth around the sun.

The case for exclusion: A job objective is too constricting and can exclude you from consideration from countless jobs you might have been interested in, and for which you are qualified. And after creating a CV with the intent of opening as many doors as possible, you wouldn't want to have half of them slammed shut. Besides, employers are not generally believed to be overly concerned about what you want from them until they have a damn good idea about what they can get out of you.

The solution: You do need an objective, but it needn't fit the traditional definition. The best CVs have objectives written in broad, non-specific terms. They are often little more than a categorization, such as:

Job Objective: Marketing Management

Sometimes these objectives appear at the top of a CV, as a headline and attention grabber. If they go beyond that, they focus on skills, achievements and relevant personal characteristics that support the argument.

Job Objective: To pursue an accounting career

STAFF ACCOUNTANT – PROPERTY MANAGEMENT

To obtain a responsible position in a company where my experience, accomplishments and proficiency will allow me the opportunity for growth.

This last approach is best, because it considers the forces at work in business these days. Including job objectives has as much to do with filing and retrieval systems and computers as it does with people. On the one hand, the CV reader is looking for a problem solver, so, by seeing that you fit into a general area, will want to rush on to the rest of the CV (where there are more specifics). Then what happens? In the best-case scenario, you will get a frantic call asking you to state your terms and a start date right away. But what happens when there isn't a need for your particular talents that day? Your CV gets filed or logged onto the company's database. The people who file CVs aren't rocket scientists, just overworked functionaries trying to dispose of a never-ending flow of paper. They want to get rid of it as quickly as possible, so they will file your CV according to your instructions. And unless you give it the right help, it may not be filed under the right category; it may never see the light of day again. The broader your objective, the greater frequency with which it will be retrieved and reviewed in the future.

The same argument holds true for CVs sent to employment agencies and executive recruiters, who have been known to keep them on file for as long as ten years.

Just recently, in fact, I heard one of those wonderful tales of an eight-year-old that landed a job for its writer because it had a general objective. Why is this relevant? Had the specific job objective of an entry-level professional been on that CV, the writer would never have been considered.

Such considerations are encouraging many job seekers to include brief and non-specific job objectives in their CVs. You will learn how to come up with the right tone for your specific needs later in the book.

Employment Dates

CV readers are often wary of CVs without employment dates. If you expect a response, you can increase your odds dramatically by including them – in one form or another.

With a steady work history and no employment gaps you can be very specific (space allowing) and write:

11 January 1997 to 4 July 1998
or
11/1/97 to 4/7/98

or, to be a little less specific:
January 1997–February 1998

But if there are short employment gaps, you can improve the look of things:

1997–1998
instead of
12 December 1997–23 January 1998

There is no suggestion here that you should lie about your work history, but it is surprising just how many interviewers will be quite satisfied with such dates. There seems to be a myth that everything written on a 20-lb rag paper needs no further inquiry.

While this technique can effectively hide embarrassing employment gaps, and may be enough to get you in for an interview, you should of course be prepared with an adequate answer to questions about your work history once you sit down with the interviewer. Even if such questions are posed, you will have the opportunity to explain yourself – _mano a mano_, as it were – and that is a distinct improvement over being peremptorily ruled out by some faceless non-entity before you get a chance to speak your piece. The end justifies the means, in this case.

Again, if you abbreviate months and years, do so consistently.

Keywords

Just as computers have helped streamline your job-hunting activities, they have done the same for the recruiting work of many human resources departments. One of the changes gaining ground in corporate UK is the use of CV screening and tracking systems. Understanding how this technology affects the way your CV is received will dramatically affect your changes for success in your job hunt.

While electronic CV distribution makes your life easier, it's created an avalanche of electronic paper on the other side of the desk. If a company once had to deal with 100 CVs a day, it now probably sees 1,000 or more. Obviously, this incredible increase in volume has to be handled more efficiently. With the high cost of human handling, the wholesale adoption of CV screening and tracking systems by businesses is a given. These systems are already in place in the most forward-looking companies – approaching 50 per cent of the total. By the time you go through your next job hunt, most likely every business will have them.

When computer screening replaces human judgement, the whole game changes. The computer program can't use human logic (although it is already getting pretty close); instead, the computer searches for keywords that describe the position and the professional skills needed to execute the duties effectively.

Your CV – and a thousand like it – can be scanned for the necessary keywords in seconds. The user receives a list of the CVs that contain the appropriate keywords. The greater the number of relevant keywords in your CV, the higher your ranking. The higher your ranking, the greater the likelihood that your CV will be rescued from the avalanche and passed along to a person for further screening.

In the CV examples you'll see a section that lumps a string of keywords together. A keyword section can be labelled with a variety of names: Special Knowledge, Keyword Preface, Keyword Section or Areas of Expertise. Here's what the keyword section of a US taxation specialist's CV looks like:

AREAS OF EXPERTISE

SBT, C-Corporation and S-Corporation State Income Tax Returns •
Vehicle Use Tax Returns • State Income Tax Budgeting and Accrual •
Multistate Property Tax Returns • Federal, State and Local Exemption
Certificates • State and Local Sales, Use and Excise Tax Management •
Tax Audit Management • Tax License and Bonding Maintenance •
Certificates of Authority and Annual Report Filing Maintenance • State
Sales and Use Tax Assessment • Federal Excise Tax Collection and
Deposits • Determination of Nexus • Tax Amnesty Programs

A section like this will become mandatory in your CV in the very near future. You would be smart to be ahead of the curve on this one! This keyword section not only dramatically increases your chances of getting the computer's attention, but HR people and line managers appreciate them as a brief synopsis of the whole CV.

Job Titles

The purpose of a job title on your CV is not to reflect exactly what you were called by a particular employer, but rather to provide a generic identification that will be understood by as many employers as possible.

A job title should give the employer 'something to hang his hat on'. So if your current title is 'Junior Accountant, Level Three', realize that such internal titling may well bear no relation to the titling of any other company on earth. I remember looking over the personnel roster of a New York bank and learning to my astonishment, that it had over 100 systems analysts. (The typical number for an outfit this size is about 12.) Then I noticed that they had no programmers. The reasoning that I eventually unearthed was remarkably simple. The human resources department, finding people to be title-conscious in this area, obligingly gave them the titles they wanted. (Another perceived benefit was that it confused the heck out of the raiding headhunters, who got disgusted with systems analysts who couldn't analyse their way out of a wet paper bag!)

This generic approach to job titles also holds true as your job takes you nearer the top of the corporate ladder. The senior executive knows that the higher up the ladder, the more rarefied the air and the fewer the opportunities. After all, a company only has one Controller or one Director of Operations. Again, to avoid painting yourself into a career corner, you can be 'specifically vague' with job titles like:

Administrative Assistant
instead of
Secretary

Accountant
instead of
Junior Accountant Level II

It is imperative to examine your current role at work, rather than relying on your starting or current title. Job titles within companies change much more slowly than the jobs themselves, so a job change can be the opportunity for some to escape stereotyping and the career stagnation that accompanies it. Take the typist hired three years ago, who has now spent two years with a word processor. Such a person could be identified thus:

Word Processor
instead of
Typist

This approach is important because of the way titles and responsibilities vary from company to company. Often, more senior titles and responsibilities are structured around a person's specific talents, especially so outside the FTSE 500.

There are two situations, however, that don't lend themselves to this technique:

▨ When you apply for a specific job where you know the title and the responsibilities, and where the position's title is similar but not the same as your own. (Then the exact title sought should be reflected in your CV – as long as you are not being misleading concerning your capabilities.)

▨ When you apply for a job in certain specific professions, such as health care. (A brain surgeon wouldn't want to be specifically vague by tagging herself as a Health Aide.)

Company Name

The names of employers should be included. There is no need to include street address or telephone number of past or present employers, although it can be useful to include the city and county. The company will find the complete address on your employment application.

When working for a multiple-division corporation you may want to list the divisional employer: 'Bell Industries' might not be enough, so you would perhaps want to add 'Computer Memory Division'. By the way, it is quite all right to abbreviate words like Corporation (Corp.), Company (Co.), Limited (Ltd), or Division (Div.). Again, be consistent.

Here is how you might combine the job title and company name and address:

DESIGN ENGINEER
Bell Industries Ltd, Computer Memory Div., Reading, Berkshire

The information you are supplying is relevant to the reader, but you don't wish it to detract from space usable to sell yourself. If, for instance, you live in a nationally known city, such as Oxford, you need not add 'Oxon'.

There is a possible exception to these guidelines. Employed professionals are justified in omitting current employers when their industry has been reduced to a small community of professionals who know, or know of, each other, and where a confidentiality breach is likely to have damaging repercussions. This usually happens to professionals on the higher rungs of the ladder. Of course, if you don't quite fit into this elite category but are still worried about identifying your firm, you are not obliged to list the name of your current employer.

One approach is simply to label a current company in a fashion that has become perfectly acceptable in today's business climate.

A National Retail Chain
An Established Electronics Manufacturer
A Major Commercial Bank

You will notice that usually a company name is followed by a brief description of the business line:

A National Retail Chain: Women and junior fashions and accessories.

An Established Electronics Manufacturer producing monolithic memories.

This requirement is obviated when the writer can get the company's function into the heading.

A Major Commercial Bank

The writer who can do this saves a line or two of precious space which can be filled with other valuable data.

Responsibilities

This is what is referred to as the meat, or body copy, of the CV, the area where not only are your responsibilities listed, but your special achievements and other contributions are also highlighted. This is one of the key areas that sets the truly great CV apart from the rest. This is a crucial part of the CV, it will be dealt with in detail in chapters 4 and 5.

Endorsements

Remember when you got that difficult job finished so quickly? And all the good things the boss said about your work? Well, in a CV you can very effectively quote him, even if the praise wasn't in writing (though of course it is best to quote directly). A line such as 'Praised as "most innovative and determined manager in the company" ' can work wonders.

These third-party endorsements are not necessary, and they most certainly shouldn't be used to excess. But one or two can be a useful addition to your

CV. Such quotes, used sparingly, can be very impressive; overkill can make you sound too self-important and reduce your chances of winning an interview.

Such endorsements become especially effective when the responsibilities have been qualified with facts, numbers and percentages.

Accreditation and Licences

Many fields of work require professional licensure or accreditation. If this is the case in your line of work, be sure to list everything necessary. If you are closer to a particular accreditation or licence (a CPA, for example), you would want to list it with information about the status:

Passed all parts of CPA exam, September 2000 (expected certification February 2001).

Professional Affiliations

Your affiliation with associations and societies dedicated to your field shows your own dedication to your career. Membership is also important for networking, so if you are not currently a member of one of your industry's professional associations, give serious consideration to joining. Note the emphasis on 'professional' in the heading. An employer is almost exclusively interested in your professional associations and societies. Omit references to any religious, political or otherwise potentially controversial affiliations. They simply do not belong on a CV; you want yours to reflect a picture of your professional, not your personal life.

An exception to this rule is in those jobs where a wide circle of acquaintances is regarded as an asset. Some examples would include jobs in public relations, sales, marketing, property management and insurance. In that case, include your membership in the Kiwanis or the Royal Lodge of the Raccoons.

By the same token, a seat on the town board, charitable cause involvement or fundraising work are all activities that show a willingness to involve oneself and can often demonstrate organizational abilities. Space permitting, these are all activities worthy of inclusion because they show you as a sober and responsible member of the community.

These activities become more important as one climbs the corporate ladder of the larger companies. Those firms that take their community responsibilities seriously look for staff who feel and act the same way – an aspect of corporate culture applying itself at the most immediate levels.

Some corporations are committed to the idea that community activities are good public relations. Accordingly, such work may mark an individual for even greater responsibilities and recognition once in the company.

As for method of inclusion, brevity is the rule.

British Heart Association: Area Fundraising Chair

My personal observation is that these activities increase in importance with the maturity of the individual. Employers, quite selfishly perhaps, like to think of their younger staff burning the midnight oil solely for them.

Civil Service Grade

With a civil service job in your background, you will have been awarded a civil service grade. So, in looking for a job with the government, be sure to list it. In transferring from the government to the private sector, you are best advised to translate it into generic terms and ignore the grade altogether, unless you are applying for jobs with government contractors, subcontractors or other specialized employers familiar with the intricacies of civil service ranking.

Publications and Patents

Such achievements, if they appear, are usually found at the end of the best CVs. Although they serve as positive means of evaluation for the reader, these achievements are of relatively minor importance in many professions.

Nevertheless, both publication and patents are manifestations of original thought and extended effort above and beyond the call of accepted professionalism. They tell the reader that you invest considerable personal time and effort in your career and are therefore a cut above the competition. Publication carries more weight in some industries and professions (where having literary visibility is synonymous with getting ahead); patents are a definite plus in the technology and manufacturing fields. You will notice in the CV examples how the writers list dates and names of publications, but do not usually include copyright information.

'New Developments in the Treatment of Chronic Pain.'
1999. *New England Journal of Medicine.*

'Radical Treatments for Chronic Pain.' 2000. *Journal of American Medicine.*

'Pain: Is It Imagined or Real?' 1998. *OMNI Magazine.*

Languages

Technology is rapidly changing our world into the proverbial global village. This means that today, as all companies are interested in client-based expansion, a linguistic edge in the job hunt could be just what you need. If you are fluent in a foreign language, you will want to mention it. Likewise if you understand a foreign language, but perhaps are not fluent, still mention it:

Fluent in French
Read and write Serbo-Croatian
Read German
Understand Spanish

Education

Educational history is normally listed whenever it helps your case, although the exact positioning of the information will vary according to the length of your professional experience and the relative strength of your academic achievements.

If you are recently out of school with little practical experience, your educational credentials, which probably constitute your primary asset, will appear near the beginning of the CV.

As you gain experience, your academic credentials become less important, and gradually slip toward the end of your CV. The exception to this is found primarily in certain professions where academic qualifications dominate a person's career – medicine, for instance.

You will notice that all examples for education are in reverse chronological order: the highest level of attainment (not necessarily a degree) always comes first, followed by the lesser levels. In this way, a doctorate will be followed by a master's degree, then a bachelor's. For degreed professionals, there is no need to go back further into educational history. (It is optional to list your prestigious prep school.) Those who attended university but did not graduate should nevertheless list the university in its proper chronological position, but should not draw attention to the fact that they did not receive a degree.

Those who did not achieve the higher levels of educational recognition will list their own highest level of attainment. A word on attainment is in order here. If you graduated from high school, attended college, but didn't graduate, you may be tempted to list your high school diploma first, followed by the name of the college you attended. That would give the wrong emphasis: it says you are a college drop-out and focuses on you as a high school graduate. In this instance you would in fact list your college and omit reference to earlier educational history.

While abbreviations are frowned on in most circumstances, it is acceptable to abbreviate educational degrees (PhD, MA, BA etc), simply because virtually everyone understands them.

Those with scholarships and awards will list them, and recent graduates will usually also list majors and minors (space permitting). The case is a little more confused for the seasoned professional. Many human resources professionals say it makes life easier for them if majors and minors are listed, so they can further sift and grade the applicants. That's good for them, but it might not be good for you. All you want the CV to do is get you in the door, not slam it in your face. So, as omitting these minutiae will never stop you from getting an interview, I strongly urge you to err on the side of safety and leave them out.

If you are a recent entrant into the workplace, both your scholastic achievements and your contributions have increased importance. Certainly you will list your position on the school newspaper or the student council, memberships in clubs and recognition for scholastic achievement; in short, anything that demonstrates your potential as a productive employee. As your career progresses, however, prospective employers care less and less about your school life and more and more about your work life. If you have five years of work experience and still feel compelled to list your chairmanship of the school's cafeteria committee, then you are not concentrating on the right achievements.

Changing times have also changed thinking about listing fraternities and sororities on CVs. A case could be made, I think, for leaving them off as a matter of course: if such organizations are important to an interviewer he or she will ask. My ruling, however, is that if the CV is tailored to an individual or company where membership in such organizations will result in a case of 'deep calling to deep', then by all means, list. If, on the other hand, the CV is for general distribution, forget it.

Professional Training

Under the educational heading on smart CVs, you will often see a section for continuing professional education, focusing on special courses and seminars attended. Specifically, if you are computer literature, list the programs you are familiar with.

Summer and Part-time Employment

This should only be included when the CV writer is either just entering the workforce or re-entering it after a substantial absence. The entry-level person can feel comfortable listing dates and places and times. The returnee should include the skills gained from part-time employment in a fashion that minimizes the 'part-time' aspect of the experience – probably by using a Functional CV format.

What Can Never Go In

Some information just doesn't belong in CVs. Make the mistake of including it, and at best your CV loses power. At worst, you fail to land the interview.

Titles: Resume, Fact Sheet, Curriculum Vitae etc

Never use any of these variations on a theme as a heading. Their appearance on a CV is redundant: if it isn't completely obvious from the very look of your piece of paper that it is a CV, go back to square one. By the way, there is no difference in meaning among the above terms.

Availability

Saying anything about your availability for employment on a CV is another redundancy. If you are not available, then why the heck are you wasting everyone's time and slowing down the process? The only justification of the item's inclusion is if you expect to be finishing a project and moving on at such and such a time, and not before. But your view should be that intelligent human beings always have their eyes and ears open for better career opportunities – because no one else is going to watch out for them. If leaving before the end of a project could affect your integrity and/or references, OK. There's a lot to be said for not burning your bridges, and as careers progress, it's surprising how many of the same people you bump into again and again.

Let the subject of availability come up at the face-to-face meeting. After meeting you, an employer will often be prepared to wait until you are available, and will probably appreciate your integrity. If, on the other hand, the employer just sees a CV that says you won't be available until next year – well, you'll just never get to a face-to-face meeting in the first place.

Reason for Leaving

There is no real point to stating your reasons for leaving a job on a CV, yet time and again they are included – to the detriment of the writer. The topic is always covered during an interview anyway. Mentioning it in advance and on paper can only damage your chances for being called in for that meeting.

References

It is inappropriate and unprofessional to list the names of references on a CV. You will never see it on a top example. Why? Interviewers are not interested in checking them before they meet and develop a strong interest in you – it's too time-consuming.

Most employers will assume that references are available anyway (and if they aren't available, boy, are you in trouble). For that reason, there's an argument to be made for leaving that famous line – References Available Upon Request – off the end of the CV. I disagree however. It may not be absolutely necessary to say that references are there for the asking, but those four extra words certainly don't do any harm and may help you stand out from the crowd. Including the phrase sends a little message:

'Hey, look, I have no skeletons in my cupboard.'

A brief but important aside. If you have ever worked under a different surname, you must take this fact into account when giving your references. A recently divorced woman wasted a strong interview performance not long ago because she was using her maiden name on her CV and at the interview. She forgot to tell the employer that her references could, of course, remember her by a different last name. The results of this oversight were catastrophic. Three prior employers denied ever having heard of anyone by the name the woman's interviewer supplied. She lost the job.

Written Testimonials

Even worse than listing references on a CV is to attach a bunch of written testimonials. It is an absolute no-no. No one believes them anyway.

Of course, that doesn't mean that you shouldn't solicit such references for your files. They can always be produced when references are requested and can be used as a basis for those third-party endorsements we talked about. This will be especially helpful to you if you are just entering the workforce, or re-entering after a long absence, because the content of the testimonials can be used to beef up your CV significantly.

Salary

Leave out all references to salary, past and present – it is far too risky. Too high or too low a salary can knock you out of the running even before you hear the starting gun. Even in responding to a help-wanted advertisement that specifically requests salary requirements, don't give them. A good CV will still get you the interview, and in the course of your discussions with the company, you'll certainly talk about salary anyway. If you somehow feel obliged to give salary requirements, simply write 'competitive' or 'negotiable' (and then only in your cover letter).

Abbreviations

With the exceptions of educational attainments, and those required by the postal service, avoid abbreviations if at all possible. Of course, space constraints might make it imperative that you write 'No. Wilshire Blvd', instead of 'North Wilshire Boulevard'. If that is the case, be sure to be consistent. If you abbreviate in one address, abbreviate in all of them. But bear in mind that you will always seem more thoughtful and professional if everything is spelt out. And anyway, your CV will be easier to read!

Jargon

A similar warning applies to industry slang. You future boss might understand it, but you can bet your boots that neither his or her boss nor the initial CV screener will. Your CV must speak clearly of your skills to many different people, and one skill that we all need today is a sensitivity to the needs of communication.

If you are in one of the high-technology industries, however, avoiding jargon and acronyms is not only impossible, it is often inadvisable. All the same, keep the non-technical CV screener in mind before you wax lyrical about bits and bytes.

Charts and Graphs

Even if charts and graphs are part of your job, they make poor use of the space available on a CV – and they don't help the reader. In fact, you should never even bring them out at an interview unless requested. The same goes for other examples of your work. If you are a copywriter or graphic artist, for example, it is all right to say that samples are available, but only if you have plenty of CV space to spare.

Mention of Age, Race, Religion, Sex, National Origin

Government legislation was enacted some years ago forbidding employment discrimination in these areas. If the government had to take action, you know things were bad. Although today it's much better, I urge you to leave out any reference to any of these areas in your CV.

Photographs

In days of old, it was the done thing to have a photograph in the top right-hand corner of the CV. So, if you are looking for a job in the 1950s, include one; if not, don't. Today, the fashion is against photographs; including them is a waste of space that says nothing about your ability to do a job.

(Obviously, careers in modelling, acting, and certain aspects of the electronic media require photos. In these instances your face is your fortune.)

Health/Physical Description

Who cares? You are trying to get a job, not a date. Unless your physical health (gym instructor, for example) and/or appearance (model, actor, media personality) are immediately relevant to the job, leave these issues alone.

Early Background

I regularly see CVs that tell you about early childhood and upbringing. To date, the most generous excuse I can come up with for such anecdotes is that the CVs were prepared by the subjects' mothers.

Weaknesses

Any weakness, lack of qualifications, or information likely to be detrimental to your cause should always be canned. Never tell CV readers what you don't have or what you can't or haven't had the opportunity to do yet. Let them find that out for themselves.

Demands

You will never see demands on a good CV. Don't outline what you feel an employer is expected to give or to provide. The time for making demands is when the employer has demonstrated sincere interest in you by extending a job offer with a salary and job description attached. That is when the employer will be interested and prepared to listen to what you want. Until then, concentrate on bringing events to that happy circumstance by emphasizing what you can bring to the employer. In your CV you should, to paraphrase President Kennedy, ask not what your employer can do for you, but rather what you can do for your employer.

Exaggerations

Avoid verifiable exaggerations of your skills, accomplishments and educational qualifications. Research has now proven that three out of every ten CVs feature inflated educational qualifications. Consequently, verification, especially of educational claims, is on the increase. If, after you have been hired, you were discovered to have told a sly one on your CV, it could cost you your job and a lot more. The stigma of deceit will very likely follow you for the rest of your professional days. On the other hand, I don't notice 30 per cent of the workforce stumbling around with crippled careers. Matters are tightening up in this area, and ultimately it will be a personal judgement call. Ask yourself, 'Do I have a defensible position, should this matter come under scrutiny now or at a later date?'

Judgement Calls

Here are some areas that fall into neither the do nor the don't camp. Whether to include them will depend on your personal circumstances.

Summary

The Summary, when it is included in a CV, comes immediately after the Objective. The point is to encapsulate your experience and perhaps highlight one or two of your skills and/or contributions. You hope, in two or three short sentences, to grab the reader's attention with a power pack of the skills and attributes you have developed throughout your career. Good summaries are short; you don't want to show all your aces in the first few lines! (You can see examples of CVs with strong summaries in the CV section of this book.)

On the other hand, many experts feel that the content of the summary must be demonstrated by the body of the CV, and that therefore summaries are pointless duplications and a waste of space. The choice is yours. Used wisely and well, they can work.

Personal Flexibility, Relocation

If you are open to relocation for the right opportunity, make it clear. It will never in and of itself get you an interview, but it won't hurt. On the other hand, never state that you aren't open to relocation. After all, that factor usually comes into play only when you have a job offer to consider. Let nothing stand in the way of a nice collection of job offers!

Career Objectives

These are okay to include at the very start of your career, before your general direction has been confirmed by experience and track record. Inclusion is also acceptable if you have very clearly defined objectives and are prepared to sacrifice all other opportunities. If that is the case, state your goals clearly and succinctly, remembering not to confuse the nature of long-term career objectives with short-term job objectives.

Beware, though, of the drawbacks. First of all, CV readers aren't famous for paying much attention to objectives. Second, I have seen these used on many occasions to make a hiring decision between two candidates. The CVs are compared, A has no objective, B has an objective that doesn't match the initial expectations. Result? A gets the job. Another consideration is that your CV may be on file for years, during which time your objectives are bound to change. You don't need last year's dusty dreams clouding over your bright tomorrows.

Marital Status

If you think mention of your marital status will enhance your chances (if you are looking for a position as a long-distance trucker, marriage counsellor or travelling salesperson, for example), include it. In all other instances leave it out. Legally, your marital status is of no consequence.

Military

Include your good military record with highest rank, especially if you are applying for jobs in the defence sector. Otherwise exclude it: it is no longer any detriment to your career not to have a military history.

Personal Interests

A recent Kom Ferry study showed that executives with team sports on their resumes were seen to be averaging US$3,000 a year more than their more sedentary counterparts. Now, that makes giving a line to your hobbies worthwhile, if they fit into certain broad categories. These would include team sports (baseball, basketball), determination activities (running, swimming, climbing, bicycling) and 'brain activities' (bridge, chess).

The rule of thumb, as always, is only to include activities that can in some way contribute to your chances. If you can draw a valid connection, include them; if not, don't.

Personal Paragraphs

Here and there throughout the CV section of this book you will see CVs that include – often toward the end – a short personal paragraph that gives you a candid snapshot of the CV writer as a person. Done well, these can be exciting, effective endings to a CV, but they are not to everyone's taste. Typically, they refer to one or two personal traits, activities, and sometimes, beliefs. These are often tied in with skills required for the particular job sought.

The idea is to make the reader say, 'Heh, there's a real person behind those Foster Grants, let's get him in here; sounds like our kind of guy.' Of course, as no one can be all things to all people, you won't want to go overboard in this area.

4

The Ultimate CV

It has been theory up to now; this is where the rubber hits the road.

You have a sound idea of why you need a CV; you've had an overview of the different types available to you; and you know what belongs in a powerful CV and what doesn't. We now move from the abstract to the intensely practical side of CV writing.

This is the part of the book that requires you to do some thinking. I will ask questions to jog your memory about your practical experience. The outcome will be a smorgasbord of your most sellable professional attributes. The work we do together in this chapter will not only form the foundation of your CV but prepare you to turn those job interviews into job offers.

People change jobs for a multitude of reasons. Perhaps your career isn't progressing as you want it. Perhaps you have gone as far as you can with your present employer, and the only way to take another career step is to change companies. Maybe you have been in the same job for three or more years, without dramatic salary increases or promotions, and you know that you are going nowhere. You have been stereotyped, classified and pigeon-holed.

Whether you are a fast-tracker, recent graduate, workforce re-entrant, career changer or what-have-you, if you are considering new horizons, you must take stock before stepping out.

You need to know where you've been, where you are, and where you're headed. Without this stock taking, your chances of reaching your ultimate goals are reduced, because you won't know how best to use what you've got to get what you want.

Believe it or not, very few people have a clear fix on what they do for a living. Oh, I know; you ask a typist what she does, and you get, 'Type, stupid.' You ask an accountant, and you hear, 'Fiddle with numbers, what do you think?' And that is the problem. Most people don't look at their work beyond these simplistic terms. They never examine the implications of their jobs in relation to the overall success of the department and company. Most people miss not only their importance to an employer as part of the business, but also, their importance to themselves. Preparing your CV will give you a fresh and more lucid view of yourself as a professional and your role in your chosen profession.

Employers all want to know the same thing: how can you contribute to keeping their ship afloat and seaworthy? No one is hired merely to be a typist or an accountant – or anything else, for that matter. Companies hire only one type of person – a problem solver. Look at your work in terms of the problems you solve in the daily round, the problems that would occur if you weren't there.

Some people find the prospect of taking stock of their skills to be an ominous one. They feel it means judging themselves by others' standards, by the job title and salary assigned to them by someone else. Then, knowing their own weaknesses too well, they look at other people in their position, of whom they see only the exterior, and are awed by those persons' seemingly superior competence, skills and professionalism.

'Seemingly' is the key word here. You are as good as the next person, and to prove it, all you have to do is look yourself squarely in the eye and learn that you have a great deal more to offer than you may ever have imagined. You have solved problems. That's what this chapter is all about.

The Secret of CV Writing

As a CV writer, you have a lot in common with journalists and novelists. Beginners in each field usually bring some basic misconceptions about how writing is done: I always thought that Stephen King or James Clavell sat down, wrote 'Page 1', then three weeks later wrote 'The End', and placidly returned the quill to the inkwell. In fact, many professional writers – and CV writers – have more in common with sculptors. What they really do to start the creative process is to write masses of notes. This great mass is the raw material, like a block of stone, at which you chip away to reveal the master-work that has been hiding there all along.

The key is that the more notes you have, the better. Just remember that whatever you write in the note-making part of your CV preparation will never suffer public scrutiny. It is for your private consumption; from these notes, the finished work of art will emerge for public view.

This chapter is going to help you write those notes, as you recapture all those forgotten moments of glory that employers love to hear about.

The only difficult step to take is the first one. So pick up a pen and some paper, and plunge ahead right now; without even pausing for breath.

Questionnaire, Part One: Raw Materials

This questionnaire is set up to follow your entire career. In answering the questions as completely as you can, you are creating the mass of raw material from which you will sculpt the final work of art.

1. *Current or last employer:* This includes part-time or voluntary employment if you are a recent graduate or about to re-enter the workforce after an absence. Try looking at your school as an employer and see what new information you reveal about yourself.

    Starting date:
    Starting salary:
    Leaving date:
    Leaving salary:

2. *Company description:* Write one sentence that describes the product(s) your company made or the service(s) it performed.

3. *Title:* Write your starting job title (the one given to you when you first signed on with the company). Then write a one- or two-sentence description of your responsibilities in that position.

4. *Duties:* What were your three major duties in this position?

5. *Methods, skills, results:* Now, for each of the above three duties, answer the following questions:

    What special skills or knowledge did you need to perform this task satisfactorily?

    What has been your biggest achievement in this area? (Try to think about money saved or made, or time saved for the employer. Don't worry if your contributions haven't been acknowledged in writing and signed in triplicate, as long as you know them to be true without exaggeration.)

    What verbal or written comments were made about your contributions in this area, by peers or managers?

    What different levels of people did you have to interact with to achieve your job tasks? How did you get the best out of superiors? Co-workers? Subordinates?

What aspects of your personality were brought into play when executing this duty? (For example, perhaps it required attention to detail, or determination, or good verbal and writing skills. Whatever, jot them all down.)

To help you address that last issue (it's a vitally important one), you should look over the following list of a number of personality traits that are in constant demand from all employers.

Analytical skills: Weighing the pros and cons. Not jumping at the first solution to a problem that presents itself.

Chemistry: Your willingness to get along with others and get the job done.

Communication skills: More than ever, the ability to talk with and write effectively to people at all levels in a company is a key to success.

Confidence: Poise, friendliness, honesty, and openness with all employees – high and low.

Dedication: Doing whatever it takes to get the job done.

Drive and determination: A desire to get things gone. Goal-oriented. Someone who does not back off when a problem or situation gets tough.

Economy: Most problems have an expensive solution and an inexpensive one that the company would prefer to implement.

Efficiency: Always keeping an eye open for inefficient uses of time, effort, resources and money.

Energy: Extra effort in all aspects of the job, the little things as well as the important matters.

Honesty/integrity: Responsibility for all your actions – both good and bad. Always making decisions in the best interests of the company, rather than on whim or personal preference.

Listening skills: Listening, rather than just waiting your turn to speak.

Motivation: Enthusiasm, finding reasons to accept challenges rather than avoid them. A company realizes that a motivated person accepts added challenges and does that little bit extra on every job.

Pride: Pride in a job well done. Paying attention to detail.

Reliability: Follow-through, a willingness to keep management informed, and a predisposition toward relying on oneself – not others – to see your job done.

Sensitivity to procedures: Following the chain of command, recognizing that procedures exist to keep a company functioning and profitable. Those who rush to implement their own 'improved procedures' wholesale, or organize others to do so, can cause untold chaos in an organization.

6. *Supporting points:* If you asked for a promotion or a raise while in this position, what arguments did you use to back up your request?

7. *Most recent position:* Write down your current (or last) job title. Then write a one- or two-sentence description of your responsibilities in that position, and repeat steps three through six. In this step it is assumed that you have a title and responsibilities that are different from those you had when you first joined the company. If this is not the case, simply ignore this step. On the other hand, many people have held three or four titles with a specific employer, and gained breadth of experience with each one. In this instance, for each different intermediary title, repeat steps one through six. The description of responsibilities should be reserved for your departing (or current) title.

8. *Reflecting on success:* Make some general observations about work with this employer. Looking back over your time with this employer, what was the biggest work-related problem that you had to face? What solution did you find? What was the result of the solution when implemented? What was the value to the employer in terms of money earned or saved and improved efficiency? What was the area of your greatest personal improvement in this job? What was the greatest contribution you made as a team player? Who are the references you would hope to use from this employer, and what do you think they would say about you?

9. *Getting all the facts:* Repeat the last eight steps for your previous employer, and then for the employer before that, and so forth. Most finished CVs focus on the last three jobs, or last ten years before that, and so forth. In this developmental portion of the process, however, you must go back in time and cover your entire career. Remember that you are doing more than preparing a CV here: you are preparing for the heat of battle. In the interview preparation, throughout any telephone screening interviews, and especially before that crucial face-to-face meeting, you can use this Questionnaire to prepare yourself for anything the interviewer might ask. One of the biggest complaints interviewers have about job candidates, and one of the major reasons for rejection, is unpreparedness: 'You know, good as some of this fellow's skills are,

something just wasn't right. He seemed – slow somehow. You know, he couldn't even remember when he joined his current employer!' You won't have that problem.

Questionnaire, Part Two: Details, Details, Details

The hard work is done and it's all downhill from here. Just fill in the facts and figures relating to the following questions. Obviously, not everything will apply to you. The key is just to put it all down; you can polish it later.

Military History

Include branch of service, rank, and any special skills that could further your civilian career.

Educational History

Start with highest level of attainment and work backward. Give dates, schools, qualifications, subjects, grades.

Specify any scholarships or other special awards.

List other school activities, such as sports, societies, social activities.

Especially important are leadership roles: any example of how you 'made a difference' with your presence could be of value to your future. Obviously, this is important for recent graduates with little work experience.

Languages

Specify fluency and ability to read and write foreign languages.

Personal Interest

List interests and activities that could be supportive to your candidacy. For example, an internal auditor who plays chess or bridge would list these and probably use them in a CV, because they support the analytical bent so necessary to work.

Technological Literacy

In this new era of work every potential employer is concerned about your ability to work with new technologies. If you are computer and Internet literate, let's hear the details. If not, it's time to catch up with today's technology – before you get left behind with the industrial era dinosaurs.

Demonstrating that you have up-to-date knowledge and are comfortable with computers and the Internet, along with understanding how they apply to your specific profession, is key to your professional survival. You should be able to identify the equipment and applications you need to function effectively in your field.

Patents

Include patents that are both pending and awarded.

Publications

If you have published articles, list the name of the publication, title of article and the publication date. If you have had books published, list the title and publisher.

Professional Associations

Include membership and the details of any offices you held.

Volunteer Work

Also include any volunteer work you performed. It isn't only paid work experience that makes you valuable.

Miscellaneous Areas of Achievement

All professions and careers are different. Use this section to itemize any additional aspects of your history where you somehow 'made a difference' with your presence.

Questionnaire, Part Three: Where Are You Going?

Knowing where you want to go will determine both the wording and the layout of your CV. There is an old saying that if you don't know where you are going, you have no hope of getting there. Remember that there is a difference between valid objectives and pipedreams. Dreams aren't bad things to have, but they mustn't be confused with making a living.

Your first step is to write down a job title that embraces your objectives. Having taken this simple step, you need to note underneath it all the skills and qualifications needed to do that job successfully. List them like this:

Job Title
1. First skill
2. Second skill
3. Third skill
4. Fourth skill
5. Fifth skill

But remember that your thoughts on what it takes may not be in accord with the employer's thoughts. And what if you are simply not sure what it takes to do the job at all? Simple. Take a trip to the library and ask to see a copy of the *Dictionary of Occupational Titles*. It gives you endless job titles, as you might expect, and brief job descriptions. Make notes by all means, but don't copy it out word for word. The book is full of dead prose that's copper-bottom guaranteed to send the average CV reader to sleep in three seconds flat. You want to avoid letting any of this soporific stuff sneak into the final draft of your CV.

When you have decided on an objective, and defined what it takes to do that job, go back through the first part of the questionnaire and flag all the entries you can use to build a viable CV. Just underline or highlight the appropriate passages for further attention when the time comes for putting pen to paper.

The chances are that you will find adequate skills in your background to qualify you for the job objective. And remember: few people have all the qualifications for the jobs they get!

If you still aren't sure, develop a 'Matching Sheet' for yourself. List the practical requirements of your job objective on one side of a piece of paper and match them on the other side with your qualifications. A senior computer programmer, looking for a step up to a systems analysis position with a new job in financial applications, might develop a Matching Sheet that looks like this:

Job Needs	*My Experience*
Mainframe IBM experience	6 yrs experience
IBM COBOL	COBOL, PL/1, Assembler
Financial experience	6 yrs in banking
Sys. dev. methodology	Major sys. dev., 3 yrs
Communication	Ongoing customer service work OS/MVS, TSO/SPF, CICS, SNAOS/MVS, TSO/SPF, ROSCOE, IMS, DB/DC, SAS

But what about the junior accountant who had VP of finance as a goal? Naturally, at this stage, many of the needed skills – and much of the experience – aren't in place. If you fall into this category, don't worry. You just happened upon a career objective rather than a job objective. To solve the dilemma, list all the title changes between your present position and your dream job. This will show you how many career steps stand between you and your ultimate goal. Your job objective is simply the title above your own, the first achievable stepping stone toward the ultimate goal.

At best, job and career objectives are simply a tool to give focus for writing the CV, and to give the reader something to take sightings on. The way the world is changing, by the time you can reasonably expect to reach your ultimate career goal, that particular position may not even exist.

Be content with a generalized objective for the next job. And don't be afraid of that objective – you aren't taking holy orders, you're identifying a job you'd like to win. Who knows what the next few years will hold for you?

Sample Questionnaire

This sample questionnaire was filled out by a fellow professional using the questionnaire guidelines on pages 38–44. Actual CV examples based on the following information – chronological, functional and combination formats – can be found on pages 9, 12 and 14.

1. Current or last employer:
   This includes part-time or voluntary employment if you are a recent graduate or about to re-enter the workforce after an absence. That does not mean you should ignore this section: try looking at your school as an employer and see what new information you reveal about yourself.

   BRANCH MANAGER
Starting Date	*11/92*
Starting Salary	*£13,000*
Leaving Date	*8/95*
Leaving Salary	*£26,000*

   AREA MANAGER
Starting Date	*8/95*
Starting Salary	*£31,200*
Leaving Date	*8/98*
Leaving Salary	*£41,600*

   DIVISION MANAGER
Starting Date	*8/98*
Starting Salary	*£62,400*
Leaving Date	*3/00*
Leaving Salary	*£62,400*

2. Write one sentence that describes the products your company made or the services it performed.

    BRANCH MANAGER through DIVISION MANAGER: MICRO/TEMPS sold software consulting services to the computer-user industry.

3. List your starting job title (the one given to you when you first signed on with the company). Then write a one- or two-sentence description of your responsibilities in that position.

    BRANCH MANAGER
    Started a new division of the Technical Aid Corporation called MICRO/TEMPS. Was responsible for developing a client and applicant database, while showing a profit for the division.

    AREA MANAGER
    Opened an additional office in the Birmingham area. Was accountable for the profitability of both the London and Birmingham offices.

    DIVISION MANAGER
    Responsible for market studies for future branches to be opened. Directly involved in choosing new locations, opening office, training staff and having the office profitable in less than one year's time.

4. What were your three major duties in this position?

    BRANCH MANAGER
    A) Selling software services to clients.
    B) Interviewing applicants and selling them on consulting.
    C) Setting up interviews for applicants and clients to meet.

    AREA MANAGER
    A) Training sales and recruiting staff.
    B) Developing and implementing goals from forecasts.
    C) Interfacing with other divisions in order to develop a working relationship between different divisions.

    DIVISION MANAGER
    A) Hired and trained Branch Managers for all new offices.
    B) Developed P & L forecasts for the BOD.
    C) Developed and implemented division policies.

5. Now, for each of the above three duties, answer the following questions:

    What special skills or knowledge did you need to perform this task satisfactorily?

    BRANCH MANAGER
    A) Knowledge of the computer industry.
    B) Key contacts in the UK computer industry.

AREA MANAGER
A)   *Knowledge and experience developing a branch.*
B)   *Experience training sales and recruiting staff.*

DIVISION MANAGER
A)   *Knowledge and understanding of developing a profitable division.*
B)   *Knowledge and experience hiring and training branch managers.*

What has been your biggest achievement in this area? (Try to think about money saved or made, or time saved for the employer. Don't worry if your contributions haven't been acknowledged in writing and signed in triplicate, so long as you know them to be true without exaggeration.)

BRANCH MANAGER
Successfully developed a new division of the Technical Aid Corporation. Now generating £18,000,000 in revenues.

AREA MANAGER
Successfully opened new branches for the division and hired and trained the staff.

DIVISION MANAGER
Built division to £20 million in annual sales.

What verbal or written comments were made about your contributions in this area, by peers or managers?

BRANCH MANAGER
Hard-working, stay-at-it attitude.

AREA MANAGER
Hires good people and knows how to get the best out of them.

DIVISION MANAGER
Her division always makes the largest gross profit out of any of the divisions.

What different levels of people did you have to interact with to get this particular duty done? How did you get the best out of each of them?

BRANCH MANAGER
A)   *Superiors – Listened to their ideas and then tried to show them I could implement them.*
B)   *Co-workers – Shared experiences and company goals – set up some competition.*
C)   *Subordinates – Acknowledged their responsibilities as very important for the team.*

AREA MANAGER
A) _Superiors – Explained situations clearly and made them understand our options._
B) _Co-workers – Challenged to reach goals._
C) _Subordinates – Complimented when and where it was necessary._

DIVISION MANAGER
A) _Superiors – Asked for their experience and advice in difficult situations._
B) _Co-workers – Set up and accepted contest between managers._
C) _Subordinates – Made them feel they were extremely important as a member of the team._

What aspects of your personality were brought into play when executing this duty?

PERSONALITY: BRANCH MANAGER TO DIVISION MANAGER
strong willpower
stick-to-it attitude
high achiever
aggressive
high goal setter

6. If you asked for a promotion or a rise while in this position, what arguments did you use to back up your request?

BRANCH MANAGER – _Increase in sales._
AREA MANAGER – _Increase in responsibility._
DIVISION MANAGER – _Increase in gross profit and responsibilities._

7. Write down your current (or last) job title. Then write a one- or two-sentence description of your responsibilities in that position, and repeat steps 3 through 6.

Current title – _Personnel Manager_

Step 3: Description of responsibilities. _Hiring all internal staff of technical managers and sales people, additionally responsible for hiring all external consultants._

Step 4: Three major duties:
A) _Hiring of all internal and external consultants._
B) _Setting up wage and salary guidelines._
C) _Establishing the London office so it could become profitable quickly._

Step 5: Skills or knowledge needed:
A) _Ability to source qualified candidates._
B) _Experience in start-up situation._
C) _Knowledge of the London marketplace._

Biggest achievement: *Helped in making the branch profitable in nine months.*

Verbal or written comments: *A no-nonsense kind of person, aggressive and hard-working; good at getting the best out of people.*

Superiors: *Was up front with any problems and clearly and concisely laid out all the alternatives.*

Co-workers: *Set up good networking of communications to have information flow quickly and easily.*

Subordinates: *Made them aware that we all had a lot to do, but that we were all important.*

Step 6: Rise or promotion.
Increase in sales figures and was responsible for hiring more consultants than we had originally discussed.

8. Make some general observations about work with this employer. Looking back over your time with this employer, what was the biggest work-related problem that you had to face?

    They wanted to grow rapidly, but didn't want to invest the money it took to recruit and attract good consultant talent.

    What solution did you find?

    Got consultants through British Computer Society and other related organizations, and set up a very aggressive referral programme.

    What was the result of the solution when implemented?

    We started to attract quality consultants, and our name was beginning to circulate.

    What was the value to the employer in terms of money earned or saved and improved efficiency?

    Company did not spent a lot of money on recruiting efforts and was able to attract quality people.

    What was the area of your greatest personal improvement in this job?

    Made many key contacts in some excellent organizations.

    What was the greatest contribution you made as a team player?

    Brought internal staff members closer together as a working team.

    Who are the references you would hope to use from this employer, and what do you think they would say about you?

Ken Shelly – He was one of our first external consultants hired. He would probably say that I identified some key consultants for this project at Sheraton, and that he could always rely on me to help him no matter what.

Dave Johnson – He was our technical manager. He would say that I did my job extremely well considering the little resources I had, and that I identified many quality applicants. He would also say that I knew how to find even difficult people.

5

Writing the Basic CV

Advertisements and CVs have a great deal in common.

You will notice the vast majority of advertisements in any media can be heard, watched or read in under 30 seconds. That is not accidental. The timing is based on studies relating to the limit of the average consumer's attention span.

And that is why you sometimes notice that both CVs and advertisements depart from the rules that govern all other forms of writing. First and last they are an urgent business communication, and business like to get to the point.

Before getting started, good advertising copywriters imagine themselves in the position of their target audience. They imagine their objective – selling something. Then they consider what features their product possesses and what benefits it can provide to the purchaser.

You will find a similar procedure beneficial in your own writing. Fortunately, your approach is simplified somewhat, because you can make certain generalizations. You can assume, for instance, that the potential employer has a position to fill and a problem to solve, and that he or she will hire someone who is able to do the job, who is willing to do it, and who is manageable.

For the next 15 minutes, imagine yourself in one of your target companies. You are in the personnel department on CV detail. Fortunately it is a slow morning, and there are only 30 that need to be read. Go straight to the example section now and read 30 CVs without a break, then return to this page.

Now you have some idea of what it feels like. Except that you had it easy – the CVs you read were good, interesting ones; CVs that got real people real jobs. Even so, you probably felt a little punch drunk at the end of the exercise. But I know that you learned a very valuable lesson: brevity is to be desired above all other things.

Preparation

Collect an old CV, some generic job descriptions and, of course, the completed Questionnaire. Then get comfortably set up at your computer (or with a pad of paper if it makes you more comfortable) and you're ready to go!

Now, just write. Don't even try for style or literacy – you can tend to that later. Think of yourself as speaking on paper. You'll find your personal speech rhythms will make for a lively CV, once they have been edited.

Choose a Layout

You have seen the basic examples of chronological, functional and combination CVs in chapter 2, and certainly you have browsed through the dozens of actual CVs. Find one that strikes your fancy and fits your needs, and use it as your model. It need not reflect your field of professional expertise. Obviously, you will have to tinker with any model, adding or deleting jobs and making other subtle adjustments as necessary, to fashion it for your background.

This first step is just like painting by numbers. Go through the model and fill in the obvious slots – name, address, telephone number(s), e-mail address, employer names, employment dates, educational background and dates, extramural activities and the like. Shazam! Now the first half of your CV is complete.

Filling in the Picture: Chronological CVs

Objectives

You can have a simple non-specific objective, one that gives the reader a general focus, such as, 'Objective: Data Processing Management'. It gets the message across succinctly; and if there is no immediate need for someone of your background, it encourages the employer to put your CV in the file where you feel it belongs. That's important, because even if you are not suitable for today's needs, there's a good chance that the CV will be pulled out when such a need does arise.

If you choose to use an expanded, detailed objective, refer to chapter 3. You will of course:

- Keep it short, just one or two sentences.

- Express your objective in the fewest possible words that can bring a picture to the reader's mind.

- Not get too specific – no one is that interested.

- Focus the objective on what you can do for the company and avoid mention of what you want in return.

- State exactly the job title you seek, if the CV is in response to a specific advertisement.

- Keep your objectives general to give yourself the widest number of employment options, if the CV will be sent out 'blind' to a number of companies.

Of course, with your CV produced on a computer, your objective can go through subtle variations for each specific job.

If you want to use both a non-specific and a detailed objective, headline the CV with the non-specific title, and then follow with the more detailed one.

Company Role

Now, for each employer, edit your response from step two of the Questionnaire, which outlines that company's services or products. Make it one short sentence. Do not exceed one line or ten words.

Job Titles

Remember what we said in chapter 3. There is nothing intrinsically wrong with listing your title as 'Fourth-Level Administration Clerk, Third Class', as long as you are prepared to wait until doomsday for it to be considered by someone who understands what it means and is able to relate it to current needs. With this in mind:

- Be general in your job title. All companies have their particular ways of dispensing job titles, and they all vary. Your title with employer A will mean something entirely different to employer B, and might not make any sense at all to employer C.

- Whenever possible, stay away from designations such as trainee, junior, intermediate, senior – as in Junior Engineer – and just designate yourself as Engineer, Designer, Editor, or what have you.

Responsibilities

In a chronological CV, the job title is often followed by a short sentence that helps the reader visualize you doing the job. Get the information from the completed questionnaire and do a rough edit to get it down to one short sentence. Don't worry about perfection now; the polishing is done later.

The responsibilities and contributions you list here are those functions that best display your achievements and problem-solving abilities. They do not necessarily correspond with how you spent the majority of your working day, nor are they related to how you might prefer to spend your working day. Problems sometimes arise by mistakenly following either of these paths. It can perhaps best be illustrated by showing you part of a CV that came to my desk recently. It is the work of a professional who listed her title and duties for one job like this:

> Sales Manager: Responsible for writing branch policy, coordination of advertising and advertising agencies. Developed knowledge of IBM PC. Managed staff of six.

Is it any wonder she wasn't getting responses to her CV-mailing campaign? Here, she has explained where she was spending her time when the CV was created. The explanation, however, has nothing to do with the major functions of her job. She has mistakenly listed everything in the reverse chronological order, not in relation to the items' relative importance to a future employer. Let's look at what subsequent restructuring achieved:

> Sales Manager: Hired to turn around stagnant sales force. Successfully recruited, trained, managed and motivated a consulting staff of six. Result: 22 per cent sales gain over first year.

In the rewrite of this particular part of the CV, notice how she thought like a copywriter and quickly identified the problem she was hired to solve.

> Hired to turn around stagnant sales force. (Demonstrates her skills and responsibilities.)

> Successfully recruited, trained, managed and motivated a consulting staff of six. Result: 22 per cent sales gain over first year. (Shows what she subsequently did about them, and just how well she did it.)

By doing this, her responsibilities and achievements become more important in the light of the problems they solved.

Some More about Contributions

Business has very limited interests. In fact, those interests can be reduced to a single phrase: making a profit. Making a profit is done in just three ways: by saving money in some fashion for the company; by saving time through some innovation at the company, which in turn saves the company money and gives it the opportunity to make more money in the time saved; or by simply making money for the company.

That's all there is to any business, when you reduce things to their simplest forms.

That does not mean that you should address only those points in your CV and ignore valuable contributions which cannot be quantified. But it does mean that you should try to quantify as much as you can.

If you find it difficult to recall and prioritize your responsibilities at a given company, go to the library and consult the *Directory of Job Descriptions*. But, as I have said before, be careful. If you do resort to this as a memory jogger be careful not to copy out the appropriate entry in its entirety – the prose is deadly boring.

Achievements

Your achievements will be listed in step five of the first part of the Questionnaire. The achievements you take from step five will not necessarily be the greatest accomplishments that can help you reach your stated (or unstated) employment objective. Concentrate solely on those topics that relate to your objectives, even if it means leaving out some significant achievement; you can always rectify the situation at the interview.

Pick two to four accomplishments for each job title and edit them down to bite-size chunks that read like a telegram. Write as if you had to pay for each entry by the word – this approach can help you pack a lot of information into a short space. The resulting abbreviated style will help convey a sense of immediacy to the reader.

> Responsible for new and used car sales. Earned 'Salesperson of the Year' awards, 2000 and 2001; Record holder for:

- Most Cars Sold in One Month

- Most Cars Sold in One Year

- Most Board Gross in One Month

- Created an annual giving programme to raise operating funds. *Raised £2,000,000.*

- Targeted, cultivated, and solicited sources including individuals, corporations, foundations and government agencies. *Raised £1,650,000.*

- Raised funds for development of the Performing Arts School facility, capital expense, and music and dance programmes. *Raised £6,356,000.*

Now, while you may tell the reader about these achievements, you should never explain how they were accomplished. After all, the idea of the CV is to pique interest and to raise as many questions as you answer. Questions means interest, and getting that interest satisfied requires talking to you!

You probably have lots of great accomplishments to share with the reader that will tempt you to add a second page, or even a third. Your CV, however, is designed to form the basis for tantalizing further discussions, so just be content with showing the reader a little glimpse of the gold vein – and let him or her discover the rest of the strike later. Very often the information discovered by the interviewer's own efforts takes on greater value than information offered free of charge on paper. Also, you have saved some of your heavy firepower for the interview, so that the meeting will not be an anticlimax for the interviewer. And that, in turn, will lend you some leverage and control in the discussions.

Prioritize the listing of your accomplishments as they relate to your job objective, and be sure to quantify your contributions (that is, put them into tangible, profit-oriented terms) wherever possible and appropriate.

Now is the time to weave in one or two of those laudatory quotes (also from step five). Don't include everyone, but do incorporate enough to show that others think well of you.

- Sales volume increased from £90 million to £175 million. Acknowledged as 'the greatest single gain of the year'.

- Earnings increased from £9 million to £18 million. Review stated, 'always a view for the company bottom line'.

- Three key stores were each developed into £30-million units. Praised for 'an ability to keep all the balls in the air, all the time'.

Functional or Combination CV

These CVs are similar to chronological ones in content; often it's just the order of information that is different. Employers and employment dates are downplayed by relegating them to the end of the paragraphs, or to the bottom of the CV. Job titles and job responsibilities for specific jobs are sometimes omitted altogether.

In a functional or combination CV, you will have identified the skills and attributes necessary to fulfil the functions of the job objective, and will highlight the appropriate attributes you have to offer. In this format, you will have headings that apply to the skill areas your chosen career path demands, such as: Management, Training, Sales etc. Each will be followed by a short paragraph packed with selling points. These can be real paragraphs, or the introductory sentence followed by the bullets usually recommended for the chronological formats. Here are examples of each style.

COLLECTIONS:

Developed excellent rapport with customers while significantly shortening pay-out terms through application of problem-solving techniques. Turned impending loss into profit. Personally salvaged and increased sales with two multi-million-pound accounts by providing remedial action for their sales/financial problems.

COLLECTIONS

Developed excellent rapport with customers while significantly shortening pay-out terms:

- Evaluated sales performance, offered suggestions for financing/merchandising.

- Performed on-the-spot negotiations; turned impending loss into profit.

- Salvaged two multi-million-pound problem accounts by providing remedial action for their sales/financial problems. Subsequently increased sales.

Keep each paragraph to an absolute maximum of four lines. This ensures that the finished product has plenty of white space so that it is easy on the reader's eye.

Editing and Polishing

Sentences gain power with verbs that demonstrate an action. For example, one client – a mature lady with ten years at the same law firm in a clerical position – had written in her original CV:

I learned to use a computer database.

After discussion of the circumstances that surrounded learning how to use the computer database, certain exciting facts emerged. By using action verbs and an awareness of employer interests, this sentence was charged up, given more punch. Not only that, for the first time the writer fully understood the value of the her contributions, which greatly enhanced her self-image:

I analysed and determined need for automation of an established law office. Responsible for hardware and software selection, installation and loading. Within one year, I had achieved a fully automated office.

Notice how the verbs show that things happen when you are around the office. These action verbs and phrases add an air of direction, efficiency and accomplishment to every CV. They succinctly tell the reader what you did and how well you did it.

Now look at the above example when a third-party endorsement is added to it:

> I analysed and determined need for automation of an established law office. Responsible for hardware and software selection, installation and loading. Within one year, I had achieved a fully automated office. Partner stated, 'You brought us out of the dark ages into the technological age, and in the process neither you nor the firm missed a beat!'

Keywords

With the advent of electronic CV screening tools, it's become more and more important to use specific keywords in your CV. Internal job descriptions are usually built of nouns and verbs that describe the skill sets required for the job. Your CV should be built the same way, with nouns that identify the skill sets and verbs/action phrases that describe your professional behaviour and achievements with these skill sets.

This is an important distinction in the initial screening process. Screening software focuses on the skill sets, which invariably are nouns. If you are a computer programmer the screening device might search for words like HTML; if you are an accountant it might search for words like 'financial analysis'. Only when the computer has identified those CVs that include matching skills do human eyes enter into the picture; and only then can the verbs/action phrases that describe your competencies and achievements have the desired impact. With an electronic CV, the nouns/skill sets are the skeleton, while the verbs/action phrases are designed to put flesh on the bones – for human eyes hungry for talent.

For our purposes the keyword nouns are the words commonly used to describe the essential skill sets and knowledge necessary to carry out a job successfully. They are likely to include:

- skill sets/abilities/competencies;

- application of these skills sets;

- relevant education and training.

As you complete the self-analysis questionnaire on pages 38–44, you will identify keywords in all of these areas.

You may also want to study the keywords that appear frequently in help-wanted ads and electronic job postings. If you do, you'll notice that different words (synonyms) are used to describe the same job or skill set. For example, one job posting might outline a need for a secretary, while another nearly identical job posting might identify the job title as administrative assistant.

Now, bring on the electronic screening tools. If you identify yourself as a secretary, a computer searching for an administrative assistant might pass you over. So if you are a secretary, you might also want to include the phrase 'administrative assistant' in your CV. Likewise, an attorney might want to include 'lawyer'; someone in HR management might want to include 'personnel administration'. You get the idea.

You'll want to weave these synonyms for job titles and skill sets into the main body of your CV as much as possible. However, that won't always be possible. The logical flow of your CV – or insufficient space – might prevent you from using the keywords in place. That's where a separate keyword section comes in handy. It is the perfect spot to list the technical acronyms and professional jargon that you can't fit into the body copy.

Here's an example of a keyword box from a sales management professional:

SPECIFIC KNOWLEDGE AND SKILLS

• Market Trend Analysis	• Profit & Loss
• Multi-Site Management	• Needs Analysis
• Budget	• Employee Motivation
• Business Savvy	• Sales
• Performance Evaluations	• Contract Negotiation
• Technical Expertise	• Team Training

This innovation in CV writing allows you to add a host of additional information to your CV in a highly space-efficient way – usually in 20 or 30 words.

Using a keyword selection will increase the odds of an electronic screening agent making multiple matches between your CV and an open job requisition. Neither will it offend human eyes, which will view the list of keywords as an expansion of the body copy – and a ready source for topics for discussion.

This compels me to offer you a warning: don't use keywords to extend the 'reach' of your CV. You must have real experience in each of the areas you include. Including keywords for areas where you have no professional expertise may get you a telephone conversation with an employer, but it will also quickly reveal you as an imposter. End of story.

Where does the keyword section go? As far as the computer is concerned it doesn't matter. The computer doesn't care about the niceties of layout and flow. However, human eyes will also see the keyword section so there is a certain logic in putting it front and centre, after any summary or objective or immediately after the contact information. The keyword section acts as a preface to the body copy, in effect saying, 'Hey, here are all the headlines. The stories behind them are immediately below.' To put it another way, the keyword section acts as a table of contents for your CV, with the body – with its action words and phrases – explaining and expanding on the list of topics.

Your keyword section can be as long as you require, though they typically don't run longer than 40 items and usually are a little shorter. There's no need to use definite or indefinite articles or conjunctions. Just list the word, starting with a capital and ending with a full stop: 'Forecasting', or a phrase, such as 'Financial modelling'.

You can also think of your keyword section as an electronic business card that allows you to network with computers!

Action Verbs

Overleaf are over 175 action verbs: see which ones you can use to give punch to your CV writing.

Use these words to edit and polish your work, to communicate, persuade, and motivate the reader to take action.

This stage is most challenging, because many people in different companies will see and evaluate your CV. Keep industry 'jargon' to a minimum; there will be some who understand the intricacies and technicalities of your profession, and some who don't. And you need to share your technical or specialist wisdom with the non-specialists, too.

Varying Sentence Structure

Most good writers are at their best when they write short punchy sentences. Keep your sentences under about 20 words; a good average is around 15. If your sentence is longer than the 20 mark, either shorten it by restructuring, or make two sentences out of one. The reader on the receiving end has neither the time nor the inclination to read your sentences twice to get a clear understanding.

At the same time, you don't want the writing to sound choppy, so vary the length of sentences when you can. You can also start with a short phrase and follow with a colon:

- followed by bullets of information;
- each one supporting the original phrase.

accepted
accomplished
achieved
acted
adapted
addressed
administered
advanced
advised
allocated
analysed
appraised
approved
arranged
assembled
assigned
assisted
attained
audited
authored
automated
balanced
budgeted
built
calculated
catalogued
chaired
clarified
classified
coached
collected
compiled
completed
composed
computed
conceptualized
conducted
consolidated
contained
contracted
contributed
controlled
coordinated
corresponded
counselled
created

critiqued
cut
decreased
defined
delegated
demonstrated
designed
developed
devised
diagnosed
directed
dispatched
distinguished
diversified
drafted
edited
educated
eliminated
emended
enabled
encouraged
engineered
enlisted
established
evaluated
examined
executed
expanded
expedited
explained
extracted
fabricated
facilitated
familiarized
fashioned
focused
forecast
formulated
founded
generated
guided
headed up
identified
illustrated
implemented
improved

increased
indoctrinated
influenced
informed
initiated
innovated
inspected
installed
instigated
instituted
instructed
integrated
interpreted
interviewed
introduced
invented
launched
lectured
led
maintained
managed
marketed
mediated
moderated
monitored
motivated
negotiated
operated
organized
originated
overhauled
oversaw
performed
persuaded
planned
prepared
presented
prioritized
processed
produced
programmed
projected
promoted
proposed
provided
publicized

published
purchased
recommended
reconciled
recorded
recruited
reduced
referred
regulated
rehabilitated
remodelled
repaired
represented
researched
resolved
restored
restructured
retrieved
revamped
revitalized
saved
scheduled
schooled
screened
set
shaped
solidified
solved
specified
stimulated
streamlined
strengthened
summarized
supervised
surveyed
systemized
tabulated
taught
trained
translated
travelled
trimmed
upgraded
validated
worked
wrote

All these different techniques are designed to enliven the reading process. Here's an example of how the above suggestions might be put into practice.

Analysed and determined need for automation of an established law office:

- responsible for hardware and software selection;
- coordinated installation of computer database and six work stations;
- operated and maintained equipment, and trained other users;
- achieved full automation in one year.

Partner stated, 'You brought us out of the dark ages, and neither you nor the firm missed a beat!'

Just as you use short sentences, use common words. They communicate quickly and are easy to understand. Stick to short and simple words wherever possible without sounding infantile. Of course, you need action words and phrases. But the real point is to stay away from obscure words.

Short words for short sentences
help make short, gripping paragraphs:
good for short attention spans!

Within your short paragraphs and short sentences, beware of name and acronym dropping, such as 'Worked for Dr A Witherspoon in Sys. Gen. SNA 2.31'. This is a good way to confuse (and lose) readers. Such coinage is too restricted to have validity outside the small circle of specialists to whom they speak. Your CV deserves the widest possible readership. Apart from the section on the CV that includes your educational qualifications, stay away from jargon unless you work in a highly technical field.

Voice and Tense

The voice you develop for your CV depends on a few important factors: getting a lot said in a small space; being factual; and packaging yourself in the best way.

The voice you use should be consistent throughout the CV. There is considerable disagreement among the experts about the best voice, and each of the leading options have both champions and detractors.

Sentences can be truncated (up to a point) by omitted pronouns – I, you, he, she, it, they – and articles – a or the. In fact, many authorities recommend the dropping of pronouns as a technique that both saves space and allows you to brag about yourself without seeming boastful. It gives the impression that another party is writing about you. Many people feel that to use the personal pronoun ('I automated the office') is naive and unprofessional. These experts suggest you use either the third person ('He automated the office') or leave the pronoun out altogether ('Automated office').

At the same time, there are others who recommend that you write in the first person because it makes you sound more human. Use whatever style works best for you. If you do use the personal pronoun, though, try not to use it in every sentence – it gets a little monotonous and takes up valuable space on the page.

A nice variation I have seen is a third-person voice used through the CV and then a final few words in the first person appended to the end of the CV, to give an insight into your values. Here is an example:

Regular third person:
James Sharpe is a professional who knows Technical Services from the ground up. He understands its importance in keeping a growing company productive, and takes pride in creating order in the chaos of technology.

Abbreviated third person:
Responsible for machine and system design, production scheduling, procurement and quality control. Redesigned conveyors and simplified maintenance while improving quality. Instituted a system of material control to account for all materials used.

First person:
I am accustomed to accepting responsibility and delegating authority, and am capable of working with, and through people at all levels. Am able to plan, organize, develop, implement, and supervise complex programmes and special projects. All of this requires a good sense of humour and a personal dedication to producing timely, cost-effective results.

Many people mistake the need for professionalism in a CV with stiff-necked formality. The most effective tone is one that mixes both the conversational and the formal, just the way we do in our offices and on our jobs. The only overriding rule is to make it readable, so that another person can see the human being shining through the pages.

Length

The accepted rules for length are one page for every 10 years of your experience. If you have more than 20 years under your belt, however, you won't want to appear to be too seeped in the annals of ancient history, and so will not want to exceed the two-page mark.

Occasionally a three- or four-page CV can be effective, but only when:

■ You have been contacted directly by an employer about a specific position and and have been asked to prepare a CV for that particular opportunity.

■ An executive recruiter who is representing you determines that the exigencies of a particular situation warrant an extensive dossier. Usually, such a CV will be prepared exclusively by the recruiter.

You'll find that thinking too much about length considerations while you write will hamper you. Think instead of the story you have to tell, then layer fact upon fact until it is sold. When that is done, you can go back and ruthlessly cut it to the bone.

Ask yourself these questions:

■ Can I cut out any paragraphs?

■ Can I cut out any sentences?

■ Can I cut out any superfluous words?

■ Where have I repeated myself?

If in doubt, cut it out – leave nothing but facts and action words!

And if you find at the end that you've cut out too much, you'll have the additional pleasure of reinstating text!

The Proofreading Checklist for Your Final Draft

There are really two proofing steps in the creation of a polished CV. The first you do at this point, to make sure that all the things that should be in are there – and that all the things that shouldn't, aren't. The final proofing is addressed later in the book.

In the heat of the creative moment, it's easy to miss critical components or mistakenly include facts that give the wrong emphasis. Check your CV against these points:

Contact Information

■ Is the pertinent personal data – name, address, personal telephone number, and e-mail address – correct? (You will want to make sure that this personal data is on every page.)

▨   Is your business number omitted unless it is absolutely necessary and safe to include it?

Objectives

▨   Does your objective briefly state your employment goals without getting too specific and ruling you out of consideration for many jobs?

▨   If you gave a detailed objective (up to – but no more than – two sentences), does it focus on what you can bring to the employer, rather than what you want from the employer?

▨   Is your stated objective supported by the facts and accomplishments stated in the rest of your CV.

Summary

▨   If you choose to include a summary, is it no more than two or three sentences long?

▨   Does it include at least one substantial accomplishment that supports your employment goals?

▨   Does it include reference to some of your personality or behavioural traits that are critical to success in your field?

Keywords

▨   If you include a keyword section, this is probably the place to put it.

▨   Do you have experience in each of the areas you've listed?

▨   Can you illustrate your experience in conversation?

▨   Does it include commonly used synonyms for your skill sets that you have not already used in the body of the CV?

▨   Are the spelling and capitalization correct? (It's easy to make mistakes here, especially with acronyms.)

▨   Are there any other justifiable keywords you should add?

Body of CV

▨   Is your most relevant and qualifying work experience prioritized throughout the CV to lend strength to your application?

▨   Have you avoided wasting space with inessential employer names and addresses?

- Have you been suitably discreet with the name of your current employer?

- Have you omitted any reference to reasons for leaving a particular job?

- Have you removed all references to past, current, or desired salaries?

- Have you removed references to your date of availability?

Education

- Is education placed in the appropriate position? (It should be at the beginning of the CV if you have little or no work experience; at the end if you are established in your field and your practical experience now outweighs your degree.)

- Is your highest educational attainment shown first?

- Have you included professional courses that support your candidacy?

Chronology

- If you've done a chronological CV, is your work history stated in reverse chronological order, with the most recent employment coming at the head of the CV?

- Within this reverse chronology, does each company history start with details of your most senior position?

- Have you avoided listing irrelevant responsibilities or job titles?

- Does your CV emphasize the contributions, achievements, and problems you have successfully solved during your career? Is this content made prominent by underlining, bolding, italicizing etc?

- Does the body copy include at least one, and possibly two or three, laudatory third-party endorsements of your work?

- Have you avoided poor focus by eliminating all extraneous information? (This category includes anything that doesn't relate to your job objective, such as captaining the tiddlywinks team in kindergarten.)

- Have you included any volunteer or community service activities that can lend strength to your candidacy?

- Is the whole thing long enough to whet the reader's appetite for more details, yet short enough not to satisfy that hunger?

- Have you left out lists of reference and only included mention of the availability of references (if, of course, there is nothing more valuable to fill up the space)?

▨ Have you avoided treating your reader like a fool by highlighting the obvious (ie, heading your CV, 'CV')?

Writing Style

▨ Have you substituted short words for long words? And one word where previously there were two?

▨ Is your average sentence 10 to 20 words? Have you made sure that any sentence of more than 20 words is shortened or broken into two sentences?

▨ Have you kept every paragraph under five lines, with many paragraphs considerably shorter?

▨ Do your sentences begin, wherever possible, with the powerful action verbs and phrases from earlier in the chapter and from the CV examples?

▨ If you are in a technical field, have you weeded out as much of the jargon as possible?

Crossing the T's, Dotting the I's

Before your CV is finished, you have to make sure that your writing is as clear as possible. Three things guaranteed to annoy CV readers are incorrect spelling, poor grammar and improper syntax. Go back and check all these areas. If you feel uneasy about your CV's syntax, you had better get a third party involved.

An acquaintance of mine recently came up with an eminently practical solution to the 'style' problem. She went around to the local library, waited for a quiet moment, and got into conversation with the librarian, who subsequently agreed to give her CV the old once-over for spelling, grammar and syntax. You say you're on bad terms with the library because of all those overdue books? Surely you know someone whose opinion you trust in these matters. Enlist him or her. The point is that you must do everything you can to make the CV a 'perfect' document before it is sent out.

It simply isn't possible for even the most accomplished professional writer to go directly from final draft to print, so don't try it. Your pride of authorship will blind you to the blemishes, and that's a self-indulgence you can't afford.

You need some distance from your creative efforts to gain detachment and objectivity. There is no hard and fast rule about how long it takes to come up with the finished product. Nevertheless, if you think you have finished, leave it alone as long as you can – at least overnight. Then you can come back to it fresh and read almost as if it were meeting your eyes for the first time.

More Than One CV

Do you need more than one type of CV? It depends. Some people have a background that qualifies them for more than one job. If this applies to you, the process is as simple as changing your objective for various employers and rewriting along the lines directed in this chapter.

There is a case for all of us having CVs in more than one format. I was once engaged in an outplacement experiment for a group of professionals. With just a little extra work, we developed chronological, functional and combination CVs for everyone. The individuals concerned sent out the CV of their choice. Then, in those instances where there was no response, a different version of the CV was sent out. The result from just a different format: 8 per cent more interviews.

What's Next?

Almost home now. Save your notes, early drafts and, of course, the completed Questionnaire. This 'legwork' represents essential material you'll need in updating or revising future versions of your CV.

6

The Final Product

When it comes to clothes, style has a certain look. It has a feel that everyone recognizes but few can define accurately. Fortunately, with CVs, the situation is considerably simplified. There are definite rules to follow.

What Do You Mean I Need TWO CVs?

One of these rules is that in today's job market you can't get by with just one perfect CV any more. Why not? Because an astounding 78 per cent of CVs are read not by humans but by machines. Your CV may be an aesthetic marvel, beautiful to behold, but if it goes into the computer as gobbledy-gook, it won't do you much good. That's why you need two. This chapter will cover 'the traditional' CV – the CV designed for human eyes. The other kind, the 'computer-friendly' CV, is custom-designed to get through a computer scanner with data intact. It is such a hot topic in today's job market that I have devoted a separate chapter to it (see chapter 7, 'Is Your CV Computer-Friendly?'). Of course, the two kinds of CV do have certain basics in common. Let's start with those.

The Circular File

A lot of CVs get discarded without ever being properly read.

The average CV arrives on a desk with dozens of others, all of which require screening. Stand in the shoes of a day-in, day-out CV reader, and you can expect that your CV will get a maximum of 30 to 40 seconds of initial attention. And that's only if it's laid out well and looks clear.

What are the biggest complaints about those CVs that reach the wastepaper basket in record time?

Impossible to read. They have too much information crammed into the space and are therefore very difficult to read and hard on the eyes.

No coherence. Their layout is unorganized, illogical and uneven. In other words, they look shoddy and slapdash – and who wants an employee like that?

Typos. They are riddled with misspellings.

Here are some tips garnered from the best CVs in the UK that will help yours rise above the rest.

Get Your Computer Ready!

If you plan to be employable in the year 2003, you'd better wake up and smell the coffee – computer literacy is a must. Typing on typewriters doesn't cut it any more. Typing your CV or using a typing service is the equivalent of carving your CV in tablets of stone. It looks old-fashioned, and it must be done from start to finish every time you need to send one to someone else to customize it for another purpose. If you cannot now prepare your CV in a computer, engage the services of a good word-processing outfit while you get up to speed.

Hard Copy

Not all printers are created equal. When you use a computer or a word-processing service, insist that your letters be printed on a letter-quality printer or laser printer; either of these will give you high-quality print.

Fonts

A laser printer gives you a vast choice of print styles and quality fonts. Business is rapidly coming to accept the likes of Bookman, New York and Palatino as the norm. By the way, when choosing your font, stay away from heavy and bold for your body copy (although you may choose to take a more dramatic approach with key words or headlines). Bold type takes up too much space, and if it needs to be copied on the receiving end, it can blur and look dreadful. Avoid 'script' faces similar to handwriting; while they look attractive to the occasional reader, they are harder on the eyes of the person who reads any amount of business correspondence. Capitalized copy is tough on the eyes too; we tend to think it makes a powerful statement when all it does for the reader is cause eye strain.

How to Brighten the Page

Once you decide on a font, stick with it, because more than one on a page looks confusing. You can do plenty to liven up the visual impact of the page within the variations of the font you have chosen.

Most fonts come in a selection of regular, bold and italic. Good traditional-style CVs try to take advantage of this – they can vary the impact of key words with italics, underline important phrases, or use boldface or capital letters in titles for additional emphasis. (Computer-friendly CVs, by contrast, keep type variations to a minimum.)

You will notice from the examples in this book that the best CVs pick two or three typographical variations and stick with them. For example, a writer who wants to emphasize personality traits might italicize only those words or phrases that describe these aspects; this way the message gets a double fixing in the reader's mind.

Proofing

When you have the printed CV in hand, you *must* proofread it. Check everything, from beginning to end.

- Is everything set up the way you want it?
- Are there any typographical errors?
- Is all the punctuation correct?
- Has everything been underlined, capitalized, emboldened, italicized and indented exactly as you specified?

Once you read the CV, try your best to get someone else to review it as well. A third party will always provide more objectivity than you can, and can catch errors you might miss.

Appearance Checklist

- Have you remembered that the first glance and the first feel of your CV can make a powerful impression?

- Have you used only one side of the page?

- If you have employed more than one page for your CV, did you check to make sure that your name, address and telephone number are on every page?

- If more than one page, did you paginate your CV ('1 of 2' at the bottom of the first page, and so on)?

Choosing Your Paper

Quality and care have a look and a feel to them that are loud and clear. Quality paper always makes a favourable impression on the person holding the page.

Beyond the aesthetics, there are plenty of reasons to use quality paper for your copies. The right paper will take the ink better, giving you clean, sharp print resolution.

While you should not skimp on paper cost, neither should you be talked into buying the most expensive available. Indeed, in some fields (health care and education come to mind), too ostentatious a paper can cause a negative impression. The idea is to create a feeling of understated quality.

Paper can come in different weights and textures. Good CV quality paper has a weight designation of between 16 and 25 lbs. Lighter, and you run the risk of appearing nonchalant, unconcerned about the personal 'I-printed-this-especially-for-you' aspect of the CV. Heavier, and the paper is unwieldly, like light cardboard.

As for colour, white is considered to be the prime choice. Cream is also acceptable, and I'm assured that some of the pale pastel shades can be both attractive and effective. Personally, I think that most professionals just don't show up in the best light when dressed in pink – call me old-fashioned if you will.

Such pastel shades were originally used to make CVs stand out. But now that everyone is so busy standing out from the crowd in Magenta and Passionate Puce, you might find it more original to stand out in white or cream. Both colours reflect the clean-cut, corporate conservatism of our time. White and cream are straightforward, no-nonsense colours.

Cover letter stationery should always match the colour and weight of your CV. To send a white cover letter – even if it is written on your personal stationery – with a cream CV is gauche, and detracts from the powerful statement you are trying to make.

A good idea, in fact, is to print some cover-letter stationery when you produce your finished CV. The letterhead should be in the same font and on the same kind of paper, and should copy the contact data from your CV.

Copies

Every CV should be printed on standard, A4-size paper. If the original is set up like this, you will be able to take it to a good-quality copy shop for photocopying. Technology has improved so much in this area that as long as the latest equipment is used, you should have no problems. (Bear in mind, though, that the computer-friendly CV is always an original – to ensure a clean scan.)

If you choose to have your CV printed – rather than photocopied – for whatever reason, you must go to a multi-lith or photo-offset printer. Both produce really smart, professional copies. Of the two – unless you are printing more than two hundred copies – photo-offset will be proportionately more expensive. Shop around for prices, as printers vary quite dramatically in their price structures. While you are shopping, ask to see samples of their CV work – they are bound to have some. If not, keep shopping.

Word-processing services can produce not only the CV and cover letter stationery but also the required number of copies of both, as can a multi-lith or offset printer. There are both local and national companies that can provide these services.

The Final Checklist

■ Have you used a good-quality paper?

■ Is the paper standard A4 size (210mm × 297mm)?

■ Have you used white, off-white or cream-coloured paper?

■ If your CV is more than one page, have you stapled the pages together (one staple in the top left-hand corner)?

■ Is your cover letter written on stationery that matches your CV?

7

Is Your CV Computer-Friendly?

Computers have infiltrated human resources offices. Here's how they'll affect your job search.

Part One: Is Your CV Scanner-Friendly?

Review Your CV

You say you already have a great CV. After all, it helped you land your most recent job, and the one before that, and the one before that. Now all you have to do is update it – add your latest job title, your responsibilities, the beginning and end dates of your employment, special projects you worked on, advanced training you received, and the like – and your CV will be ready to send in the mail, or put into your briefcase.

Right?

Well, it may not be that simple. If your CV looks exactly as it did a few years ago, then merely updating the information and keeping the old format may not be good enough. The CV that opened corporate doors for you five years ago, or even last year, may not work for you now. In fact, it *may not even get read*.

CVs in the Computer Age

Computers are being used to scan and store your CV electronically; they are being used to read help-wanted advertisements on Web site databases, and to search the CV banks on those same Web sites. In fact, the next HR professional to scan your CV is likely to be a PC or Mac instead of a mortal. The problem is that computers look at things differently than we do, which creates the new challenge of making your CV attractive to digital eyes.

Since the mid-1980s, when the technology was first introduced, the number of companies using computer-based automated tracking systems has climbed steadily. The technology has become so pervasive that by mid-1997, 85 per cent of companies surveyed had some sort of automated CV-tracking system in place.

The Way It Was

It seems like only yesterday that most companies manually read, assessed, coded, and filed all of the CVs they received. When a position opened up, an HR representative would look through all the files for likely prospects. The most promising candidates would then be invited for an interview.

In its day, this was a pretty good system. It was especially nice when you, the applicant, made the short list of prospects. Of course, sometimes the manual system didn't work in your favour. Once in a while, an HR professional who didn't like your choice of stationery, or thought that your alma mater wasn't covered in quite enough ivy, would code your CV unfavourably or even put it in the circular file. Or perhaps a recruiter thought of you immediately when a job opened up, but couldn't lay his hands on your CV quick enough to call you before the position was filled – perhaps because another supervisor, who was winging her way to Europe, had the CV in her briefcase.

Often, under the manual tracking system, CVs were misplaced, miscoded, or misfiled, never to be found again. Frequently, a perfectly good CV was buried under so much paper that it just wasn't worth anybody's trouble to unearth it. It used to be common to discard all CVs every six months.

The problems with manual CV tracking became especially apparent when corporate cutbacks caused companies to reduce their HR staff. With three people doing the job of ten, it simply wasn't possible to access, code, file, and retrieve CVs in an orderly, effective fashion. Corporations sometimes missed their chance to hire the best candidate for the job because the appropriate CV didn't make it to the top of the heap, out of the filing cabinet, or sometimes even out of the envelope.

So What's New?

These days, solicited and unsolicited CVs alike are increasingly likely to be filed in electronic databases rather than in metal cabinets. Under this system, no matter how large the computerized stack of CVs, any computer user can pull up appropriate ones with a few keystrokes or clicks of a mouse. The challenge for you is to get your CV into a shape and style that:

■ can be scanned, digitized and stored electronically, once received through the mail;

■ can be transmitted, via e-mail, to specific individuals or companies;

■ can be loaded onto public CV databases.

In the first instance, your printed/hard copy CV would wing through the mail to a company. There, a functionary in the HR department runs it through a scanner; this digitizes your CV and allows it to be stored electronically in the company's database.

In the second instance, you create a digitized CV yourself. You use this electronic/digitized version of your CV to e-mail to companies at their Web sites, to specific executives at their e-mail addresses, and to log it into the proliferating array of CV banks. We'll discuss digitized CV formats in greater detail later in this chapter.

The Computer Recruiter

What should you know about the technology that just might be responsible for deciding whether or not you're invited to that next job interview?

Like their human counterparts, computers have their good traits and their bad. The good part is that computers don't care what school you went to, whether or not you're married or how old you are. In a computerized search for qualified candidates, there's no room for human prejudice or error. Your name either pops up or it doesn't. Either way, it's nothing personal; it's strictly an automated decision. The bad news is that, if you're using a traditional CV that isn't computer-friendly (and, as you'll see, most traditional CVs aren't), you name probably won't pop up. A CV that was perfectly fine before automated tracking and the advent of the Internet will most likely leave you in the dust today.

New CV Rules

If you want to impress a human recruiter before he or she even reads your CV, make sure that your envelope matches your stationery, that the address is well typed and that the layout catches the eye. Similarly, if you want to impress a computerized recruiter, you want to first be confident that optical character recognition (OCR) software can properly read the font in which your CV was written. This is because CVs are scanned, not typed, into databases. A computer can scan a CV in a couple of minutes. The danger is that if your CV was constructed to fit the old rules of CV writing (the more eye-catching, the better), the scanner and OCR software may get confused and miss some critical information.

The human resources person who is assigned to check the CV once it's scanned may or may not have the time, or the know-how, to undo the damage; he or she may not even notice that critical elements are missing or distorted. It's therefore your responsibility to make sure the computer scans your CV properly. The rules that apply to making your CV scannable will also apply to the creation of your electronic CV; again, we'll discuss this later in the chapter.

Keep It Simple

Here's how you can help the computer (that is, the scanner and OCR software) do its job.

- Always send a clean, crisp, original CV. Even photocopies that look fine to your eye may be too fuzzy to scan.

- Put your name on the first line of your CV, with nothing else before it. If you put your address first, then your new moniker might well be '555 Bayville Drive'!

- When choosing a font, stick to common ones, such as Times, Univers, Palatino, Optima, Courier, Futura, ITC Bookman and New Century Schoolbook. Avoid exotic or serif fonts that the OCR software might confuse or might not recognize.

- Keep the point sizes between 10 and 14. Type that is too large or too small may not scan properly.

- If you want to use boldface, save it for headings. While most OCR software can read boldface, some can't, so don't take the risk of using it for your name, address, telephone number or e-mail address.

- Leave out decorative lines, particularly vertical lines. Or, if you use them, do so judiciously, leaving a least a quarter of an inch of space around them. Otherwise, you're liable to confuse the software, which often can't tell the difference between lines and letters.

Here are some things that are guaranteed to make your CVs computer-*un*friendly and that you should always avoid:

- Double columns and other complicated layouts. The scanner can only read from left to right – and it's not going to appreciate your creativity.

- Coloured paper. Use white or light beige paper; save the pink and blue stuff for personal letters announcing your new job. A key to scannability is to get the greatest possible amount of contrast between the background and the letters.

- Odd-sized paper. You should always use A4-size paper.

- Graphics, shading, ellipses, brackets or parentheses.

- Italics, script or underlining.

- Compressing letters. It isn't worth cramming a lot of information onto one page if the computer can't scan it.

- Stapling, folding or faxing your CV. Send your CV, unstapled and unfolded, in an A4-size envelope – or hand-deliver it.

Getting the Computer's Attention

If you've taken care to update your CV so that the computer can read it, the next step is to be sure the computer can find you when it's looking for somebody with your skills.

A computer isn't able to interpret your CV and make judgements about your suitability – you have to convince it. And the way to do that is by using keywords.

Here's the Key

A keyword is a word or phrase the software will search for when looking for job candidates. It is any label that can be used to describe you, or the job. The keywords are first chosen by the software user.

Also known as 'talents', keywords are not action words like 'oversaw', 'initiated', and 'installed', with which we've all saturated CVs in the past. They are nouns used to label the job and yourself. They encompass technical jargon, specific skills that relate to the job, degrees you hold, job titles, personal traits and other buzzwords.

If you're in doubt about which keywords to include on your CV, then check the classifieds for positions similar to the one you're looking for, and take note of which nouns crop up repeatedly – skills, traits and so on. Keep a running list of possibilities from which you can pick and choose, depending on the job you're applying for. Also, be open to collecting new keywords while reading the want ads (or during interviews) to add to your CV. If employers are looking for an Engineer of Excellence with a diploma in Delightfulness who can attach a Wonderwidget to a Maximachine, then those are your keywords!

How to Use Keywords

Of course, it behoves you to make sure that your keywords describe who you are and what you know, and that you're not just fudging it. Telling the computer anything it might want to hear, regardless of whether it's fact or fiction, isn't the best policy. At worst, you could tip off a prospective employer who might wonder why somebody with an engineering degree is also an expert in education, psychology, business, theatre, law and medicine.

Scanning software has limits on how many keywords it can retain, so keep the list down to a reasonable length – say, 80 words or so. And make sure the most important words go first. The scanning software won't weight your placement of keywords, but the subsequent human eyes will.

The art of making computer-friendly CVs is still brand new, and we are all feeling our way, to a certain extent. One neat technique that people are just starting to use (and are apparently finding very effective) is to place a box filled with applicable keywords/talents that might not appear in the body of your CV either near the top or at the bottom of your CV. There is absolutely no hard and fast rule on this yet, but you might find including it at the bottom of a CV less intrusive. For example, here's the talent box used by an HR professional who was able to reveal an additional bunch of skills, and make her CV more computer-friendly.

> Talents: team leader, people and communication skills, hardware needs evaluation, database management, client orientation, word-processing, spreadsheets, arbitration, manual writing, union negotiation, downsizing.

Part Two: Is Your CV Internet-Friendly?

Is the Internet the answer to a job seeker's prayer, or the emperor's new suit of clothes? Some tout it as a speedy way to end your job hunt, since it gives you global exposure. ('But,' you say, 'I only want to work in Manchester!') Others discount the Internet, claiming you have about one chance in a hundred of getting a job this way. Neither view is right; the issue isn't that simple or clear-cut, since little in the modern world of work is unarguably right or wrong.

The most practical way to look at the Internet, in the context of your job hunt, is as a means of communication that simply gives you a handful of new ways to get in contact with potential employers and headhunters. You can:

■ Meet and talk electronically with other job hunters, or even job hunting and career experts.

▨ Network with your professional peers in newsgroups. Newsgroups are ongoing discussion groups with a narrow focus aimed at people who share a common interest. There are newsgroups for every profession, from accountants to zoologists.

▨ Approach potential employers through their own Web sites. This method may get your CV closer scrutiny, since the flow of applicants online is lighter than through traditional methods. By the same token, you might also get a much swifter response, since your manipulation of the new technology can tag you as a potentially more desirable employee. Remember that even if a company has job openings but isn't advertising specifically for your skill sets, you can still query it.

▨ Scan the job banks. These are nothing more than the help-wanted section of newspapers published in an electronic medium. Instead of reading the ads for an hour, your computer can generate matching jobs in seconds or minutes, which makes life easier for you.

▨ Load your CV into a CV bank, which functions just like SITUATIONS VACANT ads in your local newspaper. Although in the past I have been strongly against advertising your availability in print, since no employer or headhunter has the time or inclination to read these ads, using this same technique in this new medium changes the picture in two ways. First, the Head of Human Resources for your local Barclays Bank is still unlikely to peruse these data banks, but he now has electronic servants who will. Second, headhunters do scan the CV banks as yet another way of digging up that hard-to-find professional for a client.

The electronic world can give you a number of practical ways to pursue your job hunt. But keep in mind that the headhunters use this new medium as just another way of completing a job search – and you should do the same.

The rest of this chapter will concern itself with how electronic CVs can help you in your job search.

The Technical Side of an Electronic CV

The oldest, most common and soon-to-be outmoded method of compiling an electronic CV is to write and save it in a text format (often referred to as ASCII). The benefit of this format is that there are no formatting commands, so anyone can read the document, regardless of the software application/program they are using. You can also cut and paste parts of a text document into the information boxes you'll find on many CV bank Web sites. To create a text/ASCII format CV, create a new CV in whatever application you are using (or make a copy of an existing one). Then, as you exit the document, use the 'Save As' option to save it in text/ASCII format. Depending on the application you are using, the computer may advise you that your actions will destroy the formatting; ignore the warning and save it as text/ASCII anyway.

After this, your CV will now look like a dog's dinner. Unfortunately, there are only a few things you can do to improve the look of a text CV. You can use a text editor to edit your CV to look more like your real CV. Since e-mail allows no more than 70 characters to a line, you will most likely have to reformat your document. Similarly, if you have created space on your CV using the tab key, you'll want to redo it using the space bar instead. Apart from these guidelines, the dos and don'ts are the same that apply to making your CV scanner-friendly, which were addressed earlier in the chapter.

HTML

HTML is the acronym for Hypertext Markup Language, the wave of the electronic CV future. HTML allows you to create sharply designed and formatted CVs. It does this by placing your wording between tags, parentheses and slashes that indicate certain kinds of formatting. These tags allow another person's (read: human resource recruiter) electronic browser to translate the accompanying data into words, graphics, format and even colour, either on a screen or as a printout. This makes HTML extremely useful in electronic CV writing since, when printed, your electronic CV will stack up against traditionally printed and mailed CVs.

HTML uses two different types of tags: those that identify and format the content of your CV so that it looks good, and those that allow you to condense your CV into its critical essentials, so that the search engines other people use when searching the CV databases will pick you out of the crowd. These condensed essentials, called metatags, will not be seen on your actual CV, and are only visible to the search engine (read: the software that searches the CV database). While HTML coding might only seem like a good idea for computer science graduates, it is in fact getting easier and easier to create your own HTML CV. (You might even remember, if not admit to, an era when 'WYSIWYG' seemed equally obscure.) Many current word processors allow you to save text in HTML format, and software developers have made a whole bunch of tools available to HTML wanna-bes.

Final Considerations

One issue to consider is that of confidentiality. As with any distribution medium, once the CV is out of your hands, you no longer have control over what happens to it. So it's wise to evaluate the relative compatibility of your needs and how they match the operational realities of the different databases.

For example, if you don't want people to know where you live, or to be able to contact you directly at home or work (it's never a good idea to have a work contact number on a CV), act accordingly. Get a voice mail service for telephone calls. Don't imagine for a moment that recruiters are going to use your e-mail address, though; if you look like a good fit, the phone is still the quickest means of cutting to the chase. Conversely, if e-mail is your only means of contact, you can expect to miss hearing about a few opportunities. And just as you would never use your current employer's time or phone to pursue a job contact, don't use their e-mail either. Depending on where you live, it is quite legal for an employer to monitor your e-mail.

If you are employed, identify your current employer as 'a major bank', a mid-sized service company', or 'an international pharmaceutical conglomerate'. Not only will you not get unwanted calls at work, but you won't run the risk of your current boss learning of your search before it suits your needs.

Other confidentiality considerations can be answered at each individual site. When you get to a particular Web site, one of the first things you will do is to look for FAQs (frequently asked questions) to find out:

- Who can access this database?

- Can you block access to certain employers or people?

- Are you notified when someone downloads your CV?

Apart from the confidentiality issue, you will want to know if you can get access to your CV to update it, change it or delete it. If not, you'll want to know the procedure for achieving each of these ends. Some CV banks will charge you for updates.

Internet Myths

This question of updating your CV brings us to three areas of Internet lore you need to be aware of:

1. You will be told that a good database will delete your CV after three to six months if you don't update it. This is absolute drivel! Constant CV updating is driven by commercial concerns. No one on God's earth needs a CV updated every 90 days! The other argument for deleting CVs that aren't updated is that, once employed, you won't want to get calls from other employers. Again, absolute drivel! Happily employed or not,

wouldn't you rather hear about exciting new jobs that fit your skill sets, and have the opportunity to pursue or reject them, *than never hear about them at all*? Of course you'll want to hear about every opportunity, if not for today, then for tomorrow, if your current employment no longer suits your career needs, or your company is about to downsize. You want to get your CV out there, full stop! And there's no reason to limit your CVs to services that limit your exposure.

2.   You will be told that a one-page CV is no longer the rule. Now, while one of the strengths of the Internet as a publishing medium is that space is limitless, that does not in any way affect the dictum that when it comes to CVs, shorter is better. Yes, your CV can be longer, but that won't stop human eyes from getting bored by the end of page two, just as CV screeners have always done. So no matter who tells you this, use your common sense and keep it short and succinct.

3.   You will also be told to put your CV on only two to four CV databases, because employers are frustrated at finding the same candidates at every database they check. Excuse me? An employer can check a hundred databases, but you can only use a maximum of four? Here are the facts: as an employer, if I like your background, I'll be happy to find you. If I like your background and I find you in a number of places, it will make recruiting you more difficult since I'll likely have more competition from other employers. On the other hand, if I keep finding your CV and you *don't* match my needs, it shouldn't matter if I find you in two or two hundred databases.

If you want to take advantage of the Internet as a means of CV creation and/or distribution, there are services out there that will take care of this business for you for a fee. If you choose to do this, there are a handful of questions you'll need to answer for yourself to make an informed decision.

■   Exactly what is the service? Will they write the CV for you? Will it be in text, HTML or multimedia? (You really don't need multimedia unless you are in graphic design and want to show your command of the new technology, in which case you'll have to walk the walk and talk the talk. On the other hand, HTML is state of the art and will show you in your best light.)

■   How much will everything cost?

■   Is there a charge to edit or update your CV once it is created, or to create a slightly different CV that emphasizes other skill sets? Once you have been in the job market for a few years, you're probably qualified for more than one job, which means that you'll need a separate CV that will highlight those skills.

How is your CV marketed? Find out how many sites the company will post your CV on, and whether or not they will repost it if that site discards your CV after a predetermined period of time.

What, if anything, will you be charged if you get a job as a result of the service?

Internet CV Etiquette

Sending out your CV through another medium (e-mail rather than regular mail) requires that you adhere to a few simple rules if you want that CV to be seen and acted upon.

1. While some companies will advertise their positions electronically, they don't all accept electronic CV submissions. So when you see a position and want to apply for it, read the instructions carefully and follow them.

2. If you are applying for a job listed in a job bank, it will always be headed with a job title, and will often have a reference number as well. Be sure to use these in your cover letter. For example:

   Ref: Internal Auditor, Ref # 123, Monster Board Job Bank

   Make reference to the same in the first paragraph of your cover letter. For example:

   Dear Ms Jones:

   I have long admired the work of Pzifer, Inc., so when I came across your job posting for an Internal Auditor (Ref # 123) on the Monster Board Job Bank, it too me two seconds to decide I had to throw my hat in the ring.

3. When you send a CV in more traditional circumstances, you will typically send two documents: the cover letter and the CV. When e-mailing two documents, they are guaranteed to become separated; so send the cover letter and CV as one document. It is also courteous and wise to mention that you will forward a copy of your communication through the mail. Remember to do so! Of course, your mail version will be compatible with its format: that is two repeat documents, a cover letter and a CV.

Still Confused?

If you are still confused, ask. Most people on the Web are new to it, and you'll find that nearly everyone (except some of those old-time elitist Web Neanderthals) is pleasant and helpful.

The best and first place to go is the site I have created to help you use the Internet effectively in your job hunt, *www.careerbrain.com*. At Careerbrain, I will answer your questions, teach you how to use the Internet, show you the most effective electronic tools, and provide you with a constantly changing menu of Internet chat, TV, radio and self-awareness tests. You can also send me questions on any aspect of CV writing, job hunting or lifetime career management. You might also use one of my other books, *Online Job Hunting: Great answers to tough questions* (£8.99, Kogan Page). This essential book takes you through an electronic jobsearch step by step and will answer all your questions.

Double Trouble

Now that you know how to get the computer's attention, be sure you don't get the computer's attention more than once because you've sent one too many CVs.

Suppose that, in the old days, you wanted to work for Big London Publishing. You might have sent one CV to the Editorial Director in application for a job as an editorial assistant; another to the Operations Manager, touting yourself as the best warehouse worker ever; and still another to the Customer Service Manager, revealing your years of intensive telemarketing experience.

So why not send three CVs to Big London Publishing now? Because the CV-tracking computer in the Human Resources Department is a know-it-all and a tattletale.

While the human supervisors of old might have read their copies of your CVs and never compared notes, the computer is all-knowing. With too many CVs and too many work histories in its files, the computer is likely to peg you as somebody who is at best unfocused about his or her career direction – and at worst a pathological liar.

If you do want to submit more than one CV in application for multiple jobs and you're unsure of whether or not the company is using a computerized tracking system, minimize the risks. Be sure that you don't follow up the CV that sells you as an experienced reference book editor with another that delineates your years of experience as an expert book packer.

8

Cover Letters

Do you ever receive junk mail? Of course you do. Who doesn't?

Junk mail. Tons of it have probably made it into your mailbox over the years. Now, what do you do with the stuff marked 'Occupant'? Either junk it without reading, or junk it after a quick glance. That's why they call it junk mail! It never gets the attention a personal letter does.

The days when you could dash your CV off to 'Personnel', with a clear conscience and no personal note, are long gone. It will be read by the lowest of the low, someone who probably can't even spell 'professional'. You will be consigning it to the mass graveyard that all other impersonally addressed CVs reach.

Your cover letter is the personalizing factor in the presentation of an otherwise essentially impersonal document – your CV. A good cover letter sets the stage for the reader to accept your CV as something special.

So your first effort with a cover letter is to find an individual to whom you can address it. That shows you have focus, and guarantees that a specific individual will open and read it. It also means you have someone to ask for by name when you do your follow-up – important when you are interviewing hunting.

Your target is someone who can either hire you or refer you to someone who can – and management rather than personnel offers you a much better chance of achieving that goal.

Your cover letter will either be sent to someone as a result of a prior conversation, or sent 'cold' – with no prior conversation. You will see how to handle both these eventualities as we progress through the chapter.

When the envelope is opened, your cover letter is the first thing seen. It can make an indelible first impression. I'm not saying that it will get you the job (or even land you the interview), but it will help you along the way by getting that CV read with something akin to serious attention.

The higher up the professional ladder you climb, the more important cover letters become. For the person using written communication in the execution of daily duties (and who doesn't these days?), this letter becomes a valuable vehicle for demonstrating needed job skills.

Cover Letter Rules

Cover letters are brief, never more than a page. Write more, and you will be labelled as an unorganized windbag. You should always try to follow accepted business letter protocol, with the date, employer's name and address first. Space can be at such a premium, however, that you can dispense with the formality and begin with a normal salutation: 'Dear _____'. Stick with the protocol when you can, ignore it when you have to.

The following four steps will help you create the body of the letter.

Step One

Grab your reader's attention. Do this by using quality stationery. If you don't have personal stationery, use some of the sheets you have bought to have your CV printed on. That way, letter and CV will match and give an impression of balance and continuity. Basic business letters should be laid out according to the accepted standards, like this:

[YOUR ADDRESS/LETTERHEAD
AND TELEPHONE NUMBER]

[DATE]

[ADDRESSEE ADDRESS]
[SALUTATION]

Recently I have been researching the leading local companies in data communications. My search has been for companies that are respected in the field, and who provide ongoing training programmes. The name of DataLink Products keeps coming up as a top company.

I am an experienced voice and data communications specialist with a substantial background in IBM environments. If you have an opening for someone in this area you will see that my CV demonstrates a person of unusual dedication, efficiency and drive.

My experience and achievements include:

■ The complete redesign of a data communications network, projected to increase efficiency companywide by some 12 per cent.

- The installation and troubleshooting of a Defender II call-back security system for a dial-up network.

I enclose a copy of my CV, and look forward to examining any of the ways you feel my background and skills would benefit DataLink Products. While I prefer not to use my employer's time taking personal calls at work, with discretion you can reach me at 020 8123 4567 to initiate contact. Let's talk!

Yours,

[SIGNATURE]
[TYPED NAME]

Step Two

Generate interest with the content. You do this by addressing the letter to someone by name and quickly explaining what you have to offer: the first sentence grabs attention, the rest of the paragraph gives the reader the old one-two punch. The rule is: say it strong and say it straight; don't pussy-foot around.

A little research, for example, can get your letter off to a fast start.

I came across the enclosed article in _Newsweek_ and thought it might interest you. It encouraged me to do a little research on your company. The research convinced me of two things: you are the kind of people I want to be associated with, and I have the kind of qualifications you can use.

Of course, in the real world, we don't all apply for jobs with companies that are featured in the big magazines. Here are some other examples:

I have been following the performance of your fund in _Mutual Funds Newsletter_. The record over the last three years shows strong portfolio management. Considering my experience with one of your competitors, I know I could make significant contributions.

Recently, I have been researching the local _____ industry. My search has been for companies that are respected in the field and that provide ongoing training programmes. The name _____ keeps coming up as a top company.

With the scarcity of qualified and motivated (_your desired job title_) that exists today, I felt sure that it would be valuable for us to communicate.

I would like the opportunity to put my _____ years of _____ experience to work for _____ .

Within the next few weeks I will be moving from London to Edinburgh. Having researched the companies in my field in my new home town, I know that you are the people I want to talk to.

The state of the art in _____ changes so rapidly that it is tough for most professionals to keep up. I am the exception. I am eager to bring my experience to bear for your company.

I am applying for a position with your company because I know you will find my background and drive interesting.

This letter and the attached CV are in application for employment with _____ .

If you are looking for summer jobs:

In six weeks I shall be finishing my second year at John Carroll University. I am interested in working for your firm during the summer because …

As the summer season gets under way, I know you will be looking for extra help.

I am an undergraduate looking for some real world experience during the summer break.

I am very interested in becoming one of your summer placements.

If you are writing as the result of a referral, say so and quote the person's name if appropriate.

Our mutual colleague, John Stanovich, felt my skills and abilities would be valuable to your company.

The manager of your Edinburgh branch, Pamela Bronson, has suggested I contact you regarding the opening for a _____ .

I received your name from Henry Charles last week. I spoke to Mr Charles regarding career opportunities with _____ and he suggested I contact you. In case the CV he forwarded is caught up in the mail, I enclose another.

Arthur Gold, your office manager and my neighbour, thought I should contact you about the upcoming opening in your accounting department.

If you are writing as the result of an online job posting or a newspaper advertisement, you should mention both the source and the date – and remember not to abbreviate advertisement to 'ad'.

I read your advertisement job posting on CareerBrain.com yesterday and after researching your company, felt I had to write.

I am responding to your recent job listing on your Web site offering the opportunity to manage accounts receivable.

In re: your advertisement in the *Glasgow Dispatch* on Sunday, the eighth of November. As you will notice, my entire background matches your requirements.

Your notice regarding a _____ in the *Liverpool News* caught my eye, and your company name caught my attention.

This letter and attached CV is in response to your advertisement in the *Times Globe*.

If you are writing to an executive search firm:

(**Note:** In a cover letter to executive search firms, unlike any other circumstances, you *must* mention your salary and, if appropriate, your willingness to relocate.)

I am forwarding my CV to you because I understand you specialize in representing clients in the _____ field.

Please find the enclosed CV. As a specialist in the _____ field, I felt you might be interested in the skills of a _____ .

Among your many clients may be one or two who are seeking a candidate for a position as a _____ .

My salary is in the mid-20s, with appropriate benefits. I would be willing to relocate for the right opportunity.

Step Three

Now turn that interest into desire. First, make a bridge that ties you to a general job category or work area. It starts with phrases like:

I am writing because …

My reason for contacting you is …

This letter is to introduce me and to explore any need you might have in the _____ area.

… should this be the case, you may be interested to know …

If you are seeking a _____ , you will be interested to know …

I would like to talk to you about your personnel needs and my ability to contribute to your department's goals.

If you have an opening for someone in this area, you will see that my CV demonstrates a person of unusual dedication, efficiency and drive.

Then call attention to your merits with a short paragraph that highlights one or two of your special contributions or achievements.

I have an economics background (LSE) and a strong analytical approach to market fluctuations. This combination has enabled me to consistently pick the new technology flotations that are the backbone of the growth-oriented mutual fund.

Similar statements applicable to your area of expertise will give your letter more personal punch. Include any qualifications, contributions and attributes that qualify you as someone with talent to offer. If an advertisement (or a conversation with a potential employer) revealed an aspect of a particular job opening that is not addressed in your CV, it can easily be covered in the cover letter.

I notice from your advertisement that audio and video training experience would be a plus. In addition to the qualifications stated in my enclosed CV, I have over five years' experience writing and producing sales and management training materials in both these media.

Whether you bullet or list your achievements in short, staccato sentences will be determined in part by the amount of space available to you on the page.

Step Four

Here's where your letter turns that desire into action. You want to make the reader dash straight to your CV, then call you in for an interview. You achieve this with brevity.

Your one-page letter shouldn't be longer than four or five paragraphs, or two hundred words. Leave the reader wanting more. This final step tells the reader that you want to talk. It explains when, where and how you can be contacted. Then tell the reader that you intend to follow up at a certain point in time if contact has not been established by then. This can encourage a decision on the reader's part to initiate action, which is what you want.

Useful phrases include:

I look forward to discussing our mutual interests further.

It would be a pleasure to give you more data about my qualifications and experience.

I will be in your area around the 20th, and will call you prior to that date to arrange a meeting.

I hope to speak with you further and will call the week of the 20th to follow up.

The chance to meet with you would be a privilege and a pleasure. To this end I will call you on the 20th.

I look forward to speaking with you further and will call in the next few days to see when our schedules will permit a face-to-face meeting.

May I suggest a personal meeting where you can have the opportunity to examine the person behind the CV?

My credentials and achievements are a matter of record that I hope you will examine in depth when we meet.

I look forward to examining any of the ways you feel my background and skills would benefit your organization. I look forward to hearing from you.

CVs help you sort out the probables from the possibles, but they are no way to judge the true calibre of an individual. I should like to meet you and demonstrate that I have the personality that makes for a successful _____ .

My CV can highlight my background and accomplishments. My drive, willingness and manageability, however, can come out only during a face-to-face meeting. With this in mind, I shall call you on the 20th, if I don't hear from you before.

After reading my CV, you will know something about my background. Yet you will still need to determine whether I am the one to help with the current problems and challenges. I would like an interview to discuss my ability to contribute.

I am anxious to meet and discuss any potential opportunities further. I will make myself available for an interview at a time convenient to you.

I expect to be in your area on Tuesday and Wednesday of next week and wonder which day would be best for you. I will call to find out.

With my training and hands-on experience, I know I can contribute to your company, and want to speak with you about it in person. When may we meet?

I feel certain that I can contribute and that I can convince you I can. I look forward to a meeting at your convenience.

You can reach me at 020 8123 4567 to arrange an interview. I know that your time investment in meeting with me will be amply repaid.

Thank you for your time and consideration. I hope to hear from you shortly.

May I call you for an interview in the next few days?

I am sure that our mutual interests will be served by speaking further, and am convinced a personal meeting will assure you of my ability, willingness and manageability. I look forward to meeting with you.

A brief phone call will establish whether or not we have mutual interest. Recognizing the demands of your schedule, I will make that call within the week.

As many employed people are concerned about their CVs going astray; you may wish to add:

In the meantime, I would appreciate my application being treated as confidential, as I am currently employed.

Just as you worked to get the opening right, labour over the close. It is the reader's last remembrance of you, so make it strong, make it tight, and make it obvious that you are serious about entering into meaningful conversation.

Writing the Cover Letter

Keep your sentences short – an average of 14 words per sentence is about right. Likewise, your paragraphs should be concise and to the point. In cover letters, paragraphs can often be a single sentence, and should never be longer than two or three sentences. This makes the page more inviting for the harried reader, by providing adequate white space to ease eye strain.

Short words work best here also. They speak more clearly than those polysyllabic behemoths that say more about your self-image problems than your abilities. A good approach is to think in terms of sending a telegram, where every word must work its hardest.

While abiding by accepted grammatical rules, you should punctuate for readability rather than strictly following E. B. White or the *Oxford Manual of Style*. Get by on commas, dashes – and full stops. And in between the punctuation marks use the action verbs and phrases that breathe life into your work.

Cover Letter Examples

Notice that the italicized areas come directly from the previous examples. You too can write a dynamic cover letter with the old 'cut and paste' technique. Then all you have to do is make the minor adjustments necessary to personalize your letter:

James Sharpe   16 November 20__
123 Anystreet
Anytown AT1 0BB

Dear Mr Bell,

Recently I have been researching the leading local companies in data communications. My search has been for companies that are respected in the field, and who provide ongoing training programmes. DataLink Products keeps coming up as a top company.

I am an experienced voice and data communications specialist with a substantial background in IBM environments. *If you have an opening for someone in this area you will see that my CV demonstrates a person of unusual dedication, efficiency and drive.*

My experience and achievements include:

- complete redesign of a data communications network, projected to increase efficiency companywide some 12 per cent;
- the installation and troubleshooting of a Defender II call-back security system for a dial-up network.

I enclose a copy of my CV, and look forward to examining any of the ways you feel my background and skills would benefit DataLink Products. While I prefer not to use my employer's time taking personal calls at work, with discretion I can be reached at 020 8123 4567 to initiate contact. Let's talk!

Yours truly

James Sharpe

James Sharpe

In response to the advertisement, here is an example using a different selection of phrases.

Jane Swift   16 November 20__
123 Anystreet
Anytown AT1 0BB

Dear Ms Pena,

I have always followed the performance of your fund in _Mutual Funds Newsletter._

Recently, your notice regarding a Market Analyst in Investors Daily caught my eye – and your company name caught my attention – because your record over the last three years shows exceptional portfolio management. With my experience with one of your competitors, I know I could make significant contributions.

I would like to talk to you about your personnel needs and how I would be able to contribute to your department's goals.

An experienced market analyst, I have an economics background and a strong analytical approach to market fluctuations. This combination has enabled me to consistently pick the new technology flotations that are the backbone of the growth-oriented mutual fund.

For example, I first recommended Fidelity Magellan six years ago. More recently, my clients have been strongly invested in Pacific Horizon Growth (in the high-risk category), and Fidelity Growth and Income (for the cautious investor).

Those following my advice over the last six years have owned shares in funds which consistently outperformed the market.

I know that CVs help you sort out the probables from the possibles, but they are no way to judge the personal calibre of an individual. I would like to meet with you and demonstrate that, along with the credentials, I have the personality that makes for a successful team player.

Yours sincerely

Jane Swift

Jane Swift

The Executive Briefing

Here is a variation on the traditional cover letter. It has been developed most effectively by the recruiting fraternity for use in relation to a specific opening.

Behind the executive briefing is the belief that the initial CV screener might have little understanding of the job in question. So a format was developed that dramatically increased the odds of your CV getting through to the right people. In addition, it customizes your general-purpose CV to each specific opening you discovered. It looks like this:

EXECUTIVE BRIEFING

for a

CREDIT/LOAN SUPERVISOR

as advertised in the *Gotham Daily News*

Jane Swift   16 November 20__
123 Anystreet
Anytown AT1 0BB
020 8123 4567

To help you evaluate the attached CV and manage your time effectively today. I have prepared this executive briefing. It itemizes your needs on the left and my skills on the right. The attached CV will give you additional details.

Job Title: CREDIT AND LOAN SUPERVISOR Required Experience:	My Current Title: CREDIT AND LOAN SUPERVISOR Relevant Experience:
▧ Five years in consumer banking	▧ Five years with a major London consumer bank
▧ Knowledge of Teller Operations	▧ Four years in Teller Operations, as teller and supervisor
▧ Three years Consumer Loans and Mortgage Loans	▧ Five years Consumer & Commercial and Mortgages
▧ Extensive Customer Service experience	▧ Four years in customer service. Reviewed as 'having superior communication skills'.

An executive briefing sent with a CV provides a comprehensive picture of a thorough professional, plus a personalized, fast and easy-to-read synopsis that details exactly how you can help with an employer's current batch of problems.

The Broadcast Letter

The broadcast letter is nothing but a simple variation on the cover letter. All the information you would need is available to you from the achievements section of your questionnaire. The intent is to get around sending a CV. Practically speaking, it can often get you into a telephone conversation with a potential employer, but that employer is usually likely to request a proper CV before seeing you anyway. A broadcast letter might have a place in your campaign, but do not use it as a CV substitute. Here is an example of a broadcast letter, in this instance sent in response to a blind newspaper advertisement:

Dear Employer,

For the past seven years I have pursued an increasingly successful career in the sales profession. Among my accomplishments I include:

SALES
As a regional representative, I contributed £1,500,000, or 16 per cent of my company's annual sales.

MARKETING
My marketing skills (based on a BA in Marketing) enabled me to increase sales 25 per cent in my economically stressed territory, at a time when colleagues here were striving to maintain flat sales. Repeat business reached an all-time high.

PROJECT MANAGEMENT
Following the above success, my regional model was adopted by the company. I trained and provided project supervision to the entire sales force. The following year, company sales showed a sales increase 12 per cent above projections.

The above was based and achieved on my firmly held zero price discounting philosophy. It is difficult to summarize my work in a letter. The only way I can think of for providing you the opportunity to examine my credentials is to talk with each other. I look forward to hearing from you.

Yours faithfully

James Sharpe

James Sharpe

As you can see, the letter is a variation on a theme, and as such might have a place in your marketing campaign.

Here is an example of a cover letter sent as a result of a conversation.

> Dear Ms _____ ,
>
> I am writing in response to our telephone conversation on Friday the 10th regarding a new- and used-car sales management position.
>
> With a successful track record in both new- and used-car sales, and as a sales manager, I believe I am ideally suited for the position we discussed. My exposure to the different levels of the sales process (I started at the bottom and worked my way up) has enabled me to effectively meet the challenges and display the leadership you require.
>
> I am a competitive person professionally. Having exercised the talents and skills required to exceed goals and set records as a Sales Manager, I believe in measuring performance by results.
>
> I would appreciate your consideration for a meeting where I could discuss in more detail my sales and management philosophy, and capabilities. Please call me at your earliest convenience to arrange a personal meeting.
>
> Sincerely yours,
>
> ## *James Sharpe*
>
> James Sharpe

Finally, here is an example of the somewhat different cover letter you would send to a corporate headhunter:

Dear Mr _____ ,

As you may be aware, the management structure at XYZ Ltd will be reorganized in the near future. While I am enthusiastic about the future of the company under its new leadership, I have elected to make this an opportunity for change and professional growth.

My many years of experience lends itself to a management position in any medium-sized service firm, but I am open to other opportunities. Although I would prefer to remain in Liverpool, I would be amenable to relocation if the opportunity warrants it. I am currently earning £65,000 a year.

I have taken the liberty of enclosing my CV for your review. Should you be conducting a search for someone with my background – at the present time or in the near future – I would greatly appreciate your consideration. I would be happy to discuss my background more fully with you on the phone or in a personal interview.

Very truly yours,

James Sharpe

James Sharpe

9

What Do You Do with It?

Creating one of the best CVs in the world is a major part of your job hunt, but nevertheless, only a part. It won't get you a job by sitting on your desk like a rare manuscript. You have to do something with it.

Companies are always looking for employees. Even a company with no growth rate can still be expected (based on national averages) to experience a 14 per cent turnover in staff over the course of a year. In other words, every company has openings, and any one of those openings could have your name on it.

The problem is, you won't have the chance to pick the very best opportunity unless you check them all out. The intelligent job hunter will use a six-pronged approach to cover all the bases. This process incorporates different ways to use:

- Internet distribution

- CV banks

- Employer Web sites

- Newspapers

- Employment agencies

- Executive recruiters

- Vocational and college placement offices

- Business and trade publications

- Personal and professional networking

Internet Distribution

The Internet provides computer-savvy professionals in all fields. If you are not Internet savvy, I cannot urge you strongly enough to take the plunge. It will only take two days (and less if you have a friend who will lend a guiding hand) to learn the ropes and get your CV loaded for distribution. A day later you'll be ready to get your CV in front of thousands of employers and recruiters. The ease with which you can reach potential employers is just impossible with more traditional methods of distribution.

Don't expect seamless perfection. The Internet is growing like a boom-town, and that means the buildings and infrastructure are under constant construction. Yet with all the problems you might encounter, the benefits far outweigh the drawbacks. Apart from the sheer volume of activity you can generate, your ability to use the Internet for CV distribution sets you apart from other candidates. All employers want technologically adept employees, so approaching them this way immediately makes a point in your favour.

There are two principal forms of electronic CV distribution:

- Posting your CV in CV banks, which are in turn searched by corporate recruiters and headhunters. These databases are rapidly becoming a major recruiting resource.

- Sending your CV directly to an employer's Web site.

CV Banks

There are literally hundreds of CV banks where you can post your CV for free. Most have CV forms where you fill in the blanks. Have your CV handy; it's easier and more accurate to cut and paste an existing document than starting from scratch every time. Your submission will look more polished (and therefore powerful) and there is less chance of spelling mistakes; with the availability of spell checking, typos are a clear sign of sloppiness.

Some of these submission forms will accept text posted from your word processing programme, while others will require an ASCII text file (addressed on pages 79–80).

Sending out 100 CVs used to be a real chore. Now, every time you post a CV it will be seen by thousands of employers. A word of caution here: in an effort to keep these CV banks fresh for the paying customers (employers pay for access to these banks) the administrators typically purge CVs over 90 days old. Every time you post to a new CV bank, make a note of its storage policies. That way you'll know when to repost your CV if you think the bank is getting you worthwhile exposure.

Employer Web Sites

While the CV banks are a godsend to people on both sides of the desk, company home pages are your very best resource, even though posting to them individually may take a little more time.

Almost every one of the millions of companies with an Internet presence uses part of their site for recruiting. By delivering your CV directly to the site you will set yourself apart from the CVs coming in from other Internet sources.

All of these sites offer information about the company (history, press clippings, even financial data in the case of public companies) so you can easily customize your cover letter and your CV to fit the company's needs.

To find e-mail addresses you can type the company name into the search engine of your choice.

A potential employer's Web site may allow you to submit a formatted CV, an ASCII version, or you may be required to cut and paste your information into a template custom-designed by the company.

If you have a strong interest in a specific company, you can usually keep your CV posted there until the right opportunity comes through. Company databases are managed pretty much the same way as the commercial ones, which means they get purged on a regular basis. Sometimes the purge comes after 90 days, other times it's six months or a year. Keep a log of the e-mail addresses you've posted to and the corresponding storage policies so that you can repost when the time comes.

Your Privacy

Unfortunately, your privacy becomes more of an issue with electronic distribution. The ease with which electronic CVs are distributed means that many more people are going to see your CV. But once it's available electronically, it also becomes almost effortless to copy or forward it. If you are currently gainfully employed, you'll need to take precautions to protect your anonymity.

First, use your own e-mail, not your employer's. If this is not possible, many CV banks will provide a 'blind' account to handle responses from their clients – but that only covers you for that specific bank. Many Internet service providers offer e-mail addresses. If your doesn't, many CV writers and career counselling firms will furnish you with a numbered account that will protect your privacy in all online job hunting scenarios.

With an electronic CV, your e-mail address can replace most of your other contact information, although you may choose to provide your home telephone number. You can replace the name of your current employer with something generic, such as 'A multinational bank' or 'a midsized telecommunications company'. 'Potential employers and headhunters don't take offence at these substitutions. They recognize that you are employed and are exercising discretion.

As you put together your electronic CV distribution programme, you will also be laying the foundations for your next job hunt, even if it's a couple of years or more down the road.

Corporate e-mail addresses don't change as often as you might think. Even if the corporation moves from 10 Main Street to 260 Centre Street, it usually keeps its 'hr@bigcompany.com' (or similar) e-mail address intact. The majority of the e-mail addresses you locate now will probably still be there the next time you are looking for a new opportunity. So don't start from scratch – you may find that by keeping a careful log this time, you've saved yourself hours of time in the future.

Newspapers

A first step for many is to go to the situations vacant ads and do a mass mailing. But beware. If this is the first idea that comes to _your_ mind, hitting the situations vacant ads will probably be at the front of everyone else's mind, too.

A single help-wanted advertisement can draw hundreds of responses. And that's not counting all the other unsolicited CVs that come in every day. So your approach must be more comprehensive than that of the average applicant. The following tips might be helpful.

- Newspapers tend to have an employment edition every week (usually Sunday, but sometimes mid-week), when in addition to their regular advertising, they have a major drive for help-wanted ads. Make sure you always get this edition of the paper.

- Look for back issues. Just because a company is no longer advertising does not necessarily mean that the slot has been filled. The employer may well have become disillusioned and gone on to hire a professional recruiter to work on the position.

- Cross-check the categories. Don't rely solely on those ads seeking your specific job title. For example, let's say you are a graphic artist looking for a job in advertising. Any advertising or public relations agency with any kind of need should be flagged. On the basis that they are actively hiring at the moment, simple logic leads you to the conclusion that their employment needs are not restricted to that particular title.

Newspapers represent an important part of your marketing campaign; you should follow up all your CVs with a phone call about a week after they have been sent.

Employment Agencies

Private Employment Agencies

Here we have a definitely for-profit sector of the employment marketplace. There are some major questions that you should get answered before signing up with any particular agency.

You are best advised to call first, and then visit. Be prepared to leave a copy of your CV for their files and for possible review by interested clients.

Here are some practical ways for you to check on the professional standing of your agent. Be sure to ask:

- When was the firm established? If the company has been in town ever since you were in nappies, the chances are good that it is reputable.

- Is the agency a member of a national employment association? National associations have strict codes of behaviour and ethics and provide ongoing training for their members. And as in all industries, people and companies who are actively involved in enhancing their profession invariably have an edge on the competition.

- Does your particular agent have a CPC designation? That stands for Certified Personnel Consultant, a title achieved only after considerable time and effort. Employment consultants with this designation come straight from the top drawer, so you can trust them and should listen attentively to their advice.

- Is the agency part of a franchise chain or independent network? Knowing this can be valuable to you, because both kinds of organizations provide considerable training for their associates, a feature that can enhance the level of service you receive. In addition, other members of the network may have a job suitable for you if the one you've located doesn't.

Finally – don't get intimidated. Remember, you are not obliged to sign anything. Neither are you obliged to guarantee an agency that you will remain in any employment for any specified length of time. Don't get taken advantage of by the occasional rogue in an otherwise exemplary and honoured profession.

Executive Recruiters

These people rarely deal at low salary levels. All the above advice regarding employment agencies applies here, although you can take it for granted that the headhunter will not charge you a fee. He or she will be more interested in your CV than in seeing you right then and there, unless you match a specific job the recruiter is trying to fill for a client. Executive recruiters are far more interested in the employed than in the unemployed. An employed person is less of a risk (headhunters often guarantee their finds to the employer for up to a year) and constitutes a more desirable commodity. Remember, these people are there to serve the client, not to find you a job. They neither want nor expect you to rely on them for employment counselling, unless they specifically request that you do – in which case you should listen to them closely.

Vocational and College Placement Offices

If you're leaving school or university, you should take advantage of this resource. (If you don't, you're crazy.) Many of the larger schools and universities have alumni placement networks, so even if you graduated some time ago, you may want to check with the alma mater and tap into the old-boy and old-girl network.

Business and Trade Publications

Two uses here. The articles about interesting companies can alert you to growth opportunities, and individually can provide neat little entrees in your cover letters. Of course, there's also the welcome fact that most of these magazines carry a help-wanted section.

Networking

A fancy word from the seventies that means talking to everyone you can get hold of in your field, whether you know them or not.

Networking at meetings and using an association's directory for contacts are wise and accepted uses of membership.

At the Library

The business reference section can give you access to numerous research books that can help.

Follow-Up

It is no use mailing off tens or even hundreds of CVs without following up on your efforts. If you are not getting a response with one CV format, you might want to consider redoing it another way, as discussed in chapter 5. Of course, in doing so, you should never mention your previous submission. Be satisfied with one of your baits catching a fish.

Always take five or six copies of your CV with you to interviews. Often you can attach it to those annoying application forms and then just write on the form 'See attached CV'. You can have one on your lap during the interview to refer to, as the interviewer does.

It is always wise to offer copies to subsequent interviewers. This is because they have very often been inadequately briefed and may have no idea about your background and skills. It's also a good idea to leave extra copies of your CV behind with managers for their personal files (which travel with them through their careers from company to company). That person may not need you today, but could come up with a dream job for your sometime in the future. I know of people who have landed jobs years later as a result of a CV left judiciously with the right person. Who is the right person? Potentially, anyone who holds on to your CV.

The job you ultimately accept may not be your picture of perfection. Nevertheless, any job can lead to great things. You can make the opportunities for yourself in any job if you make the effort. A job becomes what you choose to make it.

In the job hunt there are only two kinds of 'yes' answers: their 'yes-we-want-you-to-work-for-us', and your 'yes-I-can-start-on-Monday'. The joy is in the hunt with every 'no' bringing you closer to the big 'yes'. Never take rejections of your CV as rejections of yourself; just as every job is not for you, you aren't right for every job. Keep things in perspective.

Good luck!

10

The CVs

And now, without
further ado ... the
stars of our show.

The CVs on the following pages are based on the genuine articles, the ones that really did the trick for someone who had to translate his or her fantastic skills and background into a single, compelling document. Whether or not your background is represented in the following sample, use the CVs reproduced here as a starting point for composing your own.

Accounting Professional

Jane Swift
123 Anystreet, Anytown AT1 0BB
020 8123 4567
jane@anyaddress.co.uk

Detail-oriented, organized and efficient accounting professional with a strong background in all areas of the accounting system. Progressively responsible duties gained over the course of a career based on exceptional analytical and organizational skills. Self-motivated individual with the ability to work independently with minimal supervision and make well thought out decisions. Excellent verbal and written communications skills. Specific skills and knowledge include: accounts payable, sales and use tax, capital expenditures, accounts receivable, general ledger, cheque generation, payroll asset management, invoice verification, purchasing, requisitions, budgeting.

Technical Expertise
- Infinium Fixed Assets
- Infinium Human Resources
- Windows 95/98
- AS400 programming language
- MS Office including Excel, Word, and Access
- Oracle Financials including Accounts Payable, Purchasing, and Projects
- Internet experience
- E-mail

Professional Experience
Stewart's Retail, Salthorpe
Equipment Coordinator, 1998 to Present
- Managed purchasing, tracking, and delivery of £60 million in capital equipment for over 500 stores nationally.
- Implemented procedures to assure proper allocation of capital expenditure budget. Reviewed and analysed project documentation. Performed financial verification to determine sufficient funding prior to purchase, delivery and payment. Coordinated and processed all store equipment purchases and fixed asset improvements. Maintained property documentation of all project activity. Provided consultative, liaison and support services with vendors and management.

National Auto Parts, Beechampton, 1991–1998
Accounting Assistant – Financial Reporting Department   1996–1998
- Executed capital expenditure payments in excess of £9 million annually.
- Contributed to the development and implementation of a cost segregation programme that resulted in a £40 million disbursement to stockholders.
- Performed accounts payable functions for all construction and corporate expenses for 30 new stores nationwide as well as additional corporate projects and payables due to 250 vendors. Assisted with VAT returns and managed fixed assets for 56 locations.

Accounting Assistant – Payroll Department   1992–1996
- Generated approximately 600 on-demand and manager fund cheques monthly. Compiled total balance of employee's accounts receivable. Conducted biweekly payroll functions for 500 employees.

Computer Operator   1991–1992
- Coordinated daily and weekly jobs for payroll, accounting and warehouse. Received on-the-job training in AS400 computer language for use in daily tasks.

Education
University of the West – BSc (Hons) 2.1 – Computer Science, 1998–1991
Stanford Community College – A-levels – Maths, Computer Science, 1982–1983
Eastern Community School – 6 O-levels, including English and Maths, 1978–1982

Administrative

James Sharpe
123 Anystreet
Anytown AT1 0BB
020 8123 4567
james@anyaddress.co.uk

Summary
Administrative support professional experienced working in fast-paced environments demanding strong organizational, technical and interpersonal skills. Highly trustworthy, ethical and discreet; committed to superior customer service. Confident and poised in interactions with individuals at all levels. Detail-oriented and resourceful in completing projects; able to multitask effectively.

Key Words
Customer Service & Relations ● Word Processing ● Computer Operations
Accounts Payable/Receivable ● Filing & Data Archiving ● Office Equipment Operation
Telephone Reception ● General Accounting ● Problem Solving

Experience Highlights
Administrative Support
- Performed administrative and secretarial support functions for the Managing Director of a large sportswear manufacturer. Coordinated and managed multiple priorities and projects.
- Provided discreet secretarial and reception services for a busy family counselling centre. Scheduled appointments and maintained accurate, up-to-date confidential client files.
- Assisted with general accounting functions; maintained journals and handled A/P and A/R. Provided telephone support; investigated and resolved invoice problems for a manufacturer's buying group. Trained and supervised part-time staff and trainees.

Customer Service & Reception
- Registered incoming patients in a hospital emergency room. Demonstrated ability to maintain composure and work efficiently in a fast-paced environment while preserving strict confidentiality.
- Conducted patient interviews to elicit necessary information for registration, accurate prioritization, and to assist medical professionals in the triage process.
- Orchestrated hotel special events and reservations; managed customer relations and provided exemplary service to all customers.

Management & Supervision
- Promoted rapidly from front desk clerk to assistant front office manager at 5-star hotel. Oversaw all operations including restaurant, housekeeping and maintenance. Troubleshot and resolved problems, mediated staff disputes and handled customer complaints.
- Participated in staff recruitment, hiring, training and scheduling. Supervised front-desk staff.

Employment History
ACCOUNTING ASSISTANT, St Anne's Healthcare Trust
PATENT SERVICES REGISTRAR, University Health System Hospital, Runswick
ASSISTANT FRONT OFFICE MANAGER, Sheraton Hotel, St Anne's
RECEPTIONIST/SECRETARY, Family Counselling & Guidance Centre, Stoke Park
ADMINISTRATIVE ASSISTANT, Keen's Sportswear, Stoke Park

Education & Training
Technical College, Runswick (1999–Present)
Hazelford Community College, Runswick (1996) Introduction to Computers and MS Office
Hazelford Community College, Runswick (1988–1989) OND in Business Administration

Community Involvement
Committed to community service. Extensive volunteer history includes involvement in community school, Habitat for Humanity, children's homes, community soup run, work with the elderly, and fundraising for children with cancer.

Applications Programmer

James Sharpe
123 Anystreet
Anytown AT1 0BB
020 8123 4567
james@anyaddress.co.uk

Technical Profile
A dedicated application programmer with 3 years-hand-on experience using object-oriented (C++) and conventional languages with a Windows/DOS platform. Excellent design, coding and testing skills; pays close attention to details. Clear communication abilities and strong writing capability. A team player with cross-functional awareness and above-average work/time management skills.

Object-oriented languages:	C++, Visual C++, C-Shell, Visual Basic, HTML
Conventional languages:	C, Pascal
Database packages:	Btrieve, Oracle, SQL
Operating systems:	Windows 95/98, DOS, Unix
Professional software packages:	Word, Excel, Microsoft Project, Lotus Notes

Professional Experience   1998–Present
XTC Data, Hanford
   Programmer/Analyst
      Team development member for two banking application projects. Most recent application has been a full life cycle development project consisting of a front-end product used by bank tellers with a Btrieve database and VID-View GUI third-party interface. Second project was another front-end product used by banking counsellors and tellers.

      Team member responsibilities:
      - Gather clients' requirements
      - Prepare outline and detailed design documents
      - Code I/O interfaces to peripherals
      - Test and debug application; resolve clients' issues
      - Track and manage changes using mainframe-based impact tool

   Selected achievements:
   - Received Ovation Award (the highest level award given by XTC Data) in 1999 for meeting company's goal and receiving strongly positive customer feedback for application
   - Selected to research and resolve Y2K compliance issues
   - Implemented product to take advantage of C++ capabilities resulting in more efficient upgrades and greater flexibility to interface with different servers

Education
Bachelor of Architecture, University of the South
Certificate courses, Oracle for Developers, C++, HTML, Pascal, System Programming in C (Unix platform), Visual C++, MFC

Banking Portfolio Manager

James Sharpe
123 Anystreet, Anytown AT1 0BB. Tel: 020 8123 4567. james@anyaddress.co.uk
Page 1 of 2

SUMMARY

A track record of outstanding performance in the sophisticated environments of Trust and Investment Banking. Management of both personal and institutional portfolios with total values exceeding £300 million. An adept analyst of such diverse industries as energy, metals, automotive, insurance, banking, electrical, and consumer goods.

OBJECTIVE

An opportunity where a professional whose successful loss control/profit preservation approach to portfolio management can make a meaningful contribution.

CAREER HIGHLIGHTS

An Investment Banking Company: *Chief Executive, Institutional Portfolio Management*, 1992–Present.

Heads investment management activities of the firm's 170-account London office. Reporting to Chairman. Created more effective marketing and management of large accounts, by initiating a programme that resulted in:

- Upgrading and expansion of professional staff.
- Personal management of firm's 17 largest accounts.
- Effective supervision of all staff activities and performance.
- Elevation to position as member of Board of Directors and Chair of Investment Strategy and Policy Group.

London Trust Company: *Chief Executive & Senior Portfolio Manager*, 1988–1992.

Managed a broadly diversified account base of over 395 personal and institutional accounts with total value in excess of £450 million. Improved performance of accounts supervised, shortened turn-around time of customer requests for investment reviews, cementing relations with clients. Developed effective computerized methods for rapid analysis of investment diversification.

- Programme consistently outperformed the FT index, distilled stock guidance list of 500 firms to a value-oriented 20–85 companies.
- Reduced turn-around time on investment reviews by 30%.
- Reduced time spent in review analysis by 25% while improving review quality.

Morgan Guaranty (London): *Portfolio Manager.* 1985–1988.

Initially recruited as a Senior Investment Analyst in the energy stock area, was promoted to Portfolio Manager within 10 months.

- Hired, trained, supervised and directed activities of additional analysts in related research coverage.
- Dramatically reduced energy stock holdings in November 1988, a move that produced sizable realized capital gains while avoiding the sell-off that followed.
- Instituted automation and software for analytical staff. Increased the number of potential investment opportunities by 21% without additional cost.

EDUCATION AND PERSONAL

MBA, London School of Economics   Finance and Marketing
MSc, University of London   Economics
BSc, University of London   Economics

Willing to relocate. References are available upon request.

Broadcast Sales

James Sharpe
123 Anystreet
Anytown AT1 0BB
Tel: 020 8123 4567
james@anyaddress.co.uk

Profile

Marketing/Advertising/Sales/Corporate Development/Communications/Public
Affairs/Promotions/Non-profit Ventures/Events/Sponsorships

- Creative, results-oriented professional with 12 years of experience in broadcast sales, marketing, and corporate development. Strong track record generating revenue from existing partnerships, new customers and non-traditional sources. Oversee numerous successful promotions, projects, and special events.
- Energetic and resourceful, self-directed and innovative. Highly effective communication skills include demonstrated ability to satisfy client needs through relationship building and creative development. Career-driven, willing to relocate.

Experience

Corporate Development/Account Executive, Style Living. 1992–present
A first-class revenue producer for a leading cable/satellite station.

- Service existing accounts and generate new business. Arrange airtime through quarterly, annual and specific TV buys.
- Develop television media strategies through qualitative and quantitative research for clients in all categories, including retail, business-to-business and entertainment. Increased existing shares of local direct and agency business. Revenues: Average £1 million account list.
- Recruited Southern Power, O & P Banking as third-party co-sponsors for Junior Chef of the Year and promoted corporate image of sponsors to community. Revenues: £120,000/year (negotiated annually).
- Directed station sponsorship of the National Garden Challenge Festival. Supervised contracts, promotions, production, tickets, special events and promotional materials distributions (ads, guides, brochures, posters). Currently negotiating sponsor relationships to underwrite a documentary film on festival for distribution to schools.
- Managed creative development and revenue stream for Drive to Stay Alive, an ongoing public awareness campaign that promotes safe driving issues. Revenues: £20,000/year.
- Helped establish and promote the annual Make a Wish fundraiser and gala event. Generated incremental revenue through corporate sponsorships. Secured celebrities as spokespersons and event hosts. Event attendance grew from 75 to 600+ people in 4 years.
- Coordinated station promotion and third-party sponsorship for the South West Arts Festival, raising money for art supplies and local schools.

Account Executive, Palmer Grove Associates. 1987–1992

- Developed new business accounts for major consumer advertising agency.

Professional Affiliations

The Advertising Association. Chairman 1998–Present, Board of Directors 1995–1998, President-Elect 2000–2001: Manage public service portfolios; organize social activities; administer student services, advice and education; oversee payroll and budgets; frequent public speaker.

- Community Advisory Board, 1999–Present: Coordinate fundraising and corporate contributions for YMCA.
- South West Arts Board of Directors 1998–Present

Education

BA, Business and Communications, Midland University

Brokerage Professional

James Sharpe
123 Anystreet, Anytown AT1 0BB
020 8123 4567
james@anyaddress.co.uk

Profile

- High energy, hands-on management professional with extensive background blending operations management, high-volume brokerage information distribution and fast-paced brokerage activities.
- Employ analysis and creativity to form productive systems and interdepartmental partnerships. Cool under pressure with an excellent on-time and on-budget record.
- Hold high personal standards and consistently lead teams to achieve departmental goals. Believe that profitability, customer service, and quality work are primary factors of success in any competitive industry.

Areas of Knowledge and Ability

- stock and brokerage service ● brokerage information distribution ● proxy processing ● SIB compliance ● stock inventory management ● postal rates and requirements ● ISO-9002 ● procedure development ● budget development ● scheduling ● training ● departmental supervision ●

Career Highlights

- Selected to participate with upper management in steering committee to plan company's ISO 9002 certification process. Project was so successful that company received certification in 6 months against 12-month industry standard.
- Achieved a consistent history of promotions and excellent performance appraisals. Started with Investor Services when division employed 5 permanent operations associates; division's operations department, at peak levels, now employs over 200 associates. Have the longest service in the operations department and have hands-on knowledge of all operational procedures.
- Wrote work instruction manual for department at general level for step-by-step process of informal to formal training. Produced written instructions for training of new associates. Designed contract review process and approval.
- Developed new spreadsheet formats for Central Investments that allowed for faster, more accurate tracking of stock inventory and over-the-counter profit and loss.
- Presented stock information to Central Investments Chief Executive and Chairman. Interfaced with controller on a monthly basis to reconcile profit and loss dollars.
- Supported the fast-paced activities of 1,000 Central Investments brokers trading with a million plus shares of stock inventory.

Brokerage Services Experience

Financial Services, London	1992 to present
Manager, Data Entry and Process Control	1999 to present
Manager, Receiving	1997 to 1999
Receiving Supervisor	1995 to 1997
Data Entry Clerk	1993 to 1995

- Manage all operations of department processing over 35,000 jobs per year, peaking at more than 300 jobs per day. Mailing consists of dividend cheques, monthly brokerage statements and investor communications for 10,000 companies. Department is the hub of all the other peripheral operations.
- Control the movement of sensitive, high-profile, investment-related material. Ensure compliance with SIB, client and postal regulations. Deeply involved in productivity and quality assurance issues.
- High speed operation requires exceptional on-time/on-budget performance. Develop annual budget of £300,000 and schedule staff to cover cyclical highs and lows using historical data to project volume. Determine best postal rates and discount eligibility. Come in on or below budget on a consistent basis.

Brokerage Experience
Financial Investments, London   1992 to 1993
Assistant Manager, Trading   1993
Trading Coordinator   1992

■ Tracked millions of shares of stock inventory to determine on-demand availability of company supply.
■ Notified Chairman of levels needed for new buy. Tracked over-the-counter traders' purchases/sales and profit/loss on a daily basis.
■ Followed and analysed over-the-counter P&L and daily inventory for next days reporting and selling.

Computer Skills
Word for Windows, Excel, Windows XP, industry-specific software

Education
University of London: BSc (Hons) 2.1 Economics.
Professional Development Courses: How to Give Presentations, Priory Seminars; Business Writing

Business Development Manager/Consultant

Jane Swift
123 Anystreet
Anytown AT1 0BB
020 8123 4567
jane@anyaddress.co.uk
Page 1 of 2

Expert in the Telecommunications Industry Through 20 Years Experience

Dynamic, award-winning career reflecting pioneering expertise in consultative sales and marketing of telecommunications network infrastructure equipment and services. Offer a rare combination of superior interpersonal skills coupled with in-depth technical systems understanding. Known for innovation and lateral thinking skills; consistent success in solving a diversity of demanding business problems. Outstanding record of achievement leading to accelerated sales, improved business processes and optimized market shared.

Key Words

Business Development & Marketing	Organizational & Process Improvement
Training Programme Development & Management	Revenue, Profit & Market Share Growth
Strategic & Tactical Sales Planning	Staff Mentoring, Training & Coaching
Consultative & Solution Sales	Creative & Resourceful Problem Solving

Professional Experience

Patterson Technology, Illingford   1996–2000
SENIOR SALES TRAINER

- Rejuvenated the sales training department of this £150 million manufacturer of telecommunications switching equipment. Re-engineered methodologies and processes, instituted department goals, and established training certification programmes.
- Created a new training methodology that refocused emphasis to build consultative and solution sales competence. Transformed the sales process by empowering account executives with the knowledge and tools to assess customers' business needs and meet requirements through product solutions.
- Encouraged expansion into emerging telecommunications markets worldwide by introducing and familiarizing the sales team with various industry segments including satellite and international carriers.
- Designed and developed a critically acclaimed multimedia web-based sales training module that taught the sales force both basic and advanced selling skills. Delivered the module to the sales team at a national sales conference.

Consulting Partners, Rookwood   1992–1996
MARKETING MANAGEMENT CONSULTANT

- Contracted as an interim marketing manager. Led interdepartmental team in the creation and roll out of a precedent-setting sales initiative that drove £4.5 million in sales the first year and halted the competition, protecting an additional £1 million annual revenue.
- Coordinated with stakeholders to ensure support of a streamlined methodology that cut 50% of the time required to add capacity to the 5ESS Switch system. Managed proposal and pricing development and collaborated in the winning contract negotiations; led on-time implementation.
- Designed and deployed an innovative training programme for customer's engineers on the state-of-the-art telecommunications switch. Successfully transferred technical knowledge and established market positioning as a premier and adaptable solution to telecommunications needs.
- Honoured with the prestigious 'Technology Grows Award' for outstanding contribution. Achieved a feature story in a nationally distributed magazine that highlighted the innovative training programme.

Jane Swift 020 8123 4567
page 2 of 2

Telecom Solutions, Rackhay   1980–1992
   SALES MANAGER (1992–1996)
   DISTRICT TECHNICAL MANAGER (1989–1992)
   AREA SALES MANAGER (1984–1989)
   ACCOUNT EXECUTIVE (1982–1984)

- Promoted through a series of progressive positions, selling and supporting fibre-optic systems and telecommunications switching equipment. Led teams of up to 15 professionals and coordinated the activities of support personnel in a matrix management environment. Supported up to £150 million in annual sales and personally delivered on sales quotas of up to £25 million.
- Launched the SONET technology, building sales from the ground floor to £4.5 million within the first year of introduction. Received the 'Sales Director's Award' for valuable accomplishments.
- Delivered £25 million in new annual revenue by negotiating and closing a competitive fibre cable contract that displaced a well-entrenched, existing vendor. Recognized for top sales production with the 'Regional Director's Award'.
- Created an annual £4.5 million revenue stream by leading a team of engineers, product managers and marketing personnel that designed and brought to market a new fibre optic tie cable product in just 8 months. Honoured for achievement with a 'Sector Director's Award'.
- Initiated and acted as a change agent to support a paradigm shift in the role of sales engineers. Transformed the position from that of a 'back office' role to a customer-focused, sales support role designed to meet the unique and demanding needs of customers.
- Directed a team comprised of internal staff and customer employees in developing and implementing a new system for engineering and provisioning switching equipment that saved £500,000 annually. Awarded special appreciation honours by the customer's top management.
- Formulated and executed a strategy that achieved 88% market share for 5ESS Switching systems in spite of a price disadvantage.
- Closed the first commercial sale nationwide and managed implementation of the then cutting-edge ISDN service; earned both regional and national sales honours.
- Captured a £7.5 million account by developing an innovative warehousing service that met the customer's needs for 'just in time' product delivery.
- Increased market share 50% by closing the first multiyear contract in the company's history; led a team in improving the order realization process to optimize fulfilment times for custom orders.

Education & Training
   North West University – Business Administration
   Extensive training in:

Telecommunications Engineering & Technology	Sales & Negotiations
Leadership	Quality Management
Process Improvement	MS Office (Word, Excel, PowerPoint, Project)

Community Affiliations
   Board of Directors, The Education Foundation
   Member, School District Communications Team
   Coach and Certified Referee, Junior Football League

Buyer

James Sharpe
123 Anystreet
Anytown AT1 0BB
020 8123 4567
james@anyaddress.co.uk

EXPERIENCE

3/2000–Present Ohrbach's (York), **Buyer**, Boyswear

Responsible for purchasing boyswear sold in children's departments at 45 stores chainwide, with yearly sales exceeding £2.5 million. Branch managers report to this position. Visit wholesale showrooms on a weekly basis.

- Analyse daily sales data and inventories to plan promotions and make adjustments.
- Prepare and maintain budgets. Redistribute merchandise between stores.
- Travel to branch stores to direct departmental start-ups and solve problems.
- Train and evaluate assistant buyers.

2/1999–3/2000 **Assistant Buyer**, Silverware/Cookware/Junior Knits

- Promoted through three different lines. Consistently exceeded quota.
- Assisted buyers in selection of merchandise.
- Prepared orders, budgets and inventories.
- Planned and created newspaper advertisements.
- Organized and promoted annual Housewares Exposition.

8/1997–2/1999 **Sales Manager**

- Managed four separate departments in two stores, exceeded projections by 14%.
- Trained, scheduled, and supervised salespeople; turnover dropped 20%.
- Met daily sales quotas, handled all merchandising.

EDUCATION

B.A. Merchandising: York Institute of Technology (1996)

All education self-financed through working in retail outlets throughout college years.

Claims Representative: Loss Adjuster

Jane Swift
123 Anystreet
Anytown AT1 0BB
020 8123 4567
jane@anyaddress.co.uk

Objective: Seeking a position using my extensive knowledge and successful experience in planning, organizing and following up multi-faceted, complex activities; and a position offering opportunities for personal contribution and professional growth.

SUMMARY OF QUALIFICATIONS

Offering comprehensive experience and expertise in the following areas of responsibility:

- Extensive experience planning, organizing, evaluating and following up varied responsibilities in a timely and complete manner.
- Proficient in developing excellent/relationships with clients and consultants.
- Experienced in knowledge of and in analysing provisions and exclusions of policies in order to decide eligible benefits.
- Skilled at organizing work and resolving problems that arise in day-to-day activities.

EXPERIENCE HIGHLIGHTS

1991 to Present   **Loss Adjuster**   *Farmers Fund Insurance Co.*, North Tunshall
Responsible for meeting with policy holders, claimants and solicitors to examine, evaluate and decide upon claims for property damage and personal injury.

- Planning, organizing, evaluating and approving up to 100 active claims in process.
- Taking statements of witnesses and performing on-site inspections. Analysing reports and statements of policy holders, witnesses and claimants.
- Receiving and evaluating medical reports. Performing analytical reports on bodily injury claims.
- Negotiating claims settlements with individuals and solicitors.

1989 to 1990   **Management Trainee**   *PizzaTime*, Shepton
Participated in Management Training Programme and assisted in interviewing, hiring, training and supervising personnel. Managed operations in absence of Manager.

1988 to 1989   **Administrative Assistant**   *East Midlands University*
Responsible for assisting Fund Director in fundraising projects. Maintained daily and monthly reports of fundraising activities. Organized and coordinated meetings and luncheons.

Education: East Midlands University 1988. BA Business Studies including Communication/Business Management.

Licences: Chartered Insurance Practitioner ACII, Fellow CILA

Strengths: Highly motivated, accurate, thorough and precise in attention to details. Excellent analytical and organizational skills. Major strength is completing multi-faceted tasks within time constraints allotted. Skilled in public relations, loyal, dependable, and willing to do whatever is needed to meet established goals.

References furnished upon request

Commercial Operations Manager

Jane Swift
123 Anystreet
Anytown AT1 0BB
Tel: 020 8123 4567
jane@anyaddress.co.uk
Page 1 of 2

A highly experienced sales and marketing professional with comprehensive skills in strategic planning and implementation. Offers 6 years of combined experience in computer systems, recruiting foreign distributors, foreign sales and direct sales. Proficient in recruiting personnel, effective team management and motivating staff. Currently manages 37-strong technical sales team responsible for introducing leading US interactive software into the European market. Reputation of as hard-working and dedicated employee.

AREAS OF EXPERTISE

Computer sales – hardware, software and peripherals ● Interactive systems ● UK and European sales ● Eastern European market and culture ● Recruitment and training of technical staff ● high-level negotiation with major clients ● working in new and growing markets ● fluent business German

CAREER HIGHLIGHTS AND ACHIEVEMENTS

- Recruited, and directed training of, 37 sales and technical staff for Europe with the emphasis on the growing Eastern European market. Inculcated steady sales of original lines plus introduced new interactive software – TechNet Interactive – resulting in an initial 43% sales increase. Profit from Eastern European operation showing steady growth rate of 14% annually
- As Commercial Manager, increased European and UK sales by 27% over three years
- Increased regional UK sales from £70 million to £120 million during four years as Regional Manager
- Member of pioneering sales team in East German market – raised market share from 0% to 12% within 18 months
- Elected 'European Salesperson of the Year' 1999 by the Professional Commerce Association

COMPUTER EFFICIENCY

As well as expertise in all InterTech products, in-depth knowledge of Microsoft Word, Excel, Lotus, Windows XP, planning and presentation software, Internet and e-mail.

PROFESSIONAL EXPERIENCE

InterTech plc London   1993–Present
Commercial Operations Manager, Europe (1998–Present)
- Manage £240 million sales operation
- Responsible for all commercial and logistical operations in Europe
- Full responsibility for sales and marketing
- Recruit and ensure effective training of technical sales personnel
- Select and liaise with distributors in 14 regions in East and West Europe

Jane Swift 020 8123 4567
Page 2 of 2

- Negotiate administrative and suitable warehousing sites with authorities and property agents in each region
- Responsible for 'market preparation', induction, sales and marketing of new interactive software products

Regional Manager, UK (1994–1998)
- Managed £120 million UK sales operation
- Responsible for all sales and marketing operations in UK
- Responsible for recruiting and training sales team to the highest level in a technically demanding field
- Contracted out after-sales service to reduce overheads
- Negotiated additional technical back-up facilities for improved client service and increased client retention

Sales Manager, South of England (1992–1994)
- Increased Southern Region profits by 15% over two years
- Set team sales budgets, assigned territories and targets
- Undertook staff reviews and training
- Consistently met and exceeded personal sales targets
- Gained MBA 1994

HP&P, Birmingham   1990–1992
Sales Representative
- Exceeded target performance by 17%
- Achieved Top Ten National Sales Award and Top Regional Sales Award

EDUCATION
BA (Hons) 2.2 Economics, Birmingham University
MBA, Henbury Business School

Consultant

James Sharpe

123 Anystreet ● Anytown AT1 0BB ● Tel: 020 8123 4567
james@anyaddress.co.uk

Executive Summary

An innovative and seasoned **Senior Executive** and **Consultant** with a successful background in **crisis resolution, turnaround and start-up situations**. More than 15 years' successful, progressive experience in all phases of Strategic Planning, Operations and Financial Management. Recognized as a hands-on, proactive **troubleshooter** who can rapidly identify business problems, formulate strategic plans, initiate change and implement new processes in challenging and diverse environments. Exceptional ability to **execute income enhancement strategies** and cost control actions.

Areas of Effectiveness

- Capital & Operational Budgeting
- P&L Responsibility
- Sales/Marketing Strategies
- Financial & Operational Cost Control
- Liquidation Management
- Business Valuation
- Production & Inventory Management
- Crisis Management
- Corrective Active Planning

Significant Accomplishments

- Recruited as a **Turnaround Consultant for ATC**, to create spending accountability in all areas, resulting in cost reductions of £1 million annually. Facilitated successful negotiations with vendors, customers, the Inland Revenue, various authorities and banks for lines of credit.
- As the **Director of Zen Technologies**, orchestrated the start-up and growth of a subsidiary organization. Within just four years successfully established 18 retail stores, 3 warehousing/distribution locations and sales exceeding £5 million. Additionally created a wholly owned subsidiary for acquisitions and acquired 21 stores through bulk sale and transfer.
- Within 9 months, as the **Divisional Controller for The Electronics Store**, selected and implemented a fully integrated Purchase Order Management System enabling the centralization of national purchasing contracts and staff reductions resulting in a cost savings exceeding £1 million.
- Promoted to **Plant Manager**, for the **fifth largest facility in the UK, at Nova Computers** in less than three years (the standard was seven years). Effectively negotiated with and administered 4 unions and 15 different locals. Responsibilities for this 600-employee facility included: standard cost, budgets, sales forecasting, multi-state distribution, and capital projects.
- Developed and implemented internal controls and security measures to successfully resolve an inventory shortage that exceeded £500,000 per month. Additional operational improvements resulted in a 25% increase in deliveries as well as a 20% reduction in staff.
- As the **Acquisition Manager**, spearheaded the acquisition of a 95-unit, 350-employee organization. This included the creation of a new company for bankruptcy purchase, due diligence, negotiations with creditors, inventory valuation, employee termination and selective rehiring.
- Directed the closure of a manufacturing facility: transferred assets, handled redundancy compensation and union issues, laid off staff, shut down plant, absorbed production.

Education

BA, *Business Management & Accounting*
North West College

Consultant

Jane Swift
123 Anystreet
Anytown AT1 0BB
Tel: 020 8123 4567
jane@anyaddress.co.uk

Training Consultant

Communication skills training ● people management skills ● time management
● professional development ● customer care techniques ● IT training

Strong commitment to excellence. Dynamic presentation, communication and marketing skills. Distinguished performance over seven years' experience in the private and public sectors. Motivated, results-oriented individual. Excellent planning, organizational, development and leadership qualifications. High impact professional with a proven ability to design and deliver innovative courses and workshops right across the personal development spectrum.

PROFESSIONAL EXPERIENCE

Devised and delivered complete training programmes to organizations. Assessed training needs and negotiated package with client, including evaluation and follow-up.

Organized a series of Personal and Professional Development seminars for Voluntary Service Workers, which won the National Award for Training.

Designed and presented an Industry Award-winning Professional Development programme for fast-track graduate trainees at Langland Communications.

Devised and wrote a series of Time Management, Communication and People Skills handbooks for staff at Langland Communications.

Created, developed and led successful People Skills programme for Corbellia Counter Service staff, resulting in the placement of further workshops for managers and supervisors.

Designed and produced Customer Care training module for customer support staff, including structured workbooks and illustrative material.

Introduced Business Studies students to practical uses and benefits of office technology, including e-mail, Internet and intranet.

CAREER HISTORY

Training Associate   Keyline Training 1998–Present
Team Leader   Primary Services 1994–1998
Office Services Supervisor Primary Services 1992–1994

EDUCATION AND TRAINING

NVQ level 4 Trainer's Award
Certificate in Counselling Skills
CLAIT

Convention Sales

Jane Swift
123 Anystreet
Anytown AT1 0BB
Tel: 020 8123 4567
jane@anyaddress.co.uk

Professional Profile

Ten years' experience in hotel/convention sales with demonstrated achievements in delivering winning sales presentations, new business development, account retention and competitive marketing. Managerial background includes coordinating client services, forecasting, budgeting, personnel supervision and training sales representatives. Consistently meet and exceed sales goals. Use outstanding customer relations, negotiation and conflict resolution skills to assess clients' needs and build rewarding business relationships.

Professional Experience

Eastern Counties Conference and Exhibition Centre
National Convention Sales Manager, 1996–Present

- Successfully secured and maintained trade show, corporate meeting, convention and corporate incentive accounts; generated 30,000 to 40,000 room nights in each of the last 4 years.
- Established new key accounts including Wesley Motors, Lansdown Publishing, and Shelley Financial; coordinate with clientele regarding major convention events.
- Directed administrative staff and inter-department procedures; conducted site inspections and effectively oversaw client convention/catering/hotel services and client invoicing.
- Attend international trade and travel shows; promoted a positive public relations image and effectively developed new business leads.
- Received the National Sales award in 1998 and Top Production recognition in 1999.

Director of Agency and Tour Sales, 1994–1996

- Cultivated series accounts, wholesale contract, and leisure group clientele.
- Generated 7,500 room nights and £250,000 in food and beverage sales by securing a large domestic wholesale account.
- Created and implemented marketing programmes and promotional packages; designed marketing brochures and advertising layout.
- Developed a travel program partnership with BA to enhance room occupancy.
- Supervised sales and office personnel; assisted with departmental forecasting and budgeting.

Assistant Sales Manager, 1992–1994

Group Coordinator, 1990–1992

Education

HND – Travel and Tourism, including Hotel Administration

Affiliations

Hotel Sales & Marketing Association, Eastern Counties Tourism Council

Corporate Communications

Jane Swift
123 Anystreet, Anytown AT1 0BB
Tel: 020 8123 4567
jane@anyaddress.co.uk

Page 1 of 2

Project Management/Media Research/Client Relations

TOP-FLIGHT MANAGEMENT CAREER building high-profile organizations that have consistently enhanced competitive market positioning, won favourable media and customer recognition, and supported substantial revenue growth. Combine strong planning, organizational leadership and consensus building qualifications with creative design and writing skills. Proven effectiveness in successfully matching products and services with client needs to ensure consistent repeat business.

Work well under pressure. Thrive in atmosphere of challenge, creativity, and variety. Flexible work style – can adapt quickly to changing work and client needs. Assertive, hands-on leader with extensive publication, audio, video and broadcast studio experience. Hold BA in Communications/Broadcasting and MA in Communications Research.

Key Words

Mass media communications	Public affairs	Media relations
Strategic planning	Desktop publishing	Public relations
Video and broadcast technology	Event planning and management	Trade shows
Training and development	New business development	Conference planning
Workflow planning and coordination	Performance and profit improvement	

**Creating High-Impact Images, Concepts, Services, Programmes and Opportunities
to Improve Performance and Build Revenues**

OVERVIEW

- Organized, detail-oriented communications professional with demonstrated ability to successfully increase productivity and profitability.
- Versatile, with diversified experience in networking, business development, and training.
- Works well under pressure in demanding, time-sensitive environments.
- Achieved reputation for 'getting the job done'.
- Highly adept in developing productive internal and external business development and referral channels.

PROFESSIONAL EXPERIENCE

1999–Present
DLA Electronics, Woodbridge   Sales Support Representative

- Furnished product specifications in response to inquiries.
- Achieved reputation for matching product offerings to customer needs.

1994–1999
Professional Video, Woodbridge
Fast-track promotions through a series of increasingly responsible positions.

Production & Sales Coordinator/Account Executive   1995–1999

- Successfully directed and coordinated high-calibre efforts to both expand and maximize company's market presence while strengthening market awareness.
- Arranged for media coverage in the trade press. Coordinated large mailings to announce acquisition of the latest state-of-the-art technology.
- Posted information to ensure mention in relevant magazine articles.
- Arranged for company presence at important trade shows. Assessed and evaluated new equipment's ability to meet upcoming needs.
- Planned and hosted numerous professional trade organization meetings.

- Developed well-received media kits that included relevant article reprints.
- Effectively surveyed competitor's rate as part of a comprehensive market research project.
- Designated target audience and adapted specialized mailing lists.
- Coordinated studio operations for taping projects.
- Significantly increased repeat business through extensive consultation with clients regarding specialized needs in an effort to successfully meet those needs.
- Participated in trade meetings regarding digital technology.
- Assigned camera and audio crews to optimize resources.
- Surveyed shoot sites to establish camera placements, equipment needs and crew availability.
- Developed logistics and scheduling to maximize budgetary resources and provide maximum value for clients' money. Established prices; quoted bids for projects and negotiated consistently favourable terms.
- Conducted production meetings to facilitate crew scheduling.
- Coordinated all facets of on-location shoots, including lighting and audio.
- Performed extensive quality checks to ensure equipment's optimal operation
- Provided extensive client follow-up to ensure complete satisfaction and gain repeat business.

Office Manager   1995
- Screened and interviewed employment candidates.
- Effectively trained and supervised office personnel.

Administrative Assistant   1994
- Provided quality support for all office staff including heavy telephone support and client contact.
- Maintained all aspects of accounts payable/receivable.

1992–1993
University of London
Communications Instructor
- Instructed students in Interpersonal, Organizational, and Media Communications.
- Conducted classroom lectures, discussions, and administered tests.
- Evaluated subject-children in a classroom environment.

COMPUTER SKILLS
Highly proficient in using the following software packages:
- Microsoft Word, Excel, Access, FrontPage, and PowerPoint.
- Internet communications packages including leading search engines.
- Leading desktop publishing packages.

EDUCATION
University of London   1993
Master of Arts: Communications Research
Research:
- Media and its Effect on the Public
- Analytical research on the effects of television on children: feedforward vs. feedback theory.

University of London
Bachelor of Arts: Communications/Broadcasting   1992
- Graduated with First Class Honours

REFERENCES
                        Excellent references will be furnished on request.

Customer Operations Co-ordinator

Jane Swift
123 Anystreet
Anytown AT1 0BB

Tel: 020 8123 4567
jane@anyaddress.co.uk

PROFILE
- Self-motivated, responsible and ambitious
- Excellent communication skills at all levels
- Enjoys meeting challenges and seeing them through
- Remains good humoured and enthusiastic under pressure
- Skilled organizer and problem solver with the ability to consider options with an open mind before making a decision

AREAS OF EXPERTISE
- Identifying customer requirements
- Maintaining a high level of service
- Sourcing, ordering and delivering products
- Organizing and servicing large geographical area
- Negotiating price and quality
- Maintaining and anticipating stock levels
- Customer credit control
- Route planning

TECHNICAL SKILLS
BTEC HND Food Technology
Windows XP; Word; Excel

EXPERIENCE AND SELECTED ACCOMPLISHMENTS
Cherry Valley Farms Ltd
Customer Operations Co-ordinator (1998–Present)
Shift Supervisor (1997–1998)
Van Salesman (1995–1997)
- Increased turnover by 200% in first six months
- Increased overall turnover by £3,000 per week
- Turned a subsidized territory into a profitable area
- Reorganized two sales routes into one, reducing costs
- Developed new and existing customer accounts
- Reduced costs without reducing quality, developing a cost-effective and efficient service
- Developed and promoted mail-order and internet sales, reducing dependency on van-sales and consequently transport overheads

Sunday's (Production) Ltd
Product Development Supervisor (1993 to 1995)
Product Development Technician (1990 to 1993)

EDUCATION AND TRAINING
BTEC HND Food Technology, City University
BTEC OND Food Technology, City College

Customer Service Manager

JAMES SHARPE
123 ANYSTREET, ANYTOWN AT1 0BB. TEL: 020 8123 4567
james@anyaddress.co.uk

EXPERIENCE

CUSTOMER SERVICE MANAGER
A TELECOMMUNICATIONS COMPANY   2000 to Present
Hired and developed a staff of forty people to service the customer service needs of our highest revenue commercial accounts. Maintained an account retention percentage of 99%, while keeping revenue loss through credits to less than 2%.

CUSTOMER SERVICE – TELEMARKETING MANAGER
OMC – S.E. Region Customer Service Centre, Saintbury   1998 to 2000
Hired and developed a staff of sixty customer service – telemarketing representatives and supervisors.

Managed a mixture of inbound and outbound call activities with job responsibilities including: sales, customer service, customer correspondence and special projects.

Responsible for a budget of close to £1 million.

CUSTOMER SERVICE SUPERVISOR
X-Tel, North Ramside   1997 to 1998
Supervision of a division customer service staff. Responsibilities include: providing support for our sales force and sales management, implementing new policy and procedures for customer service, and monitoring to see that all our sales and service objectives are met.

CUSTOMER SERVICE REPRESENTATIVE
X-Tel   1992 to 1997
Involved in all aspects of customer service, including: answering questions, problem solving, interfacing with our sales force, and working with new customers to implement X-Tel services.

EDUCATION

BA 1992, South West University.

TRAINING

Leadership and Management of Change. Results Oriented Management. Managing Management Time.

REFERENCES AVAILABLE ON REQUEST

Electrical Design Engineer

Jane Swift
123 Anystreet
Anytown AT1 OBB
Tel: 020 8123 4567
jane@anyaddress.co.uk

CAREER
OBJECTIVE: Development and Design of Digital and Analogue equipment

SUMMARY: Experienced with TTL, ECL, GaAs, programmable arrays, and microprocessors. Familiar with RS-232, IEEE-488, and manchester code interfaces. Analogue design including Op-Amps, D/A's, A/D's, multiplexers and sample/holds. Secret clearance.

EXPERIENCE:
1994–Present   *ELECTRICAL ENGINEER (SOBELL)*

Designed digital and analogue equipment for Avionic Fuel Measurement and Management Systems. Prime flight hardware and support test equipment designs include:

> *Analogue Signal Conditioner* – Unit to condition analogue and digital signals provided to flight system computers. Design employed D/A converters, active filters and digital logic.

> *Digital Display Indicator* – Indicator displayed fuel quantity information to ground crew. Design consisted of LCD displays, digital logic and self-contained power supply. Dealt with small packaging requirements.

> *Analogue Tester* – Designed support test equipment to perform Acceptance Tests on Analogue Signal Conditioner.

> *Digital Tester* – Designed support test equipment to perform Acceptance Test on Digital Display Indicator.

1987–1993   *DESIGN ENGINEER (LANSDALE PRECISION)*

Member of circuit design group. Responsible for the design and debugging of various analogue and digital circuits/systems. Responsibilities included:

> Video processing portion of a radar pulse processing system. Included work with video amplifiers, track/hold amplifiers and the high-speed A/D convertors, as well as TTL (ALS, FAST, LS) and other high-speed logic.

> A servo-controller that used programmable array logic, TTL, Op-Amps and D/A convertors.

> A spread spectrum ratio that used high-speed TTL (FAST), programmable array logic and a 16-bit microprocessor, with a customer interface and a RS-232 interface.

EDUCATION: London University
BSc Electronic Engineering

Electrician

James Sharpe
123 Anystreet
Anytown AT1 0BB
Tel: 020 8123 4567
james@anyaddress.co.uk

SUMMARY

Master Electrician. Experienced in all types of electrical work – residential, commercial, industrial, electrical construction, and estimating. Six years' management experience as a Foreman.

EXPERIENCE
1996 to present

Opus Electric – Langley. Chief Electrician
Responsible for all sales, estimating, work schedule, billing, ordering of parts and equipment, maintenance of inventories, and customer service. Projects have included complete wiring of a manufacturing business after relocation, new home construction, repair of equipment, building additions. Have worked as a contractor and subcontractor.

1996

Industrial JC – Dale. Chief Electrician
Foreman on medium-sized projects, with crews of 2 to 10. Scheduled the work, checked quality and productivity, provided layouts and supervision.

1994

Longridge & Sons – Allerton. Electrician
Team member on construction of the Sheraton Hotel.

1993

CCG – Saudia Arabia. Electrician
Worked on a nuclear power plant (heavy industrial project), where safety and reliability were extremely important.

1991 to 1992

H&L Construction – Birmingham. Electrician
A variety of commercial and industrial projects (hospital, high-rise buildings, office-hotel complex).

TRAINING

North London Technical College
City & Guilds: Electrical Installation Certificate

PERSONAL

Willing to travel, relocate

References Available

Entrepreneurial

Jane Swift

123 Anystreet   Anytown   AT1 0BB   (H) 020 8123 4567   (O) 020 8123 4567
jane@anyaddress.co.uk

QUALIFICATIONS SUMMARY
Human Resource Management
Programme Development, Recruitment, Training, Quality Process Management

EXPERIENCE
Kirkdale College, Kirkdale   1993 to Present

Director, Career Planning and Placement   1998 to Present
Liaison between college and industry, building international reputation through development of
the following support and services:
- Direct professional staff of three, semi-professional staff of 10 and £85,000 operating budget in providing comprehensive placement service for 3,000 undergraduates, 250 postgraduates.
- Develop network of corporate and government employers within Business, High Tech, Creative, and Science areas.
- Annually achieve 90% placement of graduates, including hundreds at management level.
- Market on-campus recruiting programme resulting in over 200 companies visiting each season.
- Host VIP campus visits and receptions.
- Extensive travel includes organizing and supervising trade shows, attending conferences, visiting industry.
- Provide input for academic programme development through analysis of industry trends.
- Initiated seminar and workshop programmes covering all aspects of career planning and search.
- Publish bi-monthly nationally circulated *Job Opportunities Bulletin*, *Annual Placement and Salary Survey*, *CV Handbook*, and *Student Handbook on Placement*.
- Supervise work placement and summer job programmes for undergraduates.
- Directed software development and computerization of department, 1993.

Assistant Director, Placement Office   1993 to 1998

INVOLVEMENTS
- Visited/consulted with South African organizations on recruitment programme development, 1999.
- Member, College Placement Council.
- Member, Placement Association.
- Past Chairman of Membership, Publicity and Office Training Committees.
- Published articles for trade journals, appear on media, conference speaker.
- Volunteer, Youth Programme.
- Member, Toastmasters International.
- Member, Youth Resource Council.
- Accomplished photographer, enjoy painting.

EDUCATION
KIRKDALE COLLEGE
1993 to 1998, Marketing Management (part-time)
Numerous Technical and Business Seminars
Executive Management Programme
D & L Management Consultants, 2000

Entry-Level Advertising Sales

Jane Swift
123 Anystreet
Anytown AT1 0BB
Tel: 020 8123 4567
jane@anyaddress.co.uk

Strengths: Enthusiastic, creative, and hard working marketing executive with demonstrated successful sales experience. Reputation for providing excellent customer service resulting in increased sales and improved customer retention. Eager to translate solid classroom and workplace experience in advertising sales into bottom-line revenues in the radio/television industry.

Education: BA (Hons) 2.1 – Marketing, East Kent Business School – May, 2000. Coursework including advertising research & strategy, design & graphics, media planning, ad sales & campaigns.

Final year
- *Challenge:* Create an advertising campaign for the St Philip's Hospice Group.
- *Action:* As key member of a 6-person team, performed demographics survey, developed campaign strategies, created logo and slogan, authored and designed bilingual brochures, and created media kit within £100,000 budget.
- *Result:* After presenting project to 11-person panel, won first place out of 12 teams. The St Philip's Hospice Group implemented the slogan and several campaign strategies.

Work Experience
Advertising Sales Representative, Lakeland Advertising – Sept–Dec 1999
- Sold print advertising to local businesses using cold calling techniques.

Production Assistant, Community Access Broadcasting – Jan–May 1999
- Assisted with production of 2 to 3 Public Information Broadcasts a week. Accountable for delivering all technical equipment to the site and pre-production set up of lights, monitors, microphones and cameras. Worked closely with producer, learning both the technical side of production as well as client service issues.
- Handled pre-production and on-air tasks, including studio set up, script delivery, running pre-taped segments, operating on-air cameras and soundboards.

Sales/Customer Service Experience
Sales/Waiting Staff, Lakes Breweries, Boreland
- Consistently generate additional revenues using thorough product knowledge and friendly sales technique to sell house specials and add-on items. Contender for the local sales award.

Host/Waiting Staff, Jack's Seaford, Elverdale
- Developed repeat business by providing excellent customer service in fast-paced environment.

Awards/Memberships
- Won Silver Medal, an annual award for college students, 1999
- Served as Co-Director of Adwerks, developing ads for non-profit organizations, 1998
- Member and committee chairperson of the Ad Society, a college professional organization, 1998–2000

Equipment Sales

James Sharpe
123 Anystreet
Anytown AT1 0BB
Tel: 020 8123 4567
james@anyaddress.co.uk

Experience Summary
More than 15 years' customer/sales experience delivering impressive results in diverse markets and industries. Strengths include:

- Technical sales
- Banking products and services
- Contract negotiations
- Needs-specific account service
- Customer satisfactions
- Account management

Professional Experience
Customer Service/Sales Representative, Jackson's Autoparts, 1998–Present
- Secure and service field accounts. Expand customer base and increase quarterly sales 20% by winning prominent accounts. Close sales by offering unique incentives and using sales strategies to counter pricing objections. Assume control of poorly serviced accounts and rebuild relationships with customers. Prevent loss of sale by expediting turnaround time for processing product requests.
- Surpassed collections quota by 150%. Collected on difficult accounts by negotiating payment arrangements, employing refined techniques, and adhering to company policies.

Senior Technical Sales Representative, Office Electrical, 1988–1998
- Drove profitability of a nationally renowned retailer through consistent sales of high-cost industrial equipment.
- Built long-term relationships and increased sales by persuading customers to purchase warranty contracts.
- Instrumental in securing multimillion pound contracts from hotels, businesses and property owners.
- Transformed inexperienced reps into skilled technicians through comprehensive hands-on training.
- Only technical sales rep out of 19 retail locations qualified to service industrial A/C units.

Education & Training
- Certificate, Computer Technology, Institute of Data Technology; Coursework: Troubleshooting, Diagnostics, Computer Language
- Degree, Mechanical Engineering

Technical Expertise & Additional Information
- Proficient in Windows XP, MS Word and data entry
- Designed propulsions system for motorbikes (patent pending)

Executive Assistant

Jane Swift
123 Anystreet
Anytown AT1 0BB
Tel: 020 8123 4567
jane@anyaddress.co.uk
Page 1 of 2

Career and Personal Profile

Assist senior management in daily operations. Provide expert and confidential executive support and office management through experience gained in both large and small organizations. Excel in meeting objectives using independent action, prioritization, persistence, and leadership skills. Adapt quickly to diverse management and client styles. Use humour, positive attitude, continuous training and high standards to motivate staff to excellence.

Areas of Knowledge

- Executive office administration
- Fast-paced diary scheduling
- Executive-level correspondence
- Time-sensitive assignments
- Supply-inventory and purchasing
- Advanced computer applications
- Confidential materials management
- Accounts payable/receivable

Professional Highlights

- Directly contributed to company performance by offering expertise, reliability and continuity in office procedures, setting clear communication lines between clients and company, and managing all office activities on a day-to-day basis
- Managed complex planning and prioritization of workload, including secretarial duties, invoicing, accounts receivable/payable, and purchasing functions
- Designed and implemented administrative procedures in office
- Handled purchasing of office consumables, continually doing comparisons of best value. Generated thousands of pounds in savings by researching and purchasing most cost-effective office equipment, including photocopier and printers
- Monitored printing and stationery costs and implemented cost-effective measures
- Rationalized entry of information on to database with the result that the business was more accurately represented

Computer Skills

Windows XP
Word: Outlook Express; Excel; Access; PowerPoint
Dictaphone transcription

Employment

Highbury plc, Cheshire   1997 to Present
Office Manager/Executive Assistant
Highbury runs a flourishing integrated multi-utility business in the UK, including water treatment facilities serving more than 2.5 million customers in England and Wales. It provides high-quality infrastructure services, designing, developing, financing, managing and advising on infrastructure nationally.

Report directly to senior management; work independently on a daily basis.

ADMINISTRATION ACTIVITIES
- Manage comprehensive day-to-day office operations
- Maintain computer systems and confidential records
- Create and support databases, word processing and reports
- Exercise discretion regarding confidential records
- Train employees for office programmes and procedures
- Field continuous stream of phone calls while maintaining flow of daily activities
- Monitor all bank accounts and investments
- Pay all bills, do bank deposits, track all invoices and expenses
- Supervise up to ten staff
- Set up agendas and minute all departmental meetings up to, and including, board level
- Coordinate department work schedules
- Organize client preparations and corporate entertainment
- Compile monthly budget reports
- Prepare quantity audits, projections and financial statements

Somerheys & Partners Ltd, Doncaster   1994 to 1997
Office Manager

Midwich Supplies, Doncaster   1992 to 1994
Administrative Assistant

Martin J Donaldson Ltd, Ipswich   1990 to 1992
Department Secretary
Clerical Assistant

Education
North Cheshire Business College
RSA Stage II
RSA Stage III
NCBC Certificate: Finance for Administrators

Executive Management

James Sharpe
123 Anystreet
Anytown AT1 0BB
Tel: 020 8123 4567
james@anyaddress.co.uk

Page 1 of 2

Executive Management ● Financial/Business Analysis ● Consulting Energy
and High-Tech Computer/Telecom/Internet Industries

Profile
Dynamic, achievement-focused leader and manager with an established performance record and
expertise in the energy and hi-tech industries. Couple strong analytical skills with core qualifications
in accounting and administration to drive, efficiency, and financial performance improvements.

Areas of Strength

Financial and business analysis	Process Improvement
Energy Accounting	Public Speaking/Presentations
Organizing and re-engineering	Team Building and Leadership
Project management	Instruction/Training

Professional Highlights
Broadside Petroleum plc
Petroleum exploration and production company operating oil and gas wells in the North Sea and
managing outside operated investments across Northern Europe.

MANAGER, NEW BUSINESS VENTURES   1998–Present
Senior manager with an expansive scope of responsibilities including execution of
accounting, reporting, and financial functions for all operations, serving as key liaison to field
operational personnel, and evaluation and co-ordination of prospective investments.

Key Results
▪ Streamlined administrative and reporting functions
▪ Renewed investors' faith in investment management capabilities by demonstrating
  improved accounting and reporting processes; elevated the company's status when
  proposing large projects to investors
▪ Championed the consolidation of Broadside's three separate companies into a single
  company; dramatically improved efficiency by eliminating redundant administrative
  tasks.
▪ Re-engineered the Production Department for optimal efficiency; introduced
  computerized accounting and reporting and developed automated performance
  monitoring systems. Saved labour costs by eliminating and reducing staff positions
▪ Led the turnaround of the Accounting Department; redesigned processes and systems
  for efficiency and brought all accounts current less than 90 days from inception

MultiTech Ltd
   TECHNICAL SUPPORT MANAGER   1994–1998
      Developed and managed technical support division with full P&L responsibility, delivering pre- and post-sales support for the UK's leading supplier of CAD and CAM tools.

      Representative Achievements
- Managed business within budget
- Met revenue and cost objectives
- Negotiated £450,000 contract for system hardware and software upgrade

Solution Computers Ltd
   SENIOR ENGINEER   1991–1994
   SYSTEMS ENGINEER   1987–1991

Education and Training
Midlands University
BSc (Hons) 2.1 Electronic Engineering
Technical training courses covering hardware, software and networking

Recent Additional Training
Oil and Gas Accounting, Modern Petroleum
Updates:
Microsoft Networking Essentials
Microsoft Office and Advanced Microsoft Excel

Computer Skills
Advanced computer skills including both hardware and software. Demonstrated ability in applying technology to improve organizational efficiency and productivity. Extensive experience developing custom Excel applications and forms and preparing PowerPoint presentations and lectures.

Executive Marketing/Sales

JAMES SHARPE

123 Anystreet ● Anytown AT1 0BB ● Tel: 020 8123 4567
james@anyaddress.co.uk

Executive Summary

*A fast-track, highly motivated, team-oriented executive with a successful background in **turnaround situations**. More than 8 years' progressive experience in all aspects of **Market Development** and **Regional Sales Management**. Recognized for exceptional ability to develop specialized marketing strategies, sales methods and training procedures. Effectively motivates others on all levels in the achievement of individual and organizational goals.*

- P&L responsibility
- Market Optimization
- Technical Sales Support
- Operations Management
- Analysing results

- Sales Management
- Marketing/Advertising Strategy
- Training Module Development
- Interpersonal relationships
- Evaluating feedback

Selected Achievements

- Targeted technical support services and increased uptake by 85%
- Organized and established new product range from conception to completion, achieving £150,000 turnover in first year with 25% year on year growth thereafter
- Took over two new neglected ranges and revitalized them, increasing profits by 200%
- Organized ongoing training programme for internal and external sales personnel with training in sales and product knowledge, thereby decreasing staff turnover by 37% and increasing met-targets by 57%
- Planned and organized nationwide programme of exhibitions and seminars
- Prepared and delivered presentations at all levels, including hands-on product demonstrations to groups of all sizes

Employment History

Executive Regional manager   1998 to Present
Post Office Systems

Sales Manager   1993 to 1998
Direct Business Systems

Sales Representative   1991 to 1993
Dane Copiers Ltd

Education

BSc (Hons) 2.2 Economics, University of the South

Finance Executive

James Sharpe
123 Anystreet
Anytown AT1 0BB
Tel: 020 8123 4567
james@anyaddress.co.uk
Page 1 of 2

Professional Profile

Corporate Finance Executive and troubleshooting specialist with a command of operations, organization and general management. Expert competence in financial planning and analysis, cost reduction and performance/profit improvement. Excellent qualifications in managing large-scale projects from concept through planning design, development and task management. Detail-oriented and analytical. Experience in the areas of:

economic analysis ● forecasting and budgeting ● staffing and management ● quality and financial control ● sales and marketing programmes ● revenue management ● team building and leadership ● customer development ● project management ● strategic planning ● competitive pricing analysis ● diversity strategies

Performance Highlights

- Orchestrated a winning partnership between Service Parts Operations and other divisions. Supported £1 billion in annual sales business; reviewed all finance issues, provided profit & loss analysis, collaborated with six divisions to consummate alliance.
- Developed a £1 billion, five-year integrated business plan for partnership retention that included projected volume, sales, and business performance initiatives with the objective to establish profitable targets.
- Facilitated the business plan portion of 'Troubled Products' initiative (unfavourable operating profit). Generated support to make the product lines more profitable (£27 million in favourable profits) in areas of manufacturing, distribution, pricing, and other customer-driven incentives.
- Secured approval on numerous sales and marketing proposals/programmes on behalf of corporate aftermarket sales staff. Made presentations on significant programmes (exceeding £250k in operating profit impact) to the Price & Policy Review Group.
- Managed a zero-based budget as Staff Assistant to the Regional Personnel Director. Project included a £15 million operating budget (400+ security personnel, doctors, nurses and personnel benefits administration) in 11 divisions. Created budgets and forecasts for the area Personnel Directors.
- Managed various functional financial departments (Budgets, Forecasts, Payroll, Cost Accounting, Accounts Receivable, Audit, and Accounts Payable).
- Currently coordinating project to achieve market-based competitive prices (excess of £70 million) on aftermarket parts from suppliers.
- Experienced international traveller.
- Knowledge of conversational French; learning Swahili.

Education

Eastern University, MSc, Business Management
North Midlands University, BSc (Hons) 2.1, Business Administration

Experience

S&C Motor Corporation, Finance Manager – Service Operation   *1999–Present*

- Manage the Pricing and Product Programmes Group; review, analyse and report on proposals; support the sales & marketing staff; supervise and develop employees; ensure that profitability goals are met in the aftermarket channel; ensure that people development is consistent with diversity strategy; serve as financial liaison to other staffs/divisions.
- Provide financial analysis and impact on the corporation and customers; supply distribution analysis and make corporate decisions on value-added proposals.
- Currently working on introducing product lines at a national retailer/installer. Proposed package has a projected annual sales of £7.5 million in the first year and £40 million in the third year, with a margin of 10–15%. Process includes P&L analysis, customer/distributor partner interface, implementation using cross-functional workgroups, and 12–15 new product launches.
- Pricing/Product Programmes and Market Support initiatives/objectives include:
  - Improve staff efficiency/manage head count (41 employees); implement synchronous improvements.
  - Skills enhancements/employee development; apply cross-training initiatives.
  - Strategic/action-oriented analysis; administer channel/product line/customer profitability reporting processes; use common processes.
  - Enhance partnership reporting; interact with divisions to establish integrated business plan and establish profitability targets for product lines.
  - Conduct competitive price analyses, family pricing, life-cycle model strategies, elasticity analyses, profitability analysis to identify opportunities.

Regional Workforce Unit, Staff Assistant   *1997–1999*
Developed budget and forecasts. Monitored and recorded expenses. Presented statistical data on costs, head counts, and initiatives to 11 area Personnel Directors. Coordinated billing of actual costs. Performed actual vs. forecast analysis.

Automotive Glass Section, General Supervisor   *1995–1997*
Responsibilities encompassed operations analysis, payroll, receivables, and disbursement analysis; supervised 14 direct reports. Developed annual budgets and monthly plan reports; performed ad hoc analyses; reported on actual vs. budget performance. Managed all payroll, receivables and disbursement analysis liaison activities. Supervised and monitored annual £30 million inventory at glass production facility. Chief financial person who ensured accurate physical inventory count (worked with outside accounting firm of Ambit-Greenholt).

Manufacturing Section, Supervisor/Account/Senior Clerk   *1993–1995*
Managed supplier disbursement payments and the audit department. Developed plant operating budget for the Maryville Engine Section. Group leader for 40 employees in accounts payable. Generated production material cost forecasts; managed capital expenditures; recorded and audited special inventories; reconciled general ledger accounts, developed inventory forecast; recorded sales and cost of sale entries.

Financial Administrator

JAMES SHARPE

123 Anystreet
Anytown AT1 0BB

Tel: 020 8123 4567
james@anyaddress.co.uk

CAREER SUMMARY

A dedicated finance professional with 17 years' experience. Qualified Management Accountant, FMCA and Financial Administrator with expert analytical skills gained in both large and medium-sized companies. Experienced at meeting strict deadlines efficiently and effectively, with excellent communication skills and a high degree of personal commitment.

EXPERIENCE

Financial and Management Accounting
Managed day-to-day control of Finance Department. Ensured compliance with strict Accounting deadlines. VAT liaison officer. Department Budgets and Forecasts with variance reviews, including Central Distribution costing control. Fixed Assets reporting in excess of £25 million. Prepared annual Company Accounts and Tax Computations for audit. Organized and administered Period Management Accounts.

Company Administration
Attended meetings up to and including board level. Liaised with bankers, insurers and solicitors and reported accordingly.

Electronic Banking Systems and Computerized Accounting
Administered electronic and online banking functions. Controlled batch and online systems output.

Cash Management, Credit Control and Sales Ledger
Reduced Credit days from 54 to 35 days. Cash flow, Forecasting/Payment and Receivables, SWAPS and FX deals, FRAs Negotiations with banks.

Computer Skills
Mainframe – IBM, Hewlett-Packard, ICL
Windows XP, Word, Excel, Lotus 123, Supercalc

Communication Skills
Gave regular update reports to other departments including Marketing, Sales and Production. Made presentations to both executive and junior personnel.
Supervised between 12 and 24 staff, including appraisal and job evaluation

CAREER SUMMARY

Corbell Manufacturing	
FINANCIAL ADMINISTRATOR	1998 to present
FINANCIAL ACCOUNTANT	. 1990 to 1998
Impala Systems	
ACCOUNTANT	1985 to 1990

EDUCATION

HND Business Studies
FCMA

Health Care Hygienist

Jane Swift
123 Anystreet
Anytown AT1 0BB
Tel: 020 8123 4567
jane@anyaddress.co.uk

Qualifications
- Diploma in Dental Hygiene
- Certificate of Proficiency in Dental Nursing

A competent, reliable dental hygienist offers successful experience and an up-to-date, comprehensive knowledge of current dental practice. Broad scope of expertise, with experience in key areas such as:

- Assessing patient dental health
- Demonstrating oral hygiene techniques
- Taking and developing dental x-rays
- Providing temporary dressings
- Instructing patients on dental care
- Removing tartar, calculus and plaque
- Administering local anaesthesia
- Removing stitches following dental surgery
- Effecting preventative dental care procedures such as fissure and pit sealing

- Demonstrated ability to provide extensive technical support
- Experienced in preventative dental care
- Excellent interpersonal skills
- A clear understanding of the place of oral hygiene in maintaining dental health
- Confident and personable
- Resourceful and reliable under pressure
- Experience of working in both private practice and a busy health centre
- Capable of making a significant contribution to any practice

Professional Experience

The Morevale Clinic   *1998–present*
Dental Hygienist

The Hidcote Centre   *1996–1998*
Dental Hygienist

Dowery Partnership   *1993–1996*
Dental Nurse

Frencham Health Centre   *1992–1993*
Dental Receptionist

Education and Training

West of England Dental Hospital
Diploma of Dental Hygiene
Certificate of Proficiency in Dental Nursing

Hospital Trust Administrator

Jane Swift
123 Anystreet
Anytown AT1 0BB
Tel: 020 8123 4567
jane@anyaddress.co.uk

Experienced and methodical medical records administrator

- Extensive experience in the verification, storage and retrieval of records both as documents and on database
- Maintained, developed and administered medical records and data systems
- Supervised staff compiling and inputting record data, and storing documents
- Collected, stored and retrieved patient data
- Formulated strategies for handling volume records
- Implemented effective procedures for storing and retrieving
- Developed user-friendly methods of staff processing
- Undertook first-stage statistical analysis
- Prepared and supplied information for staff and departments

Professional Experience
Records Administrator, Barton and District Hospital Trust 1997 to Present
Responsible for all aspects of receiving, storing, retrieving and supplying data.
- Supervised up to ten staff
- Maintained and updated records and files
- Checked records in and out
- Noted inconsistencies and queried as necessary
- Processed both documents and computerized records and printouts

Administrative Assistant, East Holywell Health Centre 1994 to 1997
Provided clerical and administrative support to Centre Administrator.
- Maintained and updated records
- Input and retrieved data and statistical information
- Coordinated communications between staff, clinics and clinic users
- Monitored usage of consumables

Clerical Officer, Department of Employment 1992 to 1994
- Processed claims for unemployment benefit
- Maintained and updated client records

Computer Skills
Word, Outlook Express
Database and record systems:
Access database, Excel, RecordTec tailored statistical package

Education
City College
CLAIT

Human Resources Manager

Jane Swift
123 Anystreet
Anytown AT1 0BB
Tel: 020 8123 4567
jane@anyaddress.co.uk

A professional human resources manager with a fundamental interest in employee potential and workplace equality together with practical experience gained in both large and medium-sized organizations. Expertise in:

- Recruitment
- Assessment and appraisal
- Psychometric testing
- Policies and procedures

- Training
- Aptitude testing
- Careers guidance and counselling
- Employee relations

Selected Highlights
- Highly evolved personnel management skills
- Extensive experience in all facets of human resource assessment and development
- Thoroughly knowledgeable about employment law
- Widespread contacts within training agencies, Training and Enterprise Councils and recruitment agencies
- Qualified and experienced in the use of a range of psychometric and other tools for testing and selecting
- Experienced in both researching and selecting effective training programmes, and devising and delivering them from scratch
- Experienced in employee assessment and review

Relevant Career Experience
Goldman Barley
Human Resources Manager (1997 to present)
> Responsible for overall personnel function. Managed office and field staff. Developed personnel policies and procedures for financial group. Improved effectiveness of human resource development strategies. Supervised introduction of 360° performance appraisals.

The Hartshaw Partnership Ltd
Personnel Officer (1992 to 1995)
> Complete personnel function for Northern Region and Field staff. Administered records, pay and contractual documents

United Industrial
Personnel Officer (1990 to 1992)
Personnel Assistant (1987 to 1990)

Professional Memberships
Fellow of the Institute of Personnel

Education
Diploma in Personnel Management, Westgate College

Human Resources Professional

James Sharpe
123 Anystreet
Anytown AT1 0BB
Tel: 020 8123 4567
james@anyaddress.co.uk
Page 1 of 2

HUMAN RESOURCE PROFILE
Self-motivated human resource professional, successful in leading cross-functional project teams by cultivating and promoting effective working relationships. Goal-driven manager with proven track record of establishing strategic plans, priorities, work assignments and solutions within allotted time and resources. Collaborator with human resource manager, sharing restructuring and rewriting of job descriptions, performing applicant screenings and initial interviews.

KEY STRENGTHS

Career Pathing	Adult Learning Strategies
New Employee Orientation	Human Resource Partnerships
Performance Reengineering	Change Management
Corporate Technology Trainer	Curriculum Design
Train-the-Trainer	Software Applications, SAP R/3

CAREER HIGHLIGHTS
Smart Manufacturing Ltd, Chapel Hill   1991 to Present
Technology Education Manager, Human Resources (1997 to Present)
Launch, implement and coordinate companywide training programmes and curriculum for 2,400 employees. Support Information Technology Department with focus on high commitment work systems and ongoing improvement. Assess worker competencies through consultations with department and project managers to devise learning strategies and delivery methodologies.

- Joined forces with human resource management team to reorganize department.
- Oversaw design and growth of innovative curriculum with over 300 various modules addressing all aspects of new company global business processes.
- Instituted company's first online learning system for desktop applications with skills assessment and self-paced tutorial resource tools.
- Created and executed training with support efforts for new worldwide e-mail and calendar system to meet company Y2K objectives.
- Set up and led change management process from centralized computer training to decentralized environment.

Team Leader (1991 to 1997)
Hired and supervised desktop computing team, responsible for performance appraisals and advising workers on career advancement. Planned and administered special activities related to vendor negotiations on renewal agreements.

- Introduced college work placement programme that reduced workload of full-time staff without paying high cost of consultants. Benefit: Some students retained as permanent staff after graduation.
- Spearheaded development of Power Users in 'Train-the-Trainer' programmes resulting in major training cost savings and well-informed workforce.

PROFESSIONAL SYSTEMS LTD, Chapel Hill   1984 to 1990
    Reseller of personal computing products to medium to large UK companies
Area Training Manager 1986 to 1990
    Coordinated sales activities related to computer training for major and national accounts. Hired and coached instructors and administrative personnel, conducted performance reviews, and assisted workers with career development issues. Managed eight training facilities while steering activities related to class scheduling and curriculum development for each location. Constructed long-range sales quotas and plans for mid-central area, preparing and maintaining budgets and related financial reports.

- Received National Achievement Award for exceeding sales quotas by 158%, 1988–1989.
- Opened company's first satellite training facility in a secondary market, generating ⅓ of Northern Region's profits by end of first year of operation.
- Invented and installed volume purchase coupon programme, giving customers method to purchase training at volume discounted rate, redeemable at any of 126 company training facilities. Benefit: Moved company to top slot as national training vendor.
- Coordinated production of national training tool that furnished company with centralized consistent tracking and reporting system.

Sales Training Manager (1984 to 1986)
    Inaugurated and promoted sales and technical training programme activities in central region. Initiated ongoing sales development programme, cross-training store managers in delivery process.

EDUCATION
Master degree program   University of the South
Business Management
Bachelor of Arts   University of the South
Business Management/Human Relations

PROFESSIONAL CERTIFICATIONS AND AFFILIATIONS
- Certified Instructor, Human Relations and Effective Speaking
- Training and Development Certification
- Leadership Certificate, Leadership Management Course
- Certificate, Situational Interviewing Techniques, Computer Technologies Ltd
- Member, National Society of Training and Development
- Member, Continuing Education Association

Community Involvement
- Consultant, Student Achievement Program, 2000
- Participant, Everybody Wins, literacy programme for children, 1996 to 2000
- Fund raiser, National Diabetes Association, 1998 to 1999
- Fund raiser, Multiple Sclerosis Association, 1998

Human Resources Specialist

Jane Swift

123 Anystreet
Anytown AT1 0BB

Tel: 020 8123 4567
jane@anyaddress.co.uk
Page 1 of 2

Fellow of the Institute of Personnel and Development
Sixteen years' success in Corporate HR – Promoted ahead of peers – Delivered results in special assignments

---

KEY WORDS

HR administration – Employee Relations – Grievance Procedures – Arbitration – Tribunals – Team Building – Recruitment – Disciplinary Procedures – Sexual Harassment – Redundancy – Health and Safety – Psychometric Testing – Partnership Agreements – Performance Evaluation

---

Results – HR, Employee Relations and Training
- Qualified to use psychometric testing and profiling tools
- Achieved 75% staff compliance with introduction of 24-hour online and telephone customer service
- Developed comprehensive company policy on human resources
- Reduced staff turnover by 25%, reducing recruitment, induction and training costs as well as productivity loss
- Increased efficiency and productivity overall through a variety of schemes
- Negotiated Partnership Agreement between management and two on-site unions
- Introduced Quality Programme of personnel-led productivity initiatives
- Devised and delivered focused induction training courses to new employees and initiated update training programmes across the board for existing 420 employees

Leadbury Holdings plc   1996 to Present
EMPLOYEE RELATIONS MANAGER
Managed inclusive personnel function for Head Office and general staff
- Developed comprehensive knowledge of employment law, performance management, and grievance and discipline handling
- Developed personnel policies and procedures for financial group
- Liaised with specialist employment consultancies to expedite high-level technical recruitment
- Undertook project management
- Improved effectiveness of human resources development strategies
- Facilitated introduction of performance evaluation system
- Covered complete IR function
- Extended skills in all aspects of personnel management

Bower & Prince Ltd   1990 to 1996
HUMAN RESOURCES MANAGER
Organized comprehensive personnel function
- Managed personnel function for field-based staff, locally-based office and general staff
- Administered records, pay and contractual documents
- Promoted from Assistant Personnel Officer in 1993

Broadlands Ltd   1985 to 1990
PERSONNEL ADMINISTRATION SUPERVISOR
Responsible for administration of
- Records
- Information
- Pay
- Contractual documents
Promoted from Personnel Assistant in 1987

Education
BA (Hons) 2.1 Politics with Economics, Midlands University

Work-Related Training
Psychometric testing
Assessment Skills
Coaching, Mentoring and Assessing
Management Training courses

Information Technology Consultant

James Sharpe
123 Anystreet
Anytown AT1 0BB
Tel: 020 8123 4567
james@anyaddress.co.uk
Page 1 of 2

Summary
Talented, profit-driven professional qualified by nearly 10 years of visible achievements in leading-edge information technologies. Expertise in high-volume territory sales management, demonstrating skills in maintenance of revenue-generating accounts in highly competitive markets. Areas of strength include: key account management, staff recruiting/development, strategic business planning, product presentation, technical staff management, relationship building, client consulting, value-added selling, contract negotiation, project management. Technically proficient in Win98, WinXP, Windows NT Workstation, Windows NT server, Novell 3.x and 4.x, SMS, SQL, TCP/IP, cc:Mail, Microsoft Exchange and most Microsoft applications; trained in CISCO and Synoptics Design and Diagnostics.

Recent Consulting Projects
L&G Holdings. Orchestrated marketing and configuration of Compaq servers and all peripherals valued at £2.5 million annually; successfully sold and managed company-wide roll-out of new computer and software encompassing over 7,000 desktops, valued at £1 million nationwide. Accountability for placement and management of 10 technical service professionals generating £312,000 annually.
Avon Insurance. Cooperative secured £1.5+ million nationwide contract for full inventory of desktops, servers, laptops and peripherals with services including setup/configurations, depot repair and on-site support at 500 locations.
AS & P Ltd. Provided expertise in £1.2 million sale consisting of 550 computers with complete setup and configuration to desktop; successfully negotiated service agreements valued at £120,000 annually.
National Industries Ltd. Participated in sale of over 600 machines valued at £1 million with four technical professionals generating £320,000 annually.
Western Hospital Trust. Key player in successful marketing complete intranet and online policy manual (£30,000), total help desk solutions (£45,000), various service agreements (£25,000 annually), and technical personnel (£60,000 annually).
Nova Technology Centre. Successfully directed installation and configuration of all LAN/WAN equipment (3Com) purchased for two-storey building and valued at £125,000.
Green Industries Ltd. Placement and management of four technical professionals generating £175,000 annually.

Professional Experience
XL Technologies, 1996–Present
Director of Technical Services & Sales
- Managed £1.5 million full-service profit centre supporting business development and technical service efforts for computer reseller/integrator generating £6 million in annual revenues.
- Direct workflow of 12 in-house and 30 on-site technical associates involved in repair and service of hardware from all major manufacturers in addition to LAN/WAN network design, support and maintenance.
- Key member of sales function focused on new business development, client needs analysis, product/service presentation, suggestive/strategic selling, and extensive ongoing value-added selling, customer service and problem resolution.

James Sharpe 020 8123 4567
page 2 of 2

- Oversee special projects, workflow management, quality assurance, and technical troubleshooting; significant achievements managing priorities under pressure while maintaining positive client relations.
- Credited with increasing number of technicians from 17 to 42, doubling service department revenues within two years while increasing responses time to fewer than eight business hours and maintaining less than 15 per cent employee turnover.

Southeastern Technologies Ltd, 1992–1996
Senior Engineer
- Orchestrated on-site technical services at corporate headquarters for four years; instrumental in placement and management of 11 on-site technicians; spearheaded numerous special projects to assure quality and efficient information management for all accounts.
- Supported 1,200 PCs, 300 printers, 14 NT file servers and 12 Novell servers and provided support on Windows 3.x, Win95, Windows NT Workstation, Windows NT server, Novell 3.x SMS 1.1, SQL, TCP/IP, cc:Mail and all Microsoft applications.
- Managed entire quick response team for headquarters and several remote sites including all desktop and server-related hardware or software problems.
- Project manager of NT rollout team, responsible for converting over 1,200 PCs to Windows NT 3.51 workstation and 12 NT servers with back-office products.

Day Computers, 1990–1992
Technical Services Manager/Sales Representative
- Directed daily shop operations, sales, inventory control, call dispatching and weekly reporting for small organization offering full line of information technology solutions; instrumental in increasing annual revenues from £250,000 to £1.5 million.
- Gained valuable background in troubleshooting, maintenance and repair of all types of computer systems, printers, monitors; set up, supported and administered several Netware servers and supported Windows and DOS applications.

Education/Certification
North Eastern University, BSc (Hons) 2.1 Computer Information Technology
Certified in MCP, NT Workstation, NT Server

Information Technology Instructor

Jane Swift
123 Anystreet
Anytown AT1 0BB
Tel: 020 8123 4567
jane@anyaddress.co.uk

Qualified computer training specialist and information technology instructor. Trained and instructed numerous accounts for leading companies. Known for compliance and clarity; regarded for competence and creativity. Areas of expertise include:

computer training and coaching	technical writing	presentations/demonstrations
syllabus composition	resource documentation	technology instruction
Internet/e-mail	Microsoft certified	

Career Summary
Computer Trainer – certified in Microsoft products; competent in numerous Windows applications.
Technical Writer – developed user manuals, technical documentation, classroom syllabus design, presentations, and demonstrations.
Freelance Employment Columnist – for the *Business News*.
Employment Specialist – trained, evaluated and interviewed prospective employees; effectively matched qualified candidates with positions.
Guest Speaker/Facilitator – speak for various groups and organizations; facilitate job search and career enhancement workshops.
Memberships – UK Society for Training and Development (UKSTD), National Association for Job Search Training (NAJST).

Computer Expertise
Word Processing; Microsoft Word, AmiPro
Operating Systems: Windows 3.1/95/98, OS/2
Graphics: PowerPoint, Harvard Graphics
Spreadsheets: Microsoft Excel, Lotus 1-2-3
Database Management: Microsoft Access
Other: E-mail/Internet, PROFS

Experience
North East Hospital Trust, Information Analyst	1999–Present
Technical Solutions, Information Technology Trainer/Consultant	1997–1999
Offsite Resources and Services, Trainer/Staffing Specialist	1995–1997
Career Counselling Services, Owner	1995–Present
Metro Business Centre, Word Processing Specialist	1993–1995

Education and Professional Development
University of the South East, BA
CIPD Certificate in Training Practice
Associate Member CIPD

Information Technology Professional

James Sharpe
123 Anystreet, Anytown AT1 0BB
Tel: 020 8123 4567
james@anyaddress.co.uk
Page 1 of 2

Summary

- Information Technology professional with extensive knowledge of Windows NT Server 4.0 and Novell Net Ware operating systems.
- Practical, hands-on experience with assembly, troubleshooting, and repair of personal computers.
- Excellent customer relations skills, including delivery training and providing 'Help Desk' support for end users on a variety of Microsoft applications.
- Demonstrated ability to function effectively as a team player, as well as work independently to achieve organizational objectives.

TECHNICAL EXPERIENCE

Datex Systems, Tethering   1998–Present
Senior Technical Business Analyst

Provide systems technical support for multi national company's sales force throughout the UK and Europe. Configure x86 platforms, which include Windows NT Server, Windows NT Workstation Windows 95 and Windows 98, to operate with proprietary software package written for Xerox. Supported Microsoft Access database used for sales contact management.

- Provide end user/Help Desk support for PC-based systems used by company's employees.
- Train users on applications through teleconferencing, one-to-one training and on-site classes.
- Set up PC systems and configure software/hardware to meet individual users' needs.
- Diagnose software/hardware problems and address compatibility issues across Windows 3.x and Windows 95/98 platforms.
- Using Ghost application to clone PCs for use by other team members. Update and maintain hardware/software systems for 23 users.
- Administer one Novell 3.1 Server, one NT Stand-Alone Server, update all installed software, configure all software on local PCs and maintain inventory of software and licences.
- Serve as 'Subject Matter Expert' for LAN, NT and virus issues.

Major Project

Served as member of 'Travel Team' that performed remote installations and conducted on-site training for company's facilities throughout Europe. Troubleshot system problems and addressed user concerns.

Tech Solutions, Raysmill   1998
Contract Consultant

- Installed and configured NT Server Network for 25 users in an office setting. Updated software applications, wrote log scripts and installed Transaction and Index Servers.
- Adapted 386 DX platform for use with thermal camera in healthcare applications.

ADDITIONAL EXPERIENCE

Sales Associate – Telecom Cellular, Raysmill   1997–1998
Manager – The Shoe Shoppe – Raysmill   1993–1995

EDUCATION

Microsoft Certified Systems Engineer   (Anticipated) Spring 2000
Microsoft Certified Professional   1999

- Server Administration
- Windows NT Core Technician

Northlands Technical College, BSc Computer Science   1997

James Sharpe 020 8123 4567
page 2 of 2

TECHNICAL PROFICIENCIES
Operating Systems
- Windows 3.1x; Windows 98/95
- Windows NT Server: PDC, BDC and Stand-Alone Servers
- Windows NT Workstation
- Windows 2000 Beta 3
- Configured systems to run Dual boot with Windows NT and Windows 98/95
- Linux
- Solaris
- Novell 3.12

Networks
- Windows NT Networks with both PDC and Stand-Alone Servers
- Windows 98/95 peer-to-peer networks
- User and Queue Administration on Novell 3.x and NDS 4.x
- Installation and configuration of all types of network hardware including: Hubs, Cat 5 Cable, Ether Cards and Network Drops
- Configuration of TCP/IP, WINS, DNS, IPX/SPX, NetBEUI, NeBios, Gateways

Hardware
- X86-based machines from 286 to Pentium III, including Celeron and AMD CPUs
- Sparc IPX, Sparc 2 and Sparc 5
- Installation and configuration of PDC running on Compaq Proliant 1600 Dual Pentium II 450, Ultra Wide SC5I
- Installation and configuration of various hubs/Ethercards including: 3Com, Lynksys, Intel, SMC, Compaq NetFlex, Novell NE2000 compatible
- Installation and configuration of various ISA/PCI/AGP cards
- Cat5 Cabling
- APC uninterruptable power supplies
- Andataco Drive Arrays – both 27gig and 16gig
- Various CD-ROM burners including Mitsumi, Hewlett Packard and Hi-Val.

Software

Ghost	Microsoft Outlook 98/2000
Netscape	CDRWin
McAfee 4.x	Sygate
Visual C++	Rumba
PC Anywhere	Ghost Explorer
Microsoft Office 97/2000	Internet Explorer
Adaptec CD Creator	Microsoft Proxy
Microsoft Masm	Borland C++
Host Explorer	

Insurance Specialist

Jane Swift
123 Anystreet
Anytown AT1 0BB

Tel: 020 8123 4567
jane@anyaddress.co.uk

Career Profile
High-energy, cross-functional background as resourceful fast-track insurance claims specialist with an outstanding record of success in winning settlements and reducing claims payouts to acceptable and just amounts. Investigate, negotiate and settle complex claims, from beginning stages up to trial, for Hatfield and Arena.

Areas of Expertise
Administration
- organized and effective performance in high-pressure environments
- presentation development and delivery
- claims investigation with meticulous documentation
- heavy phones/switchboard
- skilled customer care
- word processing and spreadsheet development (type 60 words per minute)
- Microsoft Office, Internet and intranet proficiency

Insurance Claims
- commercial and personal liability
- property damage and bodily injury claims
- injury exposure values
- claimant, solicitor and litigation representation
- settlement and target value range setting
- medical and liability evaluation
- complex arbitration and mediation negotiation
- general liability, auto, homeowners, and products liability

Highlights
- Handle case load of up to 230 pending commercial and personal claims. Establish contact within 24 hours, maintain impeccable documentation, and determine value of case based on liability/injury. Decide claim values up to £50,000. Negotiate/settle cases in mediation, arbitration or litigation.
- Delivered a £15,000 saving to Hatfield by obtaining a defence verdict on a case that a judge suggested Hatfield 'buy out' for £15,000. Communicated with solicitors, evaluated liability/facts and determined feasibility for trial. Case went to trial and Hatfield paid nothing but legal costs.
- Saved Arena £40,000 on complex £100,000 second-degree burn claim by determining case's suitability for mediation, and meeting with judge and plaintiff's solicitors. Case was settled for a fair £60,000 without incurring major legal costs for Arena.
- Promoted onto Arena fast-track after only one year; became the youngest adjuster in company history. Track record of positive mediation, arbitration and litigation outcomes is equal to or better than that of more senior professionals.
- Possess outstanding administrative/organization skills, superior presentation and negotiation abilities, a passion for excellence and a contagious enthusiasm. Work well in independent or team environments. Tenacious, with the stamina needed to function in high-pressure environments.

Employment
Hatfield Insurance, Claims Assessor · 1998 to Present
Arena Claims Services

Claims Specialist · · · · · · · · · · 1997 to 1998
Loss Adjuster · · · · · · · · · · 1995 to 1997
Claims Assistant · · · · · · · · · · 1994 to 1995

Education and Professional Development
CICCIA
ACII
CII Insurance Foundation Certificate
CII Certificate in IT

Insurance Specialist

James Sharpe
123 Anystreet
Anytown AT1 0BB
Tel: 020 8123 4567
james@anyaddress.co.uk
Page 1 of 2

Career Profile
- Over ten years' background in Loss Control
- An experienced, accurate and tenacious Divisional Loss Control Engineer
- Extensive expertise gained through safety audits of a wide range of insured
- A confident, enthusiastic individual with a reliable sense of humour along with a keen eye for detail
- Proven ability to assess and improve safety standards and, consequently, reduce claims

Areas of Expertise
- Undertaking extensive, in-depth safety audits
- Preparing detailed and informative reports
- Identifying key opportunities for Health & Safety improvements
- Communicating effectively, positively and credibly at all levels
- Promoting Health & Safety legislation
- Supervising and training staff

Executive Highlights
- Improved company image in the broker market and with insured, resulting in retention of business, increased profits and a high profile in the broker market
- Provided detailed reports to insured with recommendations for improvements, thereby reducing claims
- Prepared detailed reports for underwriters, enabling them to set correct rates through increased knowledge

Employment
City & General Insurance
- Divisional Engineer (1997 to present)
- Senior Loss Control Engineer (1992 to 1997)

Carried out specialist surveys including employer, public and product liability safety audits. Trained survey staff for the South of England region.

Basle Insurance
- Safety Engineer (1988 to 1992)

Carried out employer liability and public audits for the London area. Prepared detailed recommendations and reports.

Key & Temple Ltd
- Manager, Internal Services Department (1984 to 1988)
- Safety, Fire and Security Officer (1980 to 1984)

Chief Officer designate for company fire brigade. Responsible for all aspects of safe working conditions along with weekly Health & Safety induction courses.

Professional Training
ONC Mechanical Engineering
ROSPA Industrial Safety Course
Southern Counties Fire Fighting Course
Safety Officers Course
Defensive Driving Course
Computer literate including use of Internet and e-mail

Professional Membership
Institute of Occupational Health and Safety
International Institute of Risk and Safety Management
Register of Safe Practitioners

International Project Manager

James Sharpe
123 Anystreet
Anytown AT1 0BB

Tel: 020 8123 4567
james@anyaddress.co.uk
Page 1 of 2

Project Manager: Industrial/Construction/Manufacturing
- Highly trained, confident and effective
- Significant experience in construction, industrial and manufacturing project both in the UK and Europe
- Established reputation for exploring, designing and implementing solutions
- Proven ability to negotiate results and an expert in the management of change

Areas of Knowledge and Expertise
- Ten years experience in project management
- Experience of a wide range of environments
- Extensive awareness of health and safety issues
- A clear understanding of staff training and motivation
- Knowledge of employment legislation and practice
- Experience of working in Europe under EU law
- A strong commitment to excellence
- An established track record in effective solutions

Career Highlights
- Revised site layout of 20-acre industrial site in Munich
- Revised traffic-handling patterns
- Managed traffic flow and resources during redevelopment
- Revisions resulted in: increased capacity; development and increased use of most valuable areas; elimination of single deliveries in favour of multiple drops; improved vehicle safety
- Devised new stock-handling system for £20 million annual turnover retail operation
- Revised system brought about: improved stock handling and rotation; reduced stock holding; safer working practices; improved storage of flammable material
- Revisions reduced stock-handling budget by £2.5 million per year

Career Development
Sutton Construction
SENIOR PROJECT MANAGER 1998 to present
PROJECT MANAGER 1995 to 1998
Projects included:
Berstatte, Munich
Eastgate Development, Colesbury
Market Precinct, Littleton

Liased with external consultants. Gathered, verified and analysed data. Maintained information flow between departments

Redmills Group
PROJECT MANAGER 1992 to 1995
Projects included:
Develop and improve stock storage and handling system

Liased with internal staff and external consultants. Researched safety regulations and legal requirements. Devised simplified visual verification system. Designed and oversaw implementation of new system

RDS Training Ltd
TRAINING MANAGER 1990 to 1992
Managed and administered training projects for local engineering companies. Researched opportunities for improved services to clients, along with industry training needs. Produced comprehensive analysis of training opportunities and skills gaps. Devised new training programmes accordingly

Education and Training
MBA, Northern University
Diploma in Supervisory Management, North Hambury College
Diploma in Operations Management, North Hambury College

Jewellery Sales

Jane Swift
123 Anystreet
Anytown AT1 0BB
Tel: 020 8123 4567
jane@anyaddress.co.uk

Professional Sales
A position to use proven sales and relationship building skills to develop new business, retain existing clients and positively affect the bottom line.

An expert professional with a passion for sales and an ability to develop rapport and trust with new clients. Cultivate existing relationships using a strong follow-up technique and gain significant add-on and repeat business. Persuade 'on the fence' clientele to make a purchase, often increasing value of sale. Participate in team selling and train new employees in consultative approach, needs identification, closing, and follow through.

- Consistently surpass monthly sales quotas by at least 50%.
- Ranked as top producer among a sales team.
- Awarded Platinum Club (or equivalent) status 3 years in a row for outstanding sales figures.
- Developed a strong following of international clientele.

Endorsements
Physician
'I have found her to be intelligent, friendly, and well spoken. She has had a remarkable grasp of understanding the medical issues we've encountered and her questions and comments showed insight. I would recommend her as an employee based on her communication skills, intellect, and motivation.'

Sales Manager
'I would highly recommend you look at her for employment with your company. She has qualities that would be an asset to you … self-motivated, self-starter, quick learner, and most important, she was my top salesperson. I could always count on her to get the job done with little supervision.'

Professional Experience
Sales Representative – Smith and Jones Jewellers, Sutton Valley   1998 to Present
- Highlights: Recruited to expand retail sales at the top selling location in area. Produce new and repeat business and train sales representative on techniques.

Sales Representative – Zachary's Jewellers, Embury   1995 to 1998
- Highlights: Led the store in sales volume. Trained new staff and shared helpful sales and marketing hints. Assumed additional responsibilities for ordering, vendor contact, and office work.

Sales Representative – Bryan's Jewellers, Embury   1994 to 1995
- Highlights: Used consultative approach to sell high-end jewellery and gems. Completed training in sales methods, gemology, and winning attitude.

Education
Bachelor of Arts in Language, University of Cairo, Egypt
English as a Second Language Programme, City University
Certified Travel Consultant

Management Consultant

James Sharpe
123 Anystreet ● Anytown AT1 0BB
Phone: 020 8123 4567 ● james@anyaddress.co.uk

Professional Profile

A seasoned, highly motivated senior executive with a successful track record in international operations and project management. Recognized for exceptional problem solving and motivational skills as well as the ability to **negotiate, deal, and close successfully across cultural barriers**. Extensive experience in management consulting in diverse industries, ranging from unit construction and mining/drilling operations to industrial equipment procurement, sales and distribution. **Bilingual with extensive international experience**, including Africa, the Middle East, South Asia, and Western Europe.

Areas of Impact

International Conflict Resolution	Worldwide Corporate Security	Risk Assessment
Operation and Project Management	New Business Development	International Law
Global Emergency Planning	International Public Relations	Recruitment/Training

Career Highlights

- Successfully providing diplomatic, risk management and crisis resolution services to a broad range of blue chip companies, Ambassadors, Heads of State, cabinet ministers, and senior government officials, UK and foreign.
- Successfully negotiated, on behalf of OCL Oil, with an East African government to resolve a cross-cultural crisis and avoid closure of a £1 billion distribution facility.
- Developed and implemented logistics and training programmes involving several thousand UK and foreign personnel and a £40 million annual budget. Effectively achieved all objectives with a budget savings of 12%.
- Directed Smith & Jones Trucks Ltd, and Haulage International in the successful negotiation of more than £15 million of capital equipment sales to a West African government.
- Conducted numerous feasibility studies and risk assessments, both political and economic forecasts, for a variety of projects including gold, platinum and diamond mining, nuclear energy development, port, railroad and packaging facilities.

Employment History

International Affairs Consultant
Professional Services Provided to: Whitway International, Vella Properties International, OCL Oil, OACH Petroleum, Haulage International, Smith & Jones Trucks Ltd, Flight Airlines, Technology Co Ltd, MSC International Ltd, National Telecommunications Co Ltd, OX Technologies

National Security Agency
Near East and Africa Referent … Chief of Station … Chief of Operations … Chief of Branch, Counterterrorism … Deputy/Chief of Station.

Education

Doctorate, *International Law*, University of London
Master of Arts, *History*, University of the South
Bachelor of Arts, *History*, New College, Oxbridge

Management Trainee

Jane Swift
123 Anystreet
Anytown AT1 0BB
Tel: 020 8123 4567
jane@anyaddress.co.uk

Objective
A MANAGEMENT TRAINING SCHEME which will make use of strong organizational skills, and the proven ability to get the job done

Overview
- Organized, highly-trained individual with exceptional follow-through abilities and a comprehensive grounding in business management
- Strong interpersonal skills; proven ability to work well with individuals at all levels
- Possessing strong problem resolution skills
- Dedicated individual; achieving reputation for consistently going beyond what is required
- Proven ability to gather, extract, and use data effectively
- Computer literate; proficient in using current business software, spreadsheets, etc

Education
HOCKLEY BUSINESS COLLEGE
- BTEC National Diploma in Business and Finance
- Current course work: Administration Systems, Human Resources, Business Environment, Financial Planning and Control, Elements of Investment, Innovation and Change, Business Statistics, Principles and Practice of Insurance, Elements of Banking, Accounting Procedures, Business Information Technology, Marketing Process

COLEDALE COLLEGE OF FURTHER EDUCATION
- BTEC First Diploma in Business and Finance
- Course work included: Insurance Proficiency, Production, Administrative Support, Business Resources and Procedures, Administrative Systems and Procedures

Achievements
- Organized guest speakers, including transport and hospitality, for quarterly Business Circle meetings at the College
- Organized 'Hockley Regatta', a two-day charity fundraising event which raised over £8,000 overall
- Planned and coordinated all details of extensive inter-college SOBAT games league
- Part of the team that wrote, edited and prepared for publication _'Orrible 'Ockley_, a history of the College

Employment
2001 to present – Amberside Stores
Cashier and Kiosk Assistant
- Handled large amounts of money; customer care; alcohol and cigarette legislation

Summers 1999 & 2001 – City & County Bank
Work Placement
- Assisted with basic office procedures and clerical work
- Observed departmental procedures including: Customer Servicing; Mortgage and Lending; Foreign Exchange; Pensions; Processing Room; High Risk Accounts

Management – Graduate Trainee

Jane Swift
123 Anystreet
Anytown AT1 0BB
Tel: 020 8123 4567
jane@anyaddress.co.uk
Page 1 of 2

Objective

MSc Economics graduate seeking a position in a major company where I can augment my knowledge of Economic Theory with practical experience, and gain understanding and expertise in the area of Development Finance and Corporate Policy.

Selected References

- '... professional in manner, dress and approach... well educated, articulate and well prepared... passionate, committed and focused on a goal or goals... ethical and honest... will make a difference wherever (she) goes...' Douglas Anders, Founder and Chairman CCRF (Childhood Cancer Relief Fund)
- '...outstanding young woman, intelligent, capable and hard-working... well respected by her peers, a team member, a natural leader who has my personal recommendation...' Ray Edwards, Sales Director Dale Systems

Education

South of England University
MSc Financial Economics
- Advanced Economic Theory
- Development Finance
- Modelling Financial Decisions and Markets
- Corporate Policy
- Uncertainty and Market Forces

South of England University
BSc (Hons) 2.1 Economics
- Business and Finance
- Econometric Theory
- Micro- and Macroeconomics
- Computer-based analysis
- Quantitative methods

Professional Experience

2000–Present – Dale Systems Ltd
Work Placement – Business Support Assistant
- Worked with Business Support Team proving administrative support to nationwide Sales Force out in the field
- Provided telephone and online instant-access information support for Sales Force
- Supplied telephone guidance to customers
- Conducted customer awareness and follow-up customer satisfaction surveys over the phone and one-to-one
- Organized materials for major trade shows
- Liaised with internal departments and contractors to ensure delivery and smooth running of exhibition
- Maintained and updated marketing database

Page 2 of Swift

- Used a range of PC software to convert raw data into charts and graphs for use by Sales Representatives and customers
- Assisted with production of reports and analyses, including data research and compiling statistics
- Achieved maximum performance rating during appraisal

Ongoing – CCRF charity
Voluntary worker
Working with children and families to provide respite care, holiday playschemes for siblings, fundraising events, Make a Wish events, ensuring hospice care, and much more. Highlights include:
- Organized Bike Ride for CCRF fundraising event which raised over £3,750 on the day and a further £470 from subsequent publicity
- Coached under-11s in tennis, squash and badminton during Holiday Playscheme
- Participated in, and completed, City Marathon 2002 for publicity and fundraising purposes

ADDITIONAL REFERENCES AND RELATED DATA AVAILABLE ON REQUEST

Marketing Analyst

Jane Swift
123 Anystreet
Anytown AT1 0BB
Tel: 020 8123 4567
jane@anyaddress.co.uk

EXPERIENCE:

Harland Ltd, London   July 1998 to Present
MARKETING ANALYST – Provide a broad-based flow of data for merchandisers, buyers, Catalogue Distribution Centre associates, and management to assure continuing high-level profitability of the company's catalogue sales. Access all databases by CRT terminal using CRIMS, an online system interfacing with ISA, IDB and MIDB. Computer Analyses focus on:

- Historical applications, such as impact of season, media ads, space, price, and colour changes
- Reliable pre-season forecasts of catalogue demand patterns and in-season revisions where necessary to maintain inventory control
- Study of inventory turnover in relation to buying estimates, commitments, and quality of merchandise
- Choice of models and development of new ones for item estimating
- Identification of systems problems in estimates above or below plan
- Establishment of recommendations for inventory surplus solutions
- Decision-marketing, planning, scheduling to meet data deadlines

Z&P Advertising Ltd   York, Summer 1997
OFFICE MANAGER – Arranged for in-house weekly newsletter and biweekly policy memos for new agency. Developed invoice system, dealt with clients and managed clerical staffing.

Tana Properties   York, Winter 1997
ASSISTANT BOOKKEEPER – Worked with accounts receivable/payable, bank reconciliations

EDUCATION:

University of the North
BA Business Administration, 1998
Concentration: Marketing and Management Information Systems

COMPUTER SKILLS:

Visual Basic, C++, FCS–EPS and SPSS software package

References Available Upon Request

Marketing Management

Jane Swift
123 Anystreet
Anytown AT1 0BB

Tel: 020 8123 4567
jane@anyaddress.co.uk
Page 1 of 2

Profile
Marketing Management ● Promotions Management ● Sales Management
A goal-oriented, decisive manager with 10+ years' experience in a corporate sales and marketing environment. Exceptionally creative with effective organizational abilities and interpersonal skills. Powerful leadership and management expertise with especially strong planning, coordinating and delegating capacities. Solid problem solving abilities. Demonstrated capacity to successfully manage multiple projects and deadlines, coming in on time and within budget.

Demonstrated Strengths
- key account development and relations
- new product introduction
- sales and trend analysis
- target market development
- software proficiency with PowerPoint, Excel, Word and FM Pro
- presentation development and delivery
- creative purchase incentives and promotions
- sales management
- distributor management
- project management

Selected Achievements
- Received Achievement Award 2 years in a row for double-digit increases in sales and development of promotional strategies and programmes.
- Selected as one of 19 managers nationwide to participate in pilot programme to restore positive sales growth in South West market areas.
- Developed numerous creative merchandising pieces throughout career that increased visibility and sales.
- Key player in several marketing initiatives such as a marketing partnership that brought several major companies together in a massive merchandising programme. Effectively managed essential initiatives that positioned product very competitively.
- Guided distributors to improve sales and marketing figures.
- Increased sales figures 50% in one year in a targeted segment. Increased sales in key accounts an average of 5% and improved feature activity and display performance from 50% to 80%.
- Counselled sales representatives and helped one improve performance from marginal to outstanding in one year.
- Met project deadlines (average lead time 4–6 weeks) 98% of the time.

Professional Experience
P&C Foods Ltd
Promotions Manager, Littledean   1998 to Present
Assist National Sales Manager and key accounts by developing customized, value-added promotions that drive volume and gain ad and display activity. Managed over 150 programmes annually. Purchase incentives include cross-merchandising programmes with other vendors, coupons, rebates, liquidators and sweepstakes. Coordinate promotional ideas and programmes with creative agencies, sports marketing, and legal departments. Manage project costs and a budget of over £2 million.

Sales and Merchandising Manager, Bolton   1997 to 1998
Supervise a team of sales and marketing specialists to increase sales in the UK and European markets. Develop distributor incentives. Work alongside distributors and corporate personnel to cultivate key retail accounts, sell product and displays, increase freezer space, and improve merchandising.

Marketing Manager, Bolton   1995 to 1997
Manage territory that generates sales of 40+ million cases of soft drinks annually – the region's largest in terms of volume and budget. Work closely with media partners to foster awareness and develop promotional lineup. Integrate regional marketing efforts with national brand strategies. Directly accountable for £300,000 budget.

Sales Manager, Bolton   1994 to 1995
Aggressively lead targeted incentive programmes and promotions. Improve distributor sales by conducting surveys and developing action plans to capitalize on sales opportunities. Make frequent calls on buyers. Increase company awareness through development of a monthly newsletter.

Sales and Marketing Planner, Bolton   1992 to 1994
Assist Regional Manager in managing sales/marketing activities. Develop 'how to' promotional manual for field personnel. Improve media support of promotions in 3 regions. Administer a £100,000 budget.

Education
BSc in Business Administration, University of the North

Medical Technology Sales

James Sharpe **123 Anystreet** **Anytown ATI 0BB** **Tel: 020 8123 4567** **james@anyaddress.co.uk**	Page 1 of 2

Summary of Qualifications

Medical Technology/Software Sales and Marketing Executive specializing in opening new markets and introducing new products. Combining strategic sales expertise, marketing creativity and clinical knowledge to communicate product benefits successfully to end users. Reputation for envisioning future client needs and translating those needs into products that provide solutions. Team player who recognizes strengths in people and corporations and brings them together to form strategic alliances to reach common objectives. Major strengths include:

- Market forecasting and new business development
- Product development (inventor of two medical products)
- Solid blend of people, sales and business skills
- Sales and distribution channels
- Strategic alliances and acquisitions
- Technically competent with many different software applications
- Communication and formal presentation skills

Employment History

MediTech Systems, Green Valley   1997–Present

Health care information systems company with a customer base of 480 hospitals throughout the United Kingdom.
Develops point-of-care software systems/databases for clinicians in various specialities.
Director of Sales

- Recruited to develop sales organization and build customer base for emerging technology.
- Instrumental in increasing annual sales from £1.5M to £6.5M over two years.
- Built sales channel operation based on nationwide reputation with distributors, enabling company to grow rapidly with minimal investment.
- Direct product managers in developing specifications and requirements for new products.

OSM Technology, Sandwell   1980–1997

Distributor specializing in introduction of new medical technology products. Recruited early on by chairman of company and promoted through several increasingly responsible positions. Instrumental in increasing annual sales from £4M to £20M with a 40% gross profit margin.
General Manager of Information Systems

- Recognized significance of emerging market for information systems within health care. Charged with creating and launching this brand new division.
- Drove sales from £0 to £2.5M within two years.
- Developed hospital client base of 100 installations.
- Helped guide product development by interpreting market trends to product managers.

Sales Manager of the Hospital Division selling 30+ different types of medical devices such as IV pumps, infusion supplies, hypo- and hyperthermia equipment. Covered six regions and managed 12 sales reps.

<u>Pain Management Specialist.</u> Developed consulting service to help hospitals establish acute pain management services. Working with pharmacies, physicians and nurses, assisted hospitals with organizing pain management committees, developing policies and procedures, and defining reimbursement protocol.

- Established 30 hospital programmes in Western Region.
- Developed Excel spreadsheet for sales force to demonstrate potential revenue stream from this new service to physicians.
- Attended national sales meetings and trained their sales reps.

<u>Southern Region for ARO Pharmaceuticals.</u> Produced £1.4M/year in personal sales while also supervising sales reps.

<u>Product Manager.</u> OSM developed and manufactured the first IV filter designed to withstand the pressure of an IV pump.

<u>Sales Representative.</u> Promoted after 9 months to Product Manager.

TAB Training, 1975–1980
<u>Sales Manager/Instructor</u>. Recruited by TAB at the age of 20 to conduct seminars after completing their Sales and Management course. Youngest instructor in history of company.

Education
University of London, Business Management courses
TAB Sales & Management course

Music Teacher

James Sharpe
123 Anystreet
Anytown AT1 0BB
Tel: 020 8123 4567
james@anyaddress.co.uk

● Music Educator ● Adjunct Professor ● Master Class Teacher ● Professional Performer ●
Arranger Composer ● Conductor ● Arts Council Consultant ●

Mission Statement
To inspire students and audiences to achieve a deep appreciation for the many aspects of music. To devote my personal passion for music performance and theory to impact students at college level. To instil a respectful dedication for the beauty and discipline of music that will enhance all aspects of academic and personal achievement.

Credentials
- Director of South East College of the Arts
- Awarded inclusion in 1998 Music Almanack
- Professional Guitarist: Classical, Jazz, and Improvisational music.
- College-level Applied Music Instructor: Classical Guitar Technique.
- Author of over 70 arrangements for guitar ensemble.
- Composer of four original works for guitar ensemble.
- Studio musician: recorded at the Music Station in London.
- Consultant to local arts councils.
- Developer of original music theory programme for South East Arts Council.
- Expert in Encore, Finale and IBIS music notation/dictation software.

Education
Master of Arts in Music Theory, University of London, 1997
Master of Music: Classical Guitar Performance, University of London, 1993
Bachelor of Arts in Music, University of London, 1989

Professional Development
Member of Guitar Foundation
Music Teachers' National Association
Master Classes and Workshops:
   Classical: Eduardo Fernandez, David Starobin, Jerry Willard.
   Jazz: Howard Morgen, Howard Roberts, Barney Kessel.
   Progressive: Robert Fripp.
   Locations: University of London, The Institute of Guitar, South East College

Nurse

JANE SWIFT, R.N., C.

123 Anystreet ● Anytown AT1 0BB ● 020 8123 4567 ● jane@anyaddress.co.uk
Page 1 of 2

CAREER PROFILE

Dedicated medical professional with nine years' practical experience in a fast-paced hospital setting. Resourceful problem-solver capable of initiating formative solutions to complex problems. Possesses special sensitivity to meeting diverse needs in varied situations. Key strengths include:

- Remain calm and professional during times of critical need.
- Strong analytical skills, easily assess conditions and implement appropriate intervention.
- Ability to motivate, produce and coordinate instructors, organize assignments, and evaluate staffing requirements.
- Relate well to people from a variety of cultures and socioeconomic conditions.
- Readily develop rapport with patients, families, staff, physicians and other health care professionals.
- Proven record of reliability and responsibility.

PROFESSIONAL EXPERIENCE AND ACCOMPLISHMENTS

1992 to Present   *ST ADAN'S MEMORIAL HOSPITAL*, Surrey

Staff Nurse–Respiratory Care
Responsible for respiratory patient care in a highly technical and complex hospital environment.
Participate in unit Quality Assurance programme and work cooperatively with physicians, medical professionals, patients, their family members and other hospitals to provide quality patient care.

Specific responsibilities:

- Alternating charge nurse accountability as assigned by nurse manager.
  - Supervise 8 to 12 staff nurses.
  - Evaluate staffing requirements, floor assignments and organize unit activities.
  - Communicate physician orders to appropriate departments using computerized data system.
- Implement total patient care (physical, psychological and cognitive aspects) for 7 to 9 patient assignment.
- Supervise Licensed Practical Nurses, non-licensed support staff and orient new staff members.
- Perform clinical skills according to hospital policies and standards of practice.
- Interact with applicable departments regarding patient care.
- Act as patient advocate; assess patient status and notify physicians of clinical changes.
- Educate patient/family members to health care needs, conditions, processes, agendas and options.
- Collaborate with case management regarding discharge needs.
- Served on Hospital Quality Assurance Committee and Task Force to develop a new care system.

_1997 to 2000_   **Instructor**
                   Developed lesson plans and curriculum for the Nurse Refresher Program and
                   Adult Respiratory Education for group of up to 35.

_1991 to 1993_   ELMLEA HEALTH CENTRE, Surrey
                   Nursing Assistant

EDUCATION

                   UNIVERSITY OF LONDON
                   MSc in _Health Care Management_, 1998

                   UNIVERSITY OF ARIZONA, Scottsdale, AZ
                   Bachelor of Science in _Nursing_, 1990

Operations and Executive Project Management

James Sharpe
123 Anystreet ● Anytown AT1 0BB ● Tel: 020 8123 4567 ● Fax: 020 8123 4567 ●
james@anyaddress.co.uk

Executive Summary

*A seasoned, team-oriented business executive with a highly successful track record with start-up and turnaround situations. More than 15 years progressive experience in all phases of **Operations and Project Management** with particular strength in feasibility analysis. Recognized for exceptional organization building skills as well as the ability to motivate others on all levels in the achievement of individual and organizational goals.*

- Business Process Re-engineering
- Feasibility Analysis/Projections
- Negotiation and Arbitration
- Project Management
- Crisis Resolution
- Start-up Management
- Business Valuation
- Liquidation Management
- P&L Responsibility

Selected Achievements

- Successfully administered a portfolio of contracts with a value exceeding £10 million. The average income of each client **increased by 15%, a gain of more than £1.5 million**.
- Provided consulting services to more than 1,090 clients from numerous parts of the UK and Europe as well as conducted numerous feasibility studies for projects valued at up to £100,000,000.
- Orchestrated a successful start-up company with responsibilities including site selection and acquisition through P&L accountability; **annual sales exceeded £50 million within ten years**.
- Aggressively negotiated, supervised, or advised in the negotiation of several contracts totalling in excess of £68 million, **savings clients at least £6.5 million**. Recent negotiations resulted in a verifiable return of **40% over current market value, a total gain of £520,000**.
- Pioneered state-of-the-art plant expansion that involved a capital investment of £500,000 and realized a **50% increase in plant capacity**.
- Successfully restarted an organization that had been shut down due to severe labour–management and production problems. Through various management techniques and styles that motivated the employees, **production increased by nearly 50% while operating costs stayed constant**.

Consulting Highlights

Wright and Mason Ltd, Northumberland   *Since 1992*
Chief Executive

Representative List of Clients

Jepson & Marks	*Ambrose Insurance*	*Ambit Technologies*
Dover Trust	*Pacific Hotels*	*Northwest Financial*
Jarvis Communications	*D&J Investments*	*Startup UK*
Holms Timber	*Heathcliffe Hydraulics*	*National Technologies Foundation*

Education

Bachelor of Science, Business Administration
University of Scotland

Interim assignments and consulting projects preferred.
Available for extensive travel in UK and abroad.
Undeterred by the most arduous conditions.

Operations Manager

JANE SWIFT
123 Anystreet
Anytown AT1 0BB
Tel: 020 8123 4567
jane@anyaddress.co.uk
Page 1 of 2

**Expert in Process Redesign, Performance Reengineering and
Productivity/Performance Improvement**

RESULTS-DRIVEN PROFESSIONAL with 15+ years' experience in industry, including 5 years at senior management level. Excellent analytical and problem-solving skills. Able to work under pressure in fast-paced, time-sensitive environments. Experienced in analysing and streamlining systems and operations to increase productivity, quality and efficiency. Proven ability to manage projects from planning through to execution. Strong database and word-processing applications.

ACHIEVEMENTS
- Coordinated activities between departments sited at four different locations to ensure efficient running of operation
- Cut annual operating costs by £150,000 by reducing doubling-up and duplications
- Devised and executed programme of change at two subsidiary sites, bringing them level in productivity and profitability with the rest of the group
- Initiated Partnership Agreement which improved industrial relations and restored management leadership profile
- Established centralized Production Support Centre
- Improved overall financial performance of group by upwards of £700,000 annually

PROFILE
- Operations Manager with a strong background in, and thorough understanding of, the engineering process
- Organized, enthusiastic professional; willing to hear new ideas and go the extra mile to improve performance
- Possess strong interpersonal skills; able to work effectively with individuals at all levels
- Demonstrated ability to develop and maintain sound employee relations
- Strong problem resolution skills; able to prioritize a broad range of responsibilities efficiently and effectively
- Catalyst for change, transformation and performance improvement
- Achieved reputation as a resource person, problem solver, trouble-shooter, and creative turnaround manager

PROFESSIONAL EXPERIENCE
The Overland Group, Leicester
Operations Manager   1997–Present
Responsible for factories and staff within the operational area.
- Coordinated and managed activities within four factories and a Production Centre
- Organized efficient running of sites
- Ensured delivery of products to internal and external customers
- Managed quality control, budget and timetable requirements
- Prepared budgets and allocated capital expenditure

Jane Swift
Page 2 of 2

Humber Industries, Hull
Factory Manager   1992–1997
Responsible for all aspects of factory management.
- Achieved budget production levels
- Administered Health & Safety legislation
- Prepared budgets
- Allocated capital expenditure
- Liaised with customers, notably MOD and Crown Suppliers

Gardner Engineering, Hull
Industrial Engineer   1987–1992
Responsible for engineering services at factory and regional level.
- Provided production engineering service with particular emphasis on product costing, pre-production engineering and methods assessment and improvement

EDUCATION
City & Guilds – Certificate in Mechanical Engineering

Supplementary Certificates: Toolroom Practices; Inspection & Quality Assurance; Health & Safety Legislation; Industrial Relations

REFERENCES
Will be furnished on request

Organizational Management

Jane Swift
123 Anystreet
Anytown AT1 0BB
Tel: 020 8123 4567
jane@anyaddress.co.uk

Organizational Manager/Programme Coordinator/Turnaround Strategist

Career Profile
Accomplished administrator with over ten years of experience in cost-effective programme development and revitalization. Work with large not-for-profit entities providing therapeutic and preventive services focusing on restoration of families to productive employment and societal relationships. Run programmes with a social worker's compassion blended with a corporate manager's productivity, fiscal responsibility, and results.

Areas of Expertise

- Total programme administration
- Cost-effective management
- Long-term strategic planning
- Team building and leadership
- Staff training and mentoring
- Fundraising and grant writing
- Multimillion pound budget responsibility
- Programme start-ups and turnarounds
- Programme development/enhancement
- Crisis intervention
- Public speaking and education
- Windows 98, Microsoft Word, Internet

Career Highlights

- **Instrumental in start-up of association formed to assist former inmates with re-establishment of family units, drug-free living, and employment.** Hired to aid in the From Prison to Paycheck start-up. Created 'preventive' element of programme, hired professional staff, constructed organizational structure, planned services, trained staff and authored treatment plans. Ensured retention of funding by meticulous following of mandates.
- **Revitalized and dramatically expanded youth programme slated for closure.** The NCH Home for very troubled children was running at less than half capacity. Immediately strengthened referring relationships and implemented new policies and procedures. Increased to 24-resident capacity within first year. Now, after five consecutive successful years, have a £3 million budget, over 80 children in programme, and substantial government funding. Programme is community-based and more cost effective than treating children in a facility.
- **Received Best Site award for successful revamping of poorly run teen group home.** Created general structure, daily living schedule, and boundaries; revised mental attitudes; established consequences; and instituted a reward system. Retrained staff and reduced turnover. Changes precipitated a stronger sense of self esteem, instilled a sense of home in the residents, reduced AWOL rate, decreased school absenteeism and raised residents' grades.
- **Restored programme suffering from lack of proper casework processing.** Recruited as Supervisor to resolve near-crisis situation. Mandated monitoring and tracking was not being performed to standard. Department was overwhelmed with new daily cases and over 100 ongoing cases requiring (by mandate) 24 hours to investigate, 7 days to recommend, and 30 days to refer. Took over, cleaned up unit, saved funding, and prevented closure of vital programme.
- **Addressed business leaders as keynote speaker.** Presented an informative presentation about the day-to-day operations of a successful therapeutic foster care programme, an overview of its management, and a perspective on its bottom-line value.

Education and Certification
DipSW University of London

Professional Development

NCH Home: Programme Director, Programme Coordinator   1998 to present

Recruited to revive ailing programme and prevent closure. Have tripled enrollment, expanded to multiple locations and obtained needed government funding. Manage overall administration and £5 million budget, supervise 32 staff members in 3 offices. Coordinate referral intake process and recruitment/training of therapeutic foster parents. Liaison with all relevant government and community agencies. Provide 24/7 crisis intervention coverage.

From Prison to Paycheque: Start-up Consultant, Case Work Supervisor   1997 to 1998

Oversaw 70 preventive cases of people involved with the criminal justice system. Supervised staff. Monitored all mandated paperwork. Coordinated workshops. Obtained linkages with community organizations. Provided emergency beeper coverage.

Family Crisis Foundation: Site Supervisor, Case Manager   1990 to 1997

Revitalized ailing group home for troubled youth, creating a model that received Best Site of the Year award. Managed total operation of home, including hiring, budgetary, physical site, casework, staff oversight, and intensive casework. Oversaw 100 active crisis and long-term cases. Supervised child protection workers and case workers. Consulted with agency solicitors. Provided 24/7 emergency coverage. Developed goals for a caseload of 33 families, using direct services, advocacy and referrals. Supervised visitation. Responded to crisis situations.

Awards and Service
- Mayor's Award for Outstanding Service
- Distinguished Service Award
- Best Site of Year Award

Outside Sales/Account Manager/Customer Service

Jane Swift
123 Anystreet
Anytown AT1 0BB
Tel: 020 8123 4567
jane@anyaddress.co.uk

Energetic and goal-focused sales professional with solid qualifications in large account management and customer relationship building/maintenance. Proven ability to develop new business and increase sales within established accounts and mature territories. Self-confident and poised in interactions across all business hierarchies; a persuasive communicator and assertive negotiator with strong deal-closing abilities. Excellent time management skills; computer literate. Areas of demonstrated value include:

- Sales Growth/Account Development
- Commercial Account Management
- Prospecting & Business Development
- Customer Liaison & Service
- Consultative Sales/Needs Assessment
- Territory Management & Growth

PROFESSIONAL EXPERIENCE

Sterling Motors, Sterling Heath   1995–Present
SALES EXECUTIVE (1997–Present)
Promoted and challenged to revitalize a large metropolitan territory plagued by poor performance. Manage, service, and build existing accounts; develop new business, establishing both regional and national accounts. Serve as key liaison for all customers and work as the only outside sales representative in the company. Produce monthly reports for major national accounts.
Selected Results

- Reversed a history of stagnant sales; delivered consistent growth and built territory sales 22%, to £4.75 million annually, in less than 2 years.
- Surpassed quota by a minimum of 20% for 14 consecutive months.
- Personally deliver 95% of all sales generated for the company's main site.
- Prospected aggressively and presented products to key decision-makers during cold calls; opened more than 60 new commercial accounts.
- Improved account service and applied consultative sales techniques; grew sales in every established account a minimum of 15%.

MANAGER, Hazeldene Motors (1995–1997)
MANAGER TRAINEE, Wilmington Store (1995)
Initially recruited as a management trainee and rapidly advanced to management of a retail location generating £1 million annually. Supervised and scheduled 12 employees. Budgeted and produced advertising, oversaw bookkeeping, and set/managed sales projections and growth objectives.

EDUCATION AND CREDENTIALS

BA BUSINESS MANAGEMENT, 1995
Wilmington College, Newcastle

Additional Training

- Building Sales Relationships, 1998
- Problem Solving Skills, 1998

Professional & Community Associations

- Member, Chamber of Commerce, 1996–Present
- Member, County Club and Women's Golf Association, 1996–Present
- Youth Soccer Coach and FIFA Certified Referee, 1999–Present

Paralegal

JAMES SHARPE
123 Anystreet
Anytown AT1 0BB
Tel: 020 8123 4567
james@anyaddress.co.uk

EXPERIENCE:
Lewis Quinn & Co., Edinburgh   1998 to present
Paralegal
Responsible for various aspects of the smooth running of the partnership.

Responsible for lodging all documents – correspondence, medical evidence, etc – in process.

Delivered instruction to counsel. Liaised with advocates' clerks. Delivered briefings.

Took notes of proceedings and reported back to law firm.

Appellate Division Municipal Court of Hong Kong   1994 to 1998
Judicial Assistant
Participated in civil and criminal trials. Took depositions. Drafted the court decisions.

EDUCATION:
Clydeside University
Paralegal Certificate

HNC Legal Services

University of Hong Kong
Faculty of Law
Master of Arts – Speciality: Law

SKILLS:
Fluent in Japanese and several Chinese dialects
Freelance writer for Asian newspapers published in the UK
Translator from above languages into English and vice versa

Pharmaceutical Sales

JANE SWIFT
123 Anystreet
Anytown AT1 0BB
Tel: 020 8123 4567
jane@anyaddress.co.uk

Professional Objective
- Position as sales representative, health care liaison, or account relationship manager in the field of pharmaceutical or medical sales
- Will make use of comprehensive health care training, proven sales expertise, excellent communication skills, self-directed prioritization, and ability to produce an immediate bottom-line impact

Career Profile
- Six years' experience as Registered Nurse caring for medical and surgical patients
- Three years' experience in Sales
- Exceptionally flexible, diplomatic, organized, dedicated, patient, calm and reliable. Eager and willing to learn new skills and knowledge to produce profitable corporate achievements

Employment
Sales Representative 1998 to present
Arden Cosmetics
Part-time job due to full-time care of two young children
- Sold Arden cosmetics products to 350 clients
- Built up own client list in local and surrounding areas
- Grossed £23,000 in product sales over current year

Registered Nurse 1992 to 1998
Hardenbrook Hospital
- Supported patients and provided patient care
- Prepared patients physically and mentally for surgery
- Provided post-operative care
- Dealt with enquiries from patients and their families
- Administered drugs
- Assisted on ward rounds
- Prepared working areas
- Updated patient records

Education and Training
Bachelor of Nursing, East England University

Probation Officer

James Sharpe
123 Anystreet
Anytown AT1 0BB

Tel: 020 8123 4567
james@anyaddress.co.uk
Page 1 of 2

Profile

- Over fifteen years NPS experience as Probation Officer. Academic and professional background in Social Services and Business. Currently enrolled in university-level Human Resource Management certificate programme.
- Use personal initiative to review operations and develop programmes that improve client services, build communication between agencies and promote efficient functioning with reduced resources.
- Recipient of two service awards. Enthusiastic and self-driven 'go-to' person with proven ability to master whatever is needed to meet goals and achieve excellence.

Areas of Expertise

programme creation and development ▪ departmental restructuring
▪ comprehensive investigative and psycho-social reporting ▪ counselling and supervision
▪ agency relations ▪ court appearances ▪

Employment

East Hampshire Probation Service
Overview

- Work in one of the nation's largest suburban areas, with a probationer population of 16,500. Currently manage a caseload of screened clients in an innovative prison alternative 'day-reporting' programme. Previously managed a 150-probationer caseload in an economically depressed, drug involved neighbourhood with limited resources. Area included large percentage of individuals with drug and alcohol involvement, educational deficits and limited job skills.
- Use social service skills and expert fieldwork as well as meticulous record keeping and timely follow-up on a daily basis. Always work with limited staff and unrelenting deadline pressure. Put in long days and do paperwork into the early hours of the morning.

Highlights

- Integral member of an award-winning probation team that was requested to become a key component of 'Weed and Seed', a government sponsored task force. In 1998, received a commendation for team's groundbreaking work with Weed and Seed programme. Original pilot programme has been so effective that it is currently in use by six additional probation teams.
- Developed innovative approach that combined caseloads with two remaining team members, in crisis response to loss of two additional members. New approach allowed processing of a greater number of clients, supported an effective network of resources and better aided high-maintenance and high-risk clients. Extensive resource network enabled team to obtain preferential client treatment as organizations became dependent on team's referrals and became more effective in developing client treatment plans.
- Currently working in prison-alternative day treatment programme that serves screened mentally ill and/or chemical-dependent abusers through medication administration, counselling, and education programmes. Centre had difficulty in maintaining schedule of medications necessary for clients' stability, as hostile and uncooperative individuals needed to be escorted to health clinics for their medication and medical needs. These patients were also unreceptive to rehabilitative programmes.
- Convinced clinics to provide an on-site registered nurse to perform home-based visits so that clients' medications could be administered, dramatically reducing client hospitalization times, keeping clients stable and making families receptive to team's efforts. Client stability now allows effective use of rehabilitative GED and counselling programmes.

Other Experience
- Worked as part-time Counsellor for the inter-schools drugs programme.
- Functioned as part-time Security for various companies.
- Provided supervision as part-time Direct Care Counsellor for mentally retarded and disabled individuals living in group homes.
- Served in the Army, Corporal, Personnel Administration Clerk/Instructor.

Education
South Midlands University, School of Management and Division for Professional Development
- Certificate programme: Human Resources Management, Summer 2000
- Certificate in Business Use of Computers, 1998
- 12 Management credits
University of the North
- BA Social Work

Technology Skills
Fluent in Windows 95/98, Knowledge of Microsoft Office Suite, WordPerfect, Internet, E-mail

Project Manager/Programmer Analyst

James Sharpe   Page 1 of 2
123 Anystreet
Anytown AT1 0BB
Tel: 020 8123 4567
james@anyaddress.co.uk

Senior project manager with nearly 20 years' experience in technical project management, systems hardware, and software applications. Skilled in day-to-day management operations of large systems support centre. Successful in developing and integrating technologies to support operational, financial and organizational needs. Recognized for excellent problem-solving skills and developing/managing various programmes and projects successfully.

TECHNICAL PROFICIENCIES
● VSE/ESA ● VM ● MVS ● VSAM ● CICS ● VOLLIE ● Librarian ● DYNAM ●
● BAL ● COBOL ● COBOL II ● Easytrieve Plus ● ORACLE ● PL/SQL ●
● SQL ● C++ ● Borland C++ Builder ● MS Windows 95/98 ●
● Windows NT ● Internet ● E-mail ●

QUALIFICATION HIGHLIGHTS
▓ Well-versed and highly skilled in system programming
▓ Exhibits excellent problem-solving and analytical skills
▓ In-depth knowledge of programming languages and hands-on experience
▓ Learns and applies new skills quickly – takes advantage of resources and tools available
▓ Demonstrates team leadership and promotes positive management style
▓ Strong ability to guide and mentor junior programmers

PROFESSIONAL EXPERIENCE
Bank Services Provider, Farrowdale   1995–Present
Data Centre Support Manager – Provide management support of retail banking system through designing and coding new programmes, resolve production issues and oversee programme maintenance.
▓ Developed SQL and PL/SQL programmes for client server programming groups
▓ Produced written procedures automating job scheduling enabling company to complete 4 conversions within a 2-day period
▓ Streamlined client acquisition process during increased acquisitions/mergers within banking industry by successfully designing, coding and implementing 'internal acquisition conversion' system
▓ Improved data mapping process by automating manual tasks by designing programme to read COBOL copy book, creating Doner File Data Directory
▓ Reduced CPU utilization by 50% through major code revisions in conversion software

Financial Management Corporation, Lincoln   1993–1995
Systems and Programming Manager – Administered project life cycle from initial systems planning and technology acquisition though installation, training, and operations.
▓ Managed and coded major system modifications
▓ Revitalized programming code, eliminating errors and improving Inland Revenue Reporting System
▓ Designed and coded data conversion algorithms, eliminating processing errors and improving reliability of Certificate of Deposit System

Prior Professional Experience
Jones Consultant – St Dunstan
      Specializing in Programme and Project Management Systems
Quick Data Processing – St Dunstan
      Retail Banking Systems Development Director
Computer Group Ltd – Rudlock
      Senior Systems Consultant

Education
Rudlock Technical College
      ▩   Network Essentials (Courses Completed), 1999
      ▩   Beginning/Advanced C++ (Courses Completed), 1998/1999
      ▩   Applied Science – General Studies, 1991

Property Management

Jane Swift
127 Anystreet
Anytown AT1 0BB
Tel: 020 8123 4567
jane@anyaddress.co.uk

OBJECTIVE
Position in Property Management

QUALIFICATION HIGHLIGHTS

- More than six years of experience assisting in the management of multiple rental properties.
- Thoroughly familiar with both tenant and landlord laws and guidelines; experienced in collections and county court procedures.
- Extensive business background in general management, customer service and support, and subcontractor supervision.
- Advanced computer skills and demonstrated proficiency in streamlining administrative tasks through the application of technology.
- Resourceful and innovative in problem solving; adapt quickly to a challenge. Strong prioritization, delegation and planning skills.
- Relate warmly to diverse individuals at all levels; respectful yet assertive communication style.

KEY SKILLS & ABILITIES

- Perform background, reference and credit checks; select quality tenants and maintain high occupancy rates.
- Show available properties to prospective tenants; negotiate lease and rental agreements.
- Handle tenant communications; respond to requests for maintenance and answer questions.
- Troubleshoot and resolve disputes, including evictions and cleaning/demand deposits.
- Research legal issues using Infolaw, file court documents and represent property owner in court.
- Schedule and supervise subcontractors; oversee upgrades, maintenance and renovations.
- Plan and manage budgets; execute general accounting functions.
- Set up and maintain computerized property management systems.
- Coordinate and track rent collection, maintenance and repairs. Proactively address security issues.

CAREER HISTORY
Assistant Property Manager (1998–Present)
     Owen & Gains, Portmere
          Assist in the management and oversight of multiple residential rental properties. Set up efficient administrative systems, coordinate rent collection, handle tenant disputes and resolve legal issues.

Owner-Manager (1996–1998)
     Computer Works, Danesford
          Founded and managed this micro/mini-computer sales and systems integration company. Achieved status as a South East Bell Master Vendor.

EDUCATION
City Technical Community College (1985–1986)
OND in Business Administration

Public Relations/Media Spokesperson

Jane Swift
123 Anystreet
Anytown AT1 0BB
Tel: 020 8123 4567
jane@anyaddress.co.uk

OBJECTIVE:

A position in Public Relations where I can use my skills as a media spokesperson and my ability to execute a variety of projects simultaneously.

EXPERIENCE:

Pubic Relations Associate/Media
A&A Media, Renton 1992 to Present

- Media spokesperson for 12 clients: interviewed and trained personnel for TV, radio and print
- Established contacts with producers and editors
- Wrote press releases
- Developed media and promotional packages
- Booked interviews with press

District Sales Manager
A&A Media, Renton. 1989–1992

- Supervised 169 representatives with a £200,000 sales volume

Account Executive/Radio Reporter
Eastern Press, Sixtree. 1986–1989

- Designed and sold advertising for Eastern Press
- Developed a £4,000 account list
- Sports and news journalist
- Feature writer

Assistant Editor
Midhampton Observer, Midhampton. Summers 1984/1985

- Feature writer, reporter, photographer, layouts and design

EDUCATION:

BA, Media and Communications, University of London, 1986

AWARDS:

1994 Business and Professional Women's 'Young Careerist' Annual Award

OTHER FACTS:

Experience as a Public Relations Seminar Leader

References/Portfolio/Video and Cassette Tapes available upon request

Publishing/Marketing Professional

Jane Swift
123 Anystreet
Anytown AT1 0BB
Tel: 020 8123 4567
jane@anyaddress.co.uk

PROFESSIONAL **EXPERIENCE:**	*Publisher of trade and academic books* **DIRECTOR OF ADVERTISING AND PROMOTION (March 1998–Present)**

Key responsibilities include: managing advertising/promotion department with staff of four; overseeing and actively engaging in all aspects of promotion, advertising, and publicity. I have established and am maintaining a 22-person national sales force and make seasonal visits to the nation's two largest bookstore chains.

Active in negotiating special sales and acquiring new titles, and as liaison with domestic and foreign rights agents. In 1998 I travelled to the United States,visited several publishers, bought and sold rights.

Frequently arrange author appearances on television and radio. As a company spokesperson, I have been interviewed numerous times by newspapers, magazines and radio stations.

ADVERTISING AND PROMOTION MANAGER (1996–1998)

Advertising and Direct Mail: created, designed and wrote copy for brochures, flyers and display ads; created direct-mail campaigns; represented company at publisher's book exhibits.

Publicity: Wrote news releases, selected media, made follow-up calls, arranged author media appearances.

ASSISTANT EDITOR (1994–1996)

Responsibilities including reading authors' manuscripts, copyediting, proofreading; writing jacket copy, coordinating and writing copy for catalogue. Some editing and proofreading was done on a freelance basis.

Comfrey & Burnage (Manchester), Advertising Copywriter (1992–1994)

Responsible for designing and writing copy for bimonthly catalogue and supplementary flyers. Created ads and brochures; wrote sales letters and edited and rewrote direct-mail pieces.

EDUCATION:	Manchester University Degree: BA (Hons) 2.1 English, 1992
SKILLS:	Word processing, working knowledge of typography, research proficiency.
REFERENCES:	Will be provided on request.

Regional Project Management Assistant

James Sharpe
123 Anystreet
Anytown AT1 0BB

Tel: 020 8123 4567
james@anyaddress.co.uk
Page 1 of 2

OBJECTIVE

A **management position** that will make use of strong analytical and organizational skills and experience of European organizations.

OVERVIEW

- A mature and reliable Project Management Assistant with valuable experience in dealing with the operational aspects of day-to-day business.
- Organized, take-charge professional with exceptional follow-through abilities and eye for detail; able to plan and oversee a full range of events from concept to successful conclusion.
- Demonstrated ability to prioritize a broad range of responsibilities efficiently in order to meet deadlines consistently.
- Demonstrated capacity to anticipate and resolve problems swiftly and independently.
- Possess strong interpersonal skills; proven ability to develop and maintain sound business relationships.
- Highly articulate effective communicator.
- Specific experience in keeping accurate computerized records; handling customer enquiries and motivating support teams.
- Consistent achievement of objectives, dedicated, experienced organizer and coordinator.
- Extensive experience liaising and planning ventures with European organizations.
- Highly adept at using state-of-the art software packages for industry-related functions.

PROFESSIONAL EXPERIENCE

2001–Present
Brown & Co., West Park, Essex
SPECIAL PROJECTS CONSULTANT for well-respected communications consulting firm. Firm's Head wrote two critically acclaimed standards in the marketing/business field: _The New Positioning_ and _The Power of Simplicity_.

- Performed directed Internet and other research in preparation for an upcoming book.
- Analysed research and draft descriptions for inclusion in articles and future book.
- Specifically recruited for special project on basis of past performance.

1999–Present
Valley Farm Products Ltd, Hemsden, Essex
REGIONAL PROJECT MANAGEMENT ASSISTANT

- Reported directly to Project Manager. Assisted coordination, implementation, administration and management of distribution of promotional material for the ongoing 'Happy Apple' campaign.
- Maintained continuous review of project development and produced status reports for senior management.
- Supervised promotional distribution from head office. Ensured computer tracking and maintenance of project.
- Input and updated scheduling data using database and word processing software.
- Planned, implemented and monitored distribution schedules throughout Southern region (over 1,500 sites).
- Verified proposed timetable and monitored progress of schedule.
- Liaised with project team, passed on and verified all modifications, updates and amendments.

1997 to 1999
Sunnyhill Products Ltd, Overhill, Essex
ADMINISTRATIVE ASSISTANT
- Monitored use of consumables
- Maintained and updated records
- Input and retrieved data using statistical software
- Coordinated communications between administrative staff, retail clients and management

1995 to 1997
JJ & T Ltd, Overhill, Essex
ADMINISTRATIVE ASSISTANT
Office Clerk

EDUCATION
ONC Business Administration
CLAIT

REFERENCES
Excellent references will be furnished on request

Retail District Manager

James Sharpe
123 Anystreet
Anytown AT1 0BB
Tel: 020 8123 4567
james@anyaddress.co.uk

Profile

Highly focused, enthusiastic and goal-driven professional with solid experience in marketing, management, sales, operations, and training. Demonstrated success in implementing test marketing programmes and promoting products that consistently increase sales. Reputation for innovative problem solving, organization and professionalism.

Employment History

G&S Convenience 1996–Present

Area Manager – Hertfordshire

Recruited to provide leadership and management for stores with high employee turnover and lagging sales. Supervised day-to-day operations of 6 retail stores with full responsibility for P&L. Hire, train and manage 60 to 70 employees. Develop and maintain vendor relations. Introduce new products and plan marketing strategies for all stores. Plan and conduct area training meetings.

Selected Accomplishments:

- Increased inside sales 15–20% over a year, and total sales by 10%, through improved management techniques, attention to detail, inventory control and developing good relationships with vendors.
- Reduced employee turnover 50% by fostering a team atmosphere through improved training, communication and motivation.
- Received five merit-based salary increases.
- The second most senior (and youngest) supervisor in the region.
- Won sales award for increased profits per store.

District Manager – Gloucestershire

Promoted from Manager. Recruited from Birmingham to work with 3 stores to improvement management, decrease turnover and increase sales. Ran several successful pilot/test programmes that were implemented throughout the company.

Manager – Birmingham

Promoted from Management Trainee.

Computer Skills

PowerPoint, MS Word, Excel, Lotus, Internet (PC and Mac)

Education

BTEC Higher National Diploma in Distribution and Retail. Courses included marketing, publicity, media, group dynamics, speech writing.

Retail Management

Jane Swift
123 Anystreet
Anytown AT1 0BB
Tel 020 8123 4567
jane@anyaddress.co.uk

Profile

Accomplished manager with more than 15 years' experience managing high-profile, upmarket operations, leading teams, and consistently delivering sales, profit and organizational improvements. Recognized for ability to achieve results through leadership, teamwork and exceptional customer service.

– Operations Management – Business Analysis & Planning – Expense Control – Inventory Management – Human Resources (interviewing, evaluating, scheduling, counselling, coaching and developing) – Buying and Merchandising (maximizing sales volume and profitability) –

Selected Achievements

Management/Leadership
- Currently managing the largest branch store with 40 executive reports and 600 staff associates.
- Brought in to turn around an underperforming back-of-house operation that was impacting negatively on profitability of entire operation. Reorganization showed immediate improvement and brought store back on plan.
- Drove sales and profits at Manchester store despite mall renovations and store's own 30,000 square foot expansion and renovation.
- Opened three new multilevel stores in major malls from the ground up. All stores exceeded plan.
- General Manager of the Year (1997) for the entire company.

Merchandising/Customer Service
- Won Chairman's Cup for sales/profitability and excellence in customer service. Shared award with 4 others out of 70 general managers.
- Took Thornley store to Top Ten status in customer service throughout chain.
- Led Hanford store to Top Ten in customer service.
- Drove Avonhill store to Number One in customer service.
- Selected to pioneer a pilot project for a Selling Skills Training Programme for all stores nationwide. Resulted in target stores all ranking highest in chain.
- Instrumental in company's customer service programme. Consistent top ten producer.
- Worked with H&B Merchandising Organization to restructure merchandise mix to better serve South Midlands market.
- As buyer, increased department 14% in first year and by 23% in second. Expanded private label programme, increasing gross margins and upgrading fashion image.

Career History

Howard Lewis plc (1990–Present)
  Director and General Manager (1999–Present)
  General Manager Divisional Director (1994–1998)
  General Manager (1992–1994)
  Buyer (1990–1992)
Lord & Taylor, Manchester
  Assistant Buyer (1985–1990)

Education

BDS National Diploma in Fashion Buying and Merchandising, London Institute of Fashion

References upon request.

Sales and Marketing Executive

Jane Swift
123 Anystreet
Anytown AT1 0BB

Tel: 020 8123 4567
jane@anyaddress.co.uk
Page 1 of 2

Business Development ● *National Accounts* ● *Government Contracts* ● *Sales Management*

Entrepreneurial executive offers accomplishments in sales/marketing of high-tech, industrial and financial products. Strong technical background with substantial knowledge of marketing using the Internet and telecommunication technologies.

SELECTED ACCOMPLISHMENTS

- Spearheaded two start-up companies into competitive enterprises. Raised capital, launched product line, and built successful sales force.
- Negotiated major contracts with government agencies and large defence contractors. Secured vendor status in record time.
- Expanded sales presence in both national and international markets. Developed niche areas based on demand.
- Consistently maintained production record within top ten per cent in highly competitive financial services industry.

Technical/Industrial

RECYCLED ENTERPRISES LTD, Moorhill   1996–2000
Director of Sales

Directed sales and marketing for this start-up company using a first-of-its-kind technology to manufacture recycled polypropylene products for cleaning oil spills. Raised £1.8 million to purchase predecessor company from bankruptcy. Negotiated 100% credit for all money due to shareholders.

- Developed and launched product line. Worked closely with DoE to ensure new standards. Generated sales of up to £300,000 by year three.
- Negotiated contract and stocking programme with Government Services Agency (GSA), which proactively advertised product. Achieved feat in year two due to intensive marketing efforts.
- Recruited and trained national sales force. Successfully penetrated government market.
- Created all marketing materials including Web site and Press advertising. Gained orders before product became available.

J&S TECHNOLOGY, Wellington Green   1990–1996
Partner/Director of Sales

Founded new firm distributing and converting high temperature alloys, titanium and exotic alloys. Established three domestic offices and three international representatives covering Europe, Israel and South America.

- Developed business with defence contractors and commercial aircraft/engine manufacturers including Boeing, General Electric and Aerospatiale/British Aerospace. Products used in production of Titan missile and Airbus.
- Grew sales by expanding sales force to 15 and securing additional distributorships from domestic and foreign mills. Generated sales of up to £4 million annually.
- Reduced turnaround delivery time by 40% as compared to industry average through use of specialized conversion technologies.
- Implemented QC programme that qualified quickly for government/corporate vendor status.

FARRER TECHNOLOGY, Sellingford   1986–1990
Marketing Director

Directed sales and marketing for this distributor and converter of high temperature, titanium
and exotic alloys with major accounts in aerospace industry.
- Developed a professional national/international sales force of 25 reps. Grew sales from
  £3.5 million to over £11 million.
- Structured sales commissions to reflect true cost of goods sold. Reduced commissions
  paid by over 20%.
- Increased mill representation, enabling company to compete more aggressively for
  larger, more lucrative orders.
- Initiated computer system to control material production, inventory, and sales
  monitoring.
- Arranged government approval for military use of foreign titanium for secret projects.
  First company to buy titanium from China.

Financial Services
C&A FINANCIAL, Leeds   1981–1986
NOVA INVESTMENT, Leeds
National Sales Manager/Branch Manager
Directed sales for two retail brokerage firms dealing in high-risk/high-reward investments to an
affluent clientele.
- Doubled monthly sales revenue (£500,000–£1 million) by expanding sales staff and
  upgrading training methods.
- Initiated a computerized commission system (Broker Portfolio) that tracked individual
  production and served as a managerial tool for monitoring sales of retail products.
- Set up training programmes, incentives, and lead systems that significantly improved
  production as well as staff morale. Emphasized one-on-one marketing.

PREVIOUS EXPERIENCE includes sales positions in dental supplies and catalogue sales of rare
coins. Among many accomplishments, negotiated a Japanese contract for equipment
manufacturing.

Education
Midland University BSc in Economics/Finance

TECHNICAL

MS-Office 97	Maximizer	QuattroPro
Quicken	MYOB	Day Timer
Pstudio	MGI Photo Suite	WinFax Pro
Netscape Communicator	MS-Internet Explorer	Corel Print & Photo House
Power Point		

References available on request.

School Psychologist

Jane Swift
123 Anystreet
Anytown AT1 0BB
Tel: 020 8123 4567
jane@anyaddress.co.uk.

Summary of Qualifications

- Experience includes 33 years within the educational system: past 21 years as Educational Psychologist, 7 years as a Guidance Counsellor, 5 years as a primary school teacher.
- Assessment of student weaknesses and strengths; preparation of written psychological reports; interpretation of psychological testing; professional presentations and workshops; curriculum development; provide recommendations to improve students' overall learning/adjustment; collaboration with teachers and parents; small group and individual counselling.
- Have the ability to work well with people; possess excellent communication skills; am considered to be energetic, results-oriented individual.

Education

MSc Educational Psychology
PGCE
BSc Psychology

Certifications/Licences

Educational Psychologist, Guidance Counsellor
Qualified Teacher
Chartered Educational Psychologist

Experience

Educational Psychologist, North Devon LEA, 1981–Present
Responsibilities: Assessment of student strengths and weaknesses. Collaboration and interpretation of psychological test results and recommendations with teachers and parents. Assist in educational planning, programming, and development of individual educational plans for special educational students and develop interventions for students who do not qualify for placement in an educational programme. Assessment of ADHD/ADD and appropriate interventive strategies. Assist in the development of behaviour and functional behaviour assessment plans, consultation (i.e. academic, social, and behaviour interventive strategies). Work directly with students and families to assist in solving conflicts and problems related to learning and adjustment. Professional presentations and workshops.

Educational Psychologist, Warwickshire LEA, 1978–1981
Served as a school psychologist in the Head Start and Migrant Education programmes, in addition to serving two primary schools. Assisted in educational programme development, using specialized knowledge of child growth and development, learning theory, personality dynamics and motivation. Presented workshops and inservice training for school personnel and parents.

Guidance Counsellor, Heath Primary School, 1971–1978
Started as guidance counsellor and eventually combined duties as school-based psychologist. Was responsible for over 750 students. Counselled students and parents; coordinated services with various community agencies. Was a facilitator in career education, early identification programme, model school programmes and drug abuse education. Taught parent workshops in the areas of learning disabilities and effective parenting.

Security/Operations Management

James Sharpe
123 Anystreet ● Anytown AT1 0BB ● Tel: 020 8123 4567
james@anyaddress.co.uk

Career Profile

- Over 14 years of management and leadership experience in security operations and related functions with prominent hotels, retailers and security providers.
- Currently functions as Director of Security for a prestigious four star hotel, earning the highest performance ranking in the company in 1998. Have directed up to 200 officers and developed/managed £500,000+ budgets. Possess an extensive knowledge of security industry standards.
- Develop and lead effective and united teams, transforming fragmented factions into a cohesive alliance of professionals producing exceptional results and adhering to strict codes of conduct. Employ a dedicated hands-on management style that has dramatically increased effectiveness and reduced turnover.
- Certified in Security Management, Hospitality Law, Hotel Security Management, Disaster Preparedness and Emergency Response, Threat Management, Workplace Violence, and HSE Regulations. Member of the British Security Industry Association.

Areas of Expertise

- Security industry standards
- Budget creation and management
- Human Resources management functions
- Recruiting, training, and development
- Interviewing, selection, performance evaluations
- Departmental turnarounds
- Programme and procedures development
- Motivational team leadership
- Coaching, counselling and motivation

Career Development

Director of Security Operations, Four Star Hotel, Irvington   1994 to Present

- Manage all aspects of the security operation of this prestigious, top-rated 600,000 square foot luxury hotel with 300 rooms, a daily roster of 1,000 employees/guests, and 14 full-time security officers.
- Dramatically reversed poor performance history of key hotel departments, achieving ranking of first in the company in 1998
  - Decreased number of security-related incidents by 30%, the lowest in hotel's history.
  - Lowered workers' compensation injuries to 7 cases (of 300 workers), the smallest in the company's history.
  - Raised quality/efficiency while reducing overtime by 65%, the lowest rate in the department's history.
  - Instituted standards that did not allow a single successful safety or security litigation in five years.
  - Earned top ranking as company's best managed department.
  - Achieved lowest employee turnover rate in the entire company.

Produced these results by creating and implementing leading-edge programmes including… Innovative training, evaluation and TQM programmes that produced employee motivation, attention, interest, cooperation, and desired response… Standard operating procedures for crisis management, disaster prevention and recovery, risk management, emergency response, incident investigation, and report writing… Detailed investigation standards for all security and safety incidents, including policy violations, and guest or employee injuries.

Chief of Security, DeLuxe Hotel, Redcliff   1993 to 1994

Directed security operations of this three star national chain hotel with 200 guest rooms, 200 employees and 6 security officers, devising effective security policies and procedures, and budgeting and monitoring department's expenditures.

- Produced a 20% decrease in security-related incidents.
- Reduced employee turnover by 50%

Established new standard operating procedures. Developed and implemented emergency action plans. Contributed to creation of multiple departments' security and safety requirement training programmes. Cooperated closely with the Human Resources department on HSE, workers' compensation, and other industrial safety matters to ensure compliance.

Operations Manager, Redwood Security, Redfield   1990 to 1992
Managed over 200 plain clothes and uniform contract security officers in multiple facilities, including defence contractors and film studios. Developed and promoted a proactive culture of risk management and prevention. Promoted through the ranks from Field Officer to Operations Manager, the highest rank within the division.
- Implemented new rewards and recognition programmes that raised morale and provided continuous feedback.
- Frequently volunteered extended hours to meet clients' needs and critical project deadlines. Acted as client liaison to develop partnerships and strategic loss prevention and asset protection programmes. Oversaw Human Resources operations, including officer selection, field deployment, training, scheduling, inspections, evaluations and disciplinary actions. Established professional ties with local police authorities.

Loss Prevention Manager, J S Hoblins, Derby   1987 to 1990
Oversaw security staff and operations at this market retailer.
- Protected assets and reduced legal liability by creating ongoing prioritized loss prevention initiatives.
- Developed effective loss countermeasure strategies and prevention awareness training programmes.
- Conducted comprehensive internal audits and investigations for external/internal sources of loss and employee misconduct.
- Minimized accidents and injuries by managing effective safety programmes.

Technology Skills
- Proficient in Microsoft Word, Excel, IRIMS and PPM2000.
- PC proficient in Windows 98/95/3.1
- Extensive knowledge of computer-based, audio/visual and access control systems.

Education and Certification
BSc Political Science, University of the Midlands
Certifications:
- Security Management (Supervisor)
- Hospitality Law
- Hotel Security Management
- Disaster Preparedness and Emergency Response
- Threat Management and Workplace Violence
- HSE Regulations and Workplace Violence
- City & Guilds: Professional Guard parts 1 & 2

Security Services Sales

Jane Swift
123 Anystreet
Anytown AT1 0BB
Tel: 020 8123 4567
jane@anyaddress.co.uk

Professional Profile

Sales ● Account Management ● New Business Development Professional

Sales and Account Management Development professional with expert qualifications in identifying and capturing market opportunities to accelerate expansion, increase revenues and improve profit contributions in highly competitive industries. Outstanding record of achievement in complex account and contract negotiations.

Key Strengths:

Account development/management	Consultative/solutions sales
Customer service/satisfaction	New market development
Bilingual English/Spanish	Account retention
Customer needs assessment	Presentation and negotiations skills
PC proficient	

Professional Experience

Key Account Executive, 1996–Present

A&L Security Services, Largest privately held security company in the UK with annual sales of over £400 million.

Recruited to start up and oversee the market development of contract security services in Northern England. Conduct in-depth client need assessments and develop technology-based security strategies to ensure maximum efficiency.

- Achieved consistent annual sales production in excess of £2.5 million
- Built territory from nowhere capturing 55% of the market share in region
- Expanded annual billable hours from 300 to more than 5,000, fostering a rapid growth in staffing from 30 to more than 300 employees in Raleigh branch
- Successfully negotiated and secured sales ranging from £300K to £1.2 million
- Earned several national and local awards for top sales performance, including the prestigious 'Salesperson of the Year' award

Account Executive/Loan Officer, 1995–1996

Equity Finance Ltd, UK's oldest finance company, a division of a Fortune 500 company.

Generated and sold bill consolidation loans through telemarketing.

- Consistently exceeded monthly sales objectives
- Received national recognition as one of the Top 10 salespeople in the nation, and Number 1 salesperson in Raleigh branch.

Education

Bachelor of Arts, Business Administration/Finance, 2.1, 1994
University of Birmingham

Senior Account Executive

Jane Swift
123 Anystreet
Anytown AT1 0BB
Tel: 020 8123 4567
jane@anyaddress.co.uk

- 15+ years' experience building partnerships with leading corporations to develop consumer packaging, sales promotions, and merchandising to strengthen brand identity and awareness. In-depth understanding of technology, household products, personal care, liquor, and food categories.
- Account management capabilities enhanced by professional design, production, printing, and technical background. Formal design education and commitment to ongoing professional development.
- Adept in Macintosh and Windows applications for graphic design, desktop publishing, word processing, spreadsheets, e-mail, database management, Web site development and multimedia presentations.

Key Words

Consultative Sales	High-Impact Presentations
Customer Service	Problem Solving & Decision Making
Project Management	Sales Closing & Negotiating
Design Process	Team Building & Leadership

Achievements

- Generated nearly £1 million in annual sales for packaging design firm by winning key accounts and cultivating relationships.
- Won four Packaging Design Council (PDC) Gold Awards for package design in personal care and household appliances categories.
- Won account with major multinational corporation and developed packaging, promotional displays, trade, and consumer material. Facilitated the national redesign (60 Product lines) in order to establish products as the technologically superior brand within the category.
- Collaborated on the national implementation of a 'company first' branding strategy. Key objective: to reinforce the brand name, weakened by a four-year trend of sub-branding. Brainstormed with marketing and creative executives to create a set of graphic standards to communicate the essence of the brand. Applied this branding system to the entire product line.
- Increased sales and distribution through development of innovative club-store packaging and promotions for a leading drinks supplier.
- Guided design and production of packaging and product launch materials for a 30-unit range of household products. Product was picked up nationally by ASCO and sales jumped 19% in an introductory period.
- Worked with a leading cereal maker to develop promotional back panel games, sweepstakes, and in-pack offers.
- Directed development of displays, brochures, and merchandising materials for Curtis Confectionary and Berry Farm Products (created through licensing agreement).
- Introduced multimedia capability to firm's new business presentations. Created Web site content, including a company tour, an interactive portfolio, and a creative access section – allowing clients online, confidential access to view work.

Career Chronology

Senior Account Executive – 1998–Present
Leading Package Design Firm, York
- Hired as a junior account executive to assist in all aspects of client services. Within seven months, promoted to account executive to develop new business in the consumer electronics category. Established key contacts with industry leaders through cold calling, direct marketing and client presentations. Consulted with clients to determine marketing objectives, packaging requirements and budgetary limitations. Directed numerous packaging, promotion, trade and consumer projects. Managed staff of five to implement the electronic design and production process.

Computer Graphics Artist – 1995–1998
Big Design Firm, York
- Worked with designers and art directors to take concepts through to highly refined computer based production. Trained members of the design and production department in the use of Adobe Illustrator. Set up a high-speed remote viewing network enabling select clients to simultaneously view design concepts.

Account Executive – 1991–1995
Freelance Placement Agency, York
- Instrumental in establishing a lucrative desktop publishing placement division. Identified and cultivated profitable markets. Managed and art directed freelancers and worked with clients through all project stages.

Graphic Designer – 1985–1990
ABC Marketing & Communications, York
- Accountable for all stages of the design and production of consumer packaging. Participated in beta testing of proprietary graphics software and various high-end peripherals, giving product reviews to manufacturers.

Education
BA Graphic Design, Industrial Design, Computer Graphics and Marketing – 1985
York University

Ongoing Professional Development
- Earned Certificate in Sales Promotion – St John's College
- Intensive seminars in Web site design, multimedia and advertising

Senior International Marketing and Business Development Executive

Jane Swift
123 Anystreet
Anytown AT1 0BB
Tel: 020 8123 4567
jane@anyaddress.co.uk

Page 1 of 2

Expertise in Product Development ● Commercialization & Global Market Expansion
Telecoms ● Consumer Electronics ● Sports & Leisure Industries

Dynamic management career leading turnaround and high-growth organizations through unprecedented profitability and explosive market growth worldwide. Combine extensive strategic planning, competitive positioning, life cycle management, channel management and product development/management qualifications with strong general management, P&L management, organizational development, workforce management, and multicultural communication skills, MBA; multilingual – fluent German, English, Italian, intermediate Japanese.

PROFESSIONAL EXPERIENCE

Major Electronics Company, Dusseldorf, Germany   1992 to 2000
The second largest electronics company worldwide ranking #15 in the Forbes International 800 ratings.
Marketing Director
Executive Board Member recruited to design marketing strategies and implement systems/processes to lead a worldwide marketing function as part of the business group's aggressive turnaround programme.

Accountable for a £250 million marketing budget. Oversee worldwide marketing operations including business strategy and benchmarking, technology strategy, market research, consumer marketing, regional marketing, Europe, Asia, USA, marketing communications, new media including Internet, intranet, and extranet, and business-to-consumer e-commerce. Manage a staff of 77 through 10 direct reports.

- Led the marketing initiatives for a successful launch of two mobile phone product lines transitioning losses of £200 million in 97/98 to profits of £30 million in 98/99 and doubling world market share to approximately 8%.
- Delivered a 5-point improvement in brand awareness, and 50% relevant set improvement for mobile and cordless phones throughout China and Europe.
- Introduced a worldwide marketing communications spending performance initiative slashing communication costs by £10 million.
- Identified and initiated business development strategies and technology vehicles instrumental in developing international marketing partnerships and equity investments.
- Established a price/value-based market analysis instrument together with the market research and consumer marketing groups to develop pricing accuracy generating revenue increases exceeding £20 million.
- Directed e-commerce marketing initiatives leading to the development of 7 operational online stores in 5 European countries generating 4 million contacts with CAGR of 20% per week, followed by development of a virtual Customer Care Centre.
- Conceived and initiated PR strategies for a new product launch generating over 130 million contracts within a few months.
- Led improvements in competitive market intelligence through enhancements to statistical reports and customer satisfaction surveys.

Jane Swift
page 2 of 2

ELECTRONICS COMPANY, Bonn, Germany   1987–1992
A leading European high-end TV, audio and consumer electronics company.

Marketing Director
Joined this privately held company to improve product life cycle management and channel marketing initiatives. Oversaw budget administration, strategic planning and market research, international communications, training and product management. Directed a staff of 21.
- Instituted a series of channel management and segmentation improvements to correct market planning and positioning initiatives and reduce price erosion throughout retail distribution channels.
- Led development of product definition, life cycle management and market launch strategies positioning company as the value-based market leader of high-end TV sets in Germany with market share exceeding 14%.

ABC BICYCLE COMPANY, Berlin, Germany   1983 to 1987
A global leading automotive, motorcycle and bicycle component equipment manufacturer.

Director of Marketing International
Led transition from an engineering-driven traditional gear hub manufacturer to a market-oriented competitor in the sport and leisure industry. Reported to Divisional Director.
- Established a marketing department, devised strategies for over 1,000 items within 6 product lines, delivered a profit for the first time in 8 years, and boosted new product sales ratios from 10% to 40%.
- Headed up a special internal R&D unit and restructuring project leading to the creation of marketing-driven product development teams. Replaced 15% of R&D personnel, established R&D controls, reduced R&D costs by £500,000, and earned a £30,000 project completion bonus.

ABC AUTOMOTIVE, Wolfsburg, Germany   1980 to 1983
Leading automotive and home appliance manufacturer.
Product Group Manager
Oversaw European product management and marketing initiatives for the £500 million Electronic Division/Successfully introduced brands in France, Italy and the UK.

EDUCATION
MBA, University of London
Diplome d'enseignement Supérieur Européen de Management, Centre d'Etudes Européennes Supérieures de Management (CESEM), France,
Diplom-Betriebswirt (FH), Business Administration, Europäisches Studienprogramm für Betriebswirschaft (ESB)

WORK EXPERIENCE PLACEMENTS
Country Chamber of Commerce, Osaka, Japan, Exchange Scholarship, counselled German and Japanese firms in all aspects of business for their respective countries. Kornwestheim Club Vertrieb GmbH, Kornwestheim, Germany, marketing concepts in direct sales.

Senior Management Executive

Jane Swift
123 Anystreet
Anytown AB1 0BB
Tel: 020 8123 4567
jane@anyaddress.co.uk

New Business Development ● Strategic Partnerships ● Product Marketing

Accomplished Senior Executive with a strong affinity for technology and a keen business sense for the application of emerging products to add value and expand markets. Proven talent for identifying core business needs and translating into technical deliverables. Launched and managed cutting-edge Internet programmes and services to win new customers, generate revenue gains and increase brand value.

Unique combination of technical and business/sales experience. Articulate and persuasive in explaining the benefits of e-commerce technologies and how they add value, differentiate offerings, and increase customer retention. Highly self-motivated, enthusiastic and profit oriented.

**Expertise in Internet services, emerging payment products,
secure electronic commerce, smart card technology, and Java.**

AREAS OF QUALIFICATION

Business
- Sales & Marketing
- Business Planning
- Business & Technical Requirements
- Relationship Management

- Business Development
- Project Management
- Revenue Generation

- Strategic Initiatives
- Strategic Partnerships
- Contract Negotiations

Technical
- Electronic Commerce
- Public Key Infrastructure
- Stored Value
- Complex Financial Systems
- Dual and Single Message

- Encryption Technology
- Firewalls
- Digital Certificates
- Authorization, Clearing, Settlement

- Key Management
- Smart Cards
- Internet & Network Security

PROFESSIONAL EXPERIENCE

ABC Credit Card, High Green   *1999 to Present*
E-COMMERCE AND SMART CARD CONSULTANT
- Developed strategic e-commerce marketing plans for large and small merchants involving Web purchases and retail transactions using a multifunctional, microcontroller smart card for both secure Internet online commerce and point-of-sale offline commerce.
- Combined multiple software products for Internet and non-Internet applications: home banking, stored value, digital certificates, key management, rewards & loyalty programme, PCS/GSM cell phone, and contactless microcontroller with RF communications without direct POS contact.
- Consulted on business and technical requirements to define new e-commerce products and essential deliverables for ABC Credit Card, values at £2.5 MM, supported and enhancing Internet transactions.
- Analysed systems relating to the point of sale environment in the physical world and at the merchant server via the Internet for real-time authorization, clearing and settlement.
- Managed projects including the requirements management system for electronic commerce products affecting core systems; authorization, clearing and settlement. Provided expertise about business and technical issues regarding SET and the Credit Card Payment Gateway Service.

Communications Technology Ltd, Heybrook Park   *1994 to 1999*
MANAGER OF WESTERN REGION CHANNEL PARTNER PROGRAMME
- Developed and maintained business relationships with large blue chip customers and partners that use or resell client-server software for applications and contracts involving e-commerce and smart card technology for a variety of Internet/intranet products: home banking, EDI, stored value, digital certificates, key management, perimeter defence with proxy firewalls, secure remote access.
- Negotiated an exclusive contract with one of the largest government and commercial contractors in the industry, projected to generate £2–4 million over a 24–36 month period. Contract includes secure remote access, telecommuting, secure health care applications.

Antava Ltd, Heybrook Park   *1990 to 1994*
SENIOR SOFTWARE ENGINEER/SOFTWARE INSTRUCTOR
- Designed new programs and trained software engineers in object-oriented analysis and design using UML Solutions that were implemented in C++ in a UNIX environment.
- Managed a software engineering group of 53 individuals. Developed in-house program that saved over £150,000 in training costs for sate-of-the-art communications system software development.
- Received Peer Award for outstanding performance; earned a performance evaluation rating of 4.2/5.0.
- Developed and maintained C and C++ communication software in a UNIX environment.
- Created curriculum and course materials that reduced overall training costs by more than £150,000. Coordinated and presented software training programmes.

EDUCATION
- BSc Electrical Engineering, University of London. Emphasis: software engineering
- Top Secret Security Clearance with Polygraph

Senior Personnel Manager

Jane Swift
123 Anystreet
Anytown AT1 0BB
Tel: 020 8123 4567
jane@anyaddress.co.uk
Page 1 of 2

PROFILE
A well-organized, disciplined individual used to working calmly, effectively and efficiently under pressure. A first-rate communicator, both orally and in writing. An outgoing personality with excellent interpersonal skills who enjoys working with a wide range of people. Self-motivated with the skill and determination to succeed.

STRENGTHS
Recruitment and Selection ● Employee Development ● Employee Relations ● Employee Services ● Motivation and Reward ● Human Resources Planning

EXPERIENCE
Montgomery Bank plc
SENIOR PERSONNEL MANAGER   1998–Present
PERSONNEL MANAGER   1995–1998
Covered all aspects of Human Resources Management from recruitment to redundancy.

- Held a senior management position in an organization employing over eight hundred staff
- Managed, organized and developed a team of six personnel managers and twenty support staff to cover all aspects of personnel management
- Developed excellent communication and motivational skills encouraging staff to achieve their objectives
- Successfully implemented an Appraisal Scheme for Head Office staff and for personnel in thirty-five branches across the UK
- Recruited specialist staff for all departments
- Introduced new and rigorous absenteeism review procedures which led to a 25% annual reduction in absentee levels
- Developed excellent working relations with the Staff Association greatly facilitating successful negotiations on matters of pay and conditions.
- Negotiated new working practices as new services introduced, resulting in a 15% increase in production with a staff reduction of 2% through natural wastage
- Resolved serious disciplinary matters not dealt with at line-manager level

SENIOR PERSONNEL ASSISTANT (EMPLOYEE SERVICES)   1992–1995

- Authorized all staff borrowing from the bank
- Authorized personal loans and overdrafts up to £50,000.
- Stood in for the Personnel Manager in their absence.
- Acted as a point of contact for staff on all account issues for managers and staff throughout the organization

PAYROLL CLERK   1989–1992
- Updated and maintained employee records
- Achieved weekly and monthly payroll deadlines
- Provided payroll assistance to bank staff
- Handled all payroll procedures, including PAYE, SMP and SSP
- Used both manual and computerized systems

EDUCATION AND TRAINING
Diploma in Personnel Management
CIPD Professional Qualification Scheme – Core Management; Core Personnel and Development
CLAIT

MEMBERSHIP OF PROFESSIONAL BODIES
Licentiate Member of the Chartered Institute of Personnel and Development (FCIPD)
Currently studying to become Graduate Member

Senior Sales and Marketing Manager

JAMES SHARPE
123 Anystreet
Anytown AT1 0BB
Tel: 020 8123 4567
james@anyaddress.co.uk
Page 1 of 2

Top-producing sales and marketing professional with nine years of management experience in world-class organizations. Consistently successful in developing new markets, penetrating new territories, identifying and capturing new business, and managing large-scale events for blue chip companies worldwide. Goal-driven manager committed to developing outcomes mutually benefiting the company and the client. Excellent qualifications in building corporate relationships with industry leaders.

Areas of expertise include:
- New Account Development
- Key Account Management
- Client Needs Assessment
- Contract Negotiations
- Competitive/Strategic Planning

- Large Scale Meeting/Event Planning
- Catering Planning/Management
- Co-Marketing Partnerships
- Relationship Management
- Customer Service/Satisfaction

PROFESSIONAL EXPERIENCE

E&R LEISURE, Hilverside   1996 to 2000
Senior Sales Manager

Joined company to lead market entry/penetration initiatives throughout the Northeast Region of the UK for this privately-held exclusive leisure complex with 800 suites, a 60,000 sq. ft. conference centre, and a full range of guest amenities. Managed business growth among blue chip corporate accounts and national association accounts.

- Developed and maintained relationships with corporate meeting planners of major accounts including FCS, TS&H, Chanteclere, Niki Portman, S&G, Kentland, Glentrich and others to develop custom-tailored business meeting packages.
- Worked closely with corporate planners throughout all phases of strategic and tactical planning, coordination, and execution of major events to ensure superior service and guest relations.
- Captured national association accounts including National Cancer Society, Heart Association, The Law Society and Chartered Institute of Psychologists.
- Sold and orchestrated multiyear bookings to numerous associations and corporate accounts.
  Achievements
  - Built territory and increased revenues from £1 million to over £7 million within first-year.
  - Achieved 157% of annual booking goals (2,500 room nights per month).

ALDEBURGH HOUSE, Aldeburg   1993 to 1996
Catering Sales Manager

Challenged to develop new markets and products for visiting multicultural groups.

- Identified target market, initiated contact with prospects, developed proposals, and forged major account relationships.
- Worked closely with corporate planners at DeLa Mere, FTA, Foresham, Newsline, and others to create unique and extravagant parties and events ranging up to £2 million per event.
- Sold, planned and coordinated catered group events for corporate accounts and private parties ranging from 2 to 19,000 guests.
- Developed comprehensive strategic and tactical plans for every phase of event including logistics, transportation, food and beverage, entertainment and gifts to create a memorable occasion.

- Oversaw scheduled events and served as troubleshooter and liaison between staff, event managers and corporate clients to resolve issues and ensure guest satisfaction and loyalty.
- Compiled planning, tracking and forecasting reports using proprietary computer system.
  Achievements
  - Achieved 130% of Catering Sales & Service Team Goals, 1996.
  - Consistently exceeded individual annual sales goals.

INTERNATIONAL HOTEL, Southgate   1985 to 1993
Fast track promotions through a series of increasingly responsible positions based on business growth and improved sales revenue for this high-volume airport property.
Sales Manager-North (1992 to 1993)
Sales Manager-South (1989 to 1992)
Associate Director of Catering (1985 to 1988)
Catering Manager (1985)

- Created innovative guest packages for corporate accounts locally and nationally for this first-rate property with 300 rooms, a 12,000 sq. ft. conference centre and several guest services facilities.
- Developed corporate and professional relationships throughout the industry and coordinated with other properties to accommodate extremely large groups.
- Identified target accounts and consistently developed new business driving increased revenues.
- Promoted property through trade show and convention participation, including public speaking engagements for large groups.
- Planned and coordinated exclusive large-scale intimate client events for the affluent.
  Achievement
  - Achieved 131% of sales goals throughout the Northern Region, 1993

CHINESE COURT RESTAURANT, Midvale   1983 to 1985
Catering/Sales Manager
Successfully sold Chinese themed parties to international wholesale and corporate convention groups.

EDUCATION
Diploma in Marketing – Institute of Marketing
Diploma in Multinational Business Operations – Institute of Marketing
Diploma, Certificat de Langue Francaise, Institut Catholique De Paris, 1983 (Study Abroad Programme)

PROFESSIONAL DEVELOPMENT
Sales Training:
International Hotel, BEST progams (Building Effective Sales Techniques), Top Achiever Sales, Travel Management Companies, Best Practices
Designation
Certified Meeting Professional (CMP)
Affiliations
Meeting Planners International, Member
Society of Association Executives, Member

Senior Technology Executive

James Sharpe
123 Anystreet
Anytown AT1 0BB
Tel: 020 8123 4567
james@anyaddress.co.uk

Page 1 of 2

Accomplished Management Executive with 15+ years of experience and a verifiable record of delivering enhanced productivity, streamlined operations and improved financial performance. Natural leader with strong entrepreneurial spirit and a special talent for transitioning strategy into action and achievement. Highly effective team building and motivational skills.

Multifunctional expertise includes:

- Corporate Information Technology
- Staffing & Management Development
- Quality & Productivity Improvement
- Marketing Strategy & Management
- Strategic & Business Planning
- Customer Service & Satisfaction
- Operations Management
- Team Building & Leadership

PROFESSIONAL EXPERIENCE

InterTech Group plc
1992–Present
CHIEF INFORMATION OFFICER (1997–Present)
CHAIRMAN, Martins Systems (InterTech subsidiary) (1997–Present)

Appointed to these dual senior-level positions and challenged to create and execute technology strategy for InterTech and subsidiaries of the £700 million Information Services Group. Concurrently provide executive oversight for the development and deployment of software products/services and MIS solutions for Martins Systems, affiliate offices, and 3,900 independent agents.

Provide leadership for a team of 200 management and support personnel. Administer a £16 million annual budget. Scope of accountabilities is expansive and includes planning and strategy, operations management, human resource affairs, customer service, marketing, management reporting, and communications.

Key Management Achievements

- Built the complete corporate technology infrastructure from the ground up. Developed techology strategies and tactical plans mapped to align with corporate goals.
- Served as a member of the corporate Leadership Council. Defined corporate vision; developed business plans, created strategies and establish tactical goals for all business units.
- Established a high-performance management staff and created a team-based work atmosphere that promotes cooperation to achieve common corporate objectives. Instituted a series of initiatives that substantially improved communications between staff and management.
- Developed and integrated programmes to maximize productive and efficient use of technology throughout the corporation. Instituted 'user champions' to serve as technical experts within each business unit, launched executive 'boot camps' to train management in aggressive computer use, and built responsive help centres for technical support.
- Spreadheaded creation and implementation of a customer information and marketing team responsible for developing an award-winning marketing programme, promotions, direct-mail campaigns, and demonstrations and tours.
- Created innovative processes using product specialists for management of sales leads and distributor networks, resolution of customer escalated issues, and provision of work-flow and engineering consulting for company offices and agents.

Key Technical Achievements
- Led implementation of client/server software suite that won the industry's 1996 and 1998 Title Tech Discovery Award for best and most innovative title industry software.
- Spreadheaded development of numerous technical infrastructure projects, including the corporate Internet presence, corporate intranet, Web hosting solutions for independent agents, and electronic commerce solutions for offices, agents and service providers in the property management industry.
- Orchestrated development of an award-winning marketing programme, Power Tools for the Modern World, that won the local and district awards for best overall marketing programme.
- Guided development and implementation of a title industry software suite installed in 400 systems throughout the distributor network. Designed and deployed training programmes to ensure high quality service levels.
- Managed creation of an Electronic Underwriting Manual that was selected as best policies and procedures implementation in the National Awards competition, 1996.
- Led design and implementation of a 1,200-user corporate WAN, a centralized help desk, a 2000-user corporate e-mail system, and a comprehensive training centre for desktop applications.

CHIEF EXECUTIVE, InterTech (1988–1992)
Promoted to manage all operations for this subsidiary. Took over leadership for a staff of 25 and recruited/built to 90+ personnel. Oversaw all management reporting, finances, marketing, product delivery, and closing services.

Key Management Achievements
- Delivered profits throughout a severe recession.
- Maintained a consistent 15% market share despite a tripling in the local competition.
- Achieved standing in the top 15% in profitability and revenues across all company offices nationwide.
- Created and deployed a marketing programme including a series of 20 seminars; built strong industry relationships and established a reputation as the area's premier experts.
- Pioneered innovative marketing strategies to reach new markets and build a network of industry professionals.

COMMERCIAL SALES (1985–1988)
Hired to develop and manage a commercial closing division. Achieved the highest market share of commercial closings in the local market.

EDUCATION
MBA, University of the West (1985)
Bachelor of Arts, Business, University of the West (1982)

PROFESSIONAL ACTIVITIES
Frequent Lecturer, Technology Conferences, 1995–Present
Member, Systems Committee, Technical Association, 1994–Present
Member, 'Technology 2000' Planning Committee, 1994–Present

Senior Technology Executive

Jane Swift   Page 1 of 2
123 Anystreet
Anytown AT1 0BB
Tel: 020 8123 4567
jane@anyaddress.co.uk

SENIOR TECHNOLOGY EXECUTIVE
Project Management ● *Multimedia Communications & Production* ● *MIS Management*

Exceptionally creative management executive uniquely qualified for a digital media technical production position by a distinctive blend of hands-on technical, project management and advertising/communications experience. Offer a background that spans broadcast, radio and print media; fully fluent and proficient in interactive and Internet technologies and tools.

Proven leader with a strength for identifying talent, building and motivating creative teams that work cooperatively to achieve goals. Highly articulate with excellent interpersonal skills and a sincere passion for blending communications with technology. Capabilities include:

- Project Planning & Management
- Account Management & Client Relations
- Multimedia Communications & Production
- Information Systems & Networking
- Conceptual & Creative Design
- Work Plans, Budgets & Resource Planning
- Department Management
- Interactive/Internet Technologies
- Technology Needs Assessment & Solutions
- Team Building & Leadership

PROFESSIONAL EXPERIENCE
LTR Investments, Inc., St Mary's   1986–Present
DIRECTOR OF MIS (1997–Present)
ASSISTANT DIRECTOR OF IT/CORPORATE COMMUNICATIONS (1992–1997)
CORPORATE COMMUNICATIONS OFFICER (1988–1992)
ASSOCIATE (1986–1988)

Advanced rapidly through a series of increasingly responsible positions with this UK based, European investment group. Initially hired to manage market research projects, advanced to plan and execute corporate communications projects, and in 1992, assumed responsibility for spearheading the introduction of emerging technologies to automate the entire company.

Current scope of responsibility is expansive and focuses on strategic planning, implementation and administration of all information systems and technology. Lead technical staff members, manage budgets, select and oversee vendors, define business requirements, and produce deliverables through formal project plans. Manage systems configuration and maintenance, troubleshoot problems, plan and direct upgrades, and test operations to ensure optimum systems functionality and availability.

Technical Contributions
- Pioneered the company's computerization from the ground floor; led the installation and integration of a state-of-the-art and highly secure network involving 50+ workstations running on 6 LANs interconnected by V-LAN switching technology.
- Defined requirements; planned and accelerated the implementation of advanced technology solutions, deployed on a calculated timeframe, to meet the short- and long-term needs of the organization.
- Orchestrated the introduction of sophisticated applications and multimedia technology to streamline workflow processes, expand presentation capabilities and keep pace with the competition.
- Administered the life cycle of multiple projects from initial systems/network planning and technology acquisition through installation, training and operation. Saved hundreds of thousands in consulting fees by managing IS and telecommunication issues in-house.

Business Contributions
- Created and produced high-impact multimedia presentations to communicate the value and benefits of individual investment projects to top-level company executives. Tailored presentations to appeal to highly sophisticated, multicultural audiences.
- Assembled and directed exceptionally well qualified project teams from diverse creative disciplines; collaborated with and guided photographers, videographers, copywriters, script writers, graphic designers and artists to produce innovative presentations and special events.
- Performed market research and analyses to determine risks and feasibility of multiple investment projects valued at up to £150 million. Developed and recommended tactical plans to transform vision into achievement.

Broadcast, Print and Radio Advertising & Production   *(1971–1985)*
DIRECTOR OF ADVERTISING, Blackwell Advertising Associates   (1983–1985)
ADVERTISING ACCOUNT EXECUTIVE, Vividian Press (1984) / Rainbow Advertising (1981–1983) /
M&K Advertising (1980–1981) / Wells Publishing (1979–1980) / Image Advertising (1971–1978)
WRITER/PRODUCER, Radio Programming, Southern Counties Radio (1971)
    Early career involved a series of progressive creative and account management positions spanning all advertising media: multimedia, television, radio and print. Worked directly with clients to assess complex and often obscure needs, conceptualized and developed advertising campaigns to communicate the desired message in an influential manner.
Achievement Highlights
- Designed, wrote, produced and launched advertising campaigns that consistently positioned clients with a competitive distinction. Developed a reputation for ability to accurately intuit and interpret clients' desires and produce deliverables that achieved results.
- Hand-selected and led creative teams consisting of graphic designers, artists, musicians, talent, cartoonists, animators, videographers, photographers, and other freelancers and third-party creative services to develop and produce multimillion pound advertising campaigns.
- Won accolades for the creation, production and launch of a 4-colour fractional-page advertisement that generated the greatest response in the history of the publication. Honoured with a featured personal profile recognizing achievements.
- Developed and applied a unique style and advertising philosophy that accounted for the nuances of human psychology and used innovative, intelligent, and sometimes startling techniques to capture attention and influence the target market.

EDUCATION & TRAINING
HND Media Studies, Irvington College
Continuing education in Marketing Research and Broadcast Production, 1981–1983
Northern College of Arts

TECHNICAL QUALIFICATIONS
Innate technical abilities and interest in emerging technologies and digital communications. Trained and fully versed in all aspects of network design, implementation, installation and maintenance. Advanced skill in the installation, configuration, customization and troubleshooting of software suites and applications, hardware and peripherals within the Windows environment (3.x, 95, 98, NT 3.5, NT 3.51, NT 4). Proficient with most Web development, multimedia, word processing, spreadsheet, graphic/presentation and database tools and applications.

Software Development

James Sharpe
123 Anystreet
Anytown AT1 0BB
Tel: 020 8123 4567
james@anyaddress.co.uk

Summary
IS professional recognized for broad-based skills encompassing Web, hardware and software solutions. Move effortlessly through and adapt readily to ever changing technologies. Areas of expertise encompass: project management, team leadership, staff supervision, coding, design, testing, user training/support, troubleshooting, customer relations.

Technical Skills
Software: MS Office Suites, Quattro Pro, DacEasy, Act!, Premier, Avid Cinema, Authorware, Director, PhotoShop, CorelDraw, VoicePad, Naturally Speaking Impromptu, PowerPlay, Visio
Hardware: SCSI, RAID Systems, IDE, NIC's, video/audio network hubs, switches, and routers
Web/Internet: Netscape Commerce Sever, MS IIS, HTML, CGI, ISAPI
Databases & Technologies: Dbase, Paradox, MS Access, MS SQL Server, Progress, DDE, OLE, OLE2, ActiveX, Automations Servers (in and out of process), Active Forms, DCOM, Memory Mapped Files, Compound Files, MS Transaction Server (version 1.0), NT Services, Named Pipes, Thunking, Multiheaded applications and libraries (Win32), WinSock, mail services, HTTP, FTP, NNTP, TCP, UDP, SMTP, POP3
Operating Systems/Services: MS DOS, MS Windows 3.11, 95, 98, NT Server/Workstation, UNIX, MS Exchange, MS SQL Server, WINS, RAS, DHCP, IIS
Programming Languages: Delphi, Pascal, Progress, C/C++, VB, Fortran, PowerBuilder, Perl, Assembly

Career Highlights
- Recruited to manage several major projects at Technical Services (TS):
    - Reconfigured entire IS department. Developed specifications for new servers for file sharing, Web and database. Redesigned network 100 Base T; installed T1; and enabled WINS, DHCP, Exchange Server, MS SQL Server and IIS.
    - Revamped networks, servers and Internet connections to resolve the weekly, sometimes daily, crashing of network.
    - Project manager for medical/Internet project that was designed to provide continuing education courses online.
    - Supervised two professionals in IS and Web development.
    - Wrote several interfaces for authorware, I.E. 4.0 and Exchange, and created Intranet as dynamic pages from MSQL database.

- Founded Holbrook Software, with sole responsibility for account development, project planning, staffing, and customer relations. Developed software solutions for several public agencies and private firms:
    - Created an employee scheduling software, married filing status software with yearly upgrades and conversion programme.
    - Developed a criminal history database, investigation and complaint software packages for South Gloucester and Somerset Police.
    - Developed a UCR (uniform criminal reporting) software package. Program enables small cities, villages, and towns to participate in computerized national UCR.
    - Created software to accommodate membership database, account histories, invoices, membership functions, bank deposits, reports, and rosters for the J&B Association.

▨ Designed Vortex Computer Systems Web site, applying knowledge of HTML/CGI, security and interactive pages, among other functions.
   ▨ Developed user-defined help feature for online help
   ▨ Provided HTML CGI and Winhelp training
   ▨ Created interfaces to third-party products
   ▨ Gained extensive expertise with large relational databases

Professional Experience
Holbrook Software   *1997–Present*
Software Developer/Proprietor

Electronic Systems   *1994–1996*
Director of IS, Programming and Web Development

CIM   *1992–1993*
Software Developer

Vortex Computer Systems   *1990–1991*
Interface Developer/Web Programmer/Webmaster; Online Help Programmer

Verso & Co.   *1985–1990*
Regional Computer Coordinator

TechuStat   *1984–1985*
Customer Service Representative

Professional Development
Coursework in Advanced Programming, Pascal and Fortran

Store Manager

James Sharpe
123 Anystreet
Anytown AT1 0BB
Tel: 020 8123 4567
james@anyaddress.co.uk

WORK
EXPERIENCE

Manager, A National Kitchen Utensil Retailer. 1997–Present
Manage daily operations of a £2-million annual business. Staff of 12 people. Responsible for increasing sales and profitability and decreasing expenses.

Increased gross margin by 25% and net contribution by 105% on a 3% sales increase.

Senior Assistant Buyer, Turner's, Brent Green. 1993–1997
Controlled purchasing – profitability reports, weekly three-month estimate of sales, stocks, and markdown items. Planned and negotiated sales promotions, advertising and special purchases.

Coordinated training and teamwork with managers and merchants in the 22 stores.

Increased department sales 18% more than the Division's increase.

Assistant Buyer. Assisted selection and distribution of merchandise. Managed all buying office functions while learning to plan sales and control stocks. Created weekly, monthly and seasonal financial plans.

Developed all systems to support the growth of the branch from a £1-million volume to a £4-million annual volume.

Buyer/Manager, Green Gifts. 1990–1993

Bought merchandise for two different gift stores. Directed daily store operations and sales. Directed merchandise presentation, inventory control and customer service. Scheduled and supervised a 7-person staff.

Increased sales volume 22% more than corporate projection.

Manager, Webb & Grant. 1987–1990

Directed daily store operations. Analysed trends in fashion, merchandise and consumer needs. Planned effective marketing strategy, displays, advertising and an employee sales programme.

Increased annual net sales volume by 33%.

EDUCATION

Institute of Purchasing and Supply: Diploma in Purchasing and Supply.

Supermarket Management

James Sharpe
123 Anystreet ● Anytown AT1 0BB ● Tel: 020 8123 4567 ● james@anyaddress.co.uk

Career Profile

▪ Extensive experience in the speciality and natural foods industries serving as consultant, manager, store designer, buyer and lecturer.

▪ Expert in wholesale and retail sale of conventional and organic produce with total annual volume as high as £2.5 million. Achieve produce profit margins of up to 42 per cent.

▪ Working background in South East, Midlands and Scottish markets; understand regional variances in food products, growing seasons, local economies and consumer buying patterns.

▪ Active proponent of sustainable farming methods and profitable organic market development. Keen interest in historical and political perspectives on food and food production. Believe that eating is a political act.

▪ Recognized by the *York Courier* for establishing the best organic products in the city.

Representative Customers and Clients

▪ Cornucopia
▪ Farm Markets
▪ Organic Specialities
▪ Lakeland Diners' Club

▪ Riverbank
▪ Berry Farms
▪ The Gourmet Market

Achievements and Qualifications

▪ Expert in forecasting, planning, trend spotting, and creating new opportunities. Specialist in cost and inventory control. Have increased product movement and reduced spoilage at every retail or wholesale client/employer.

▪ Increase typical produce department percentage of store sales from 15% to 25–35%. Run a profit margin usually 6 to 8 points over regional average. Total annual volume in produce has been £250,000 to £2.5 million.

▪ Experienced buyer with wide knowledge of farmers and wholesalers in key growing areas of the UK and Europe. Understand regional and cultural negotiating and buying patterns. Expert in foraging for the freshest and most unusual produce.

▪ Adept in the innovative and profitable presentation of produce and all types of speciality foods. Create effective and prize-winning displays using unusual props; mix texture and colour, identify and react to food and visual trends.

▪ Directed design, construction and opening management of £1 million annual sales, 4,000 square foot, full-line speciality foods store. Determined floor layout, product placement, lighting, fixturing, signage, and back-room production arrangements/equipment. Scouted for antiques and unusual fixtures to enhance store concept.

▪ Facility for selling to the speciality and organics customer and to the customer with a highly developed palate and a sense of aesthetic character – food stylists, personal and professional chefs, world travellers, society figures, and international clients. Develop and maintain an excellent rapport with customers accustomed to the best in quality and service.

▪ Interact with customers on a personal and instructional level that creates a redirected purchasing pattern based on a seasonal sensibility for produce and an understanding of ingredients. Direct total purchase for a loyal following of customers who shop with an 'open list' and ask 'What's today's special?'

Experiences as Manager, Buyer, and Consultant

City Foods: Produce Manager and Buyer, 1998–Present
Organic Specialities: Store Designer, Construction Project Manager, Store Opening Manager, 1997
South East Farmers Market: Produce Consultant, 1996
Nurture by Nature: Produce Manager, 1995
Salad Days: Produce Consultant, 1994
Farm Markets: Produce Consultant, Manager/Buyer, 1993
Cornucopia: Produce Manager, 1992

Supervisor

James Sharpe
123 Anystreet
Anytown AT1 0BB

Tel: 020 8123 4567
james@anyaddress.co.uk

Career Focus
A position in management where communication, organizational and people-management skills can be developed and used to their fullest extent.

Profile
- An excellent manager with more than seven years' supervisory experience in a demanding industrial environment.
- Communicates well at all levels and has developed a wide range of management expertise on a firm foundation of practical skills.
- Capable and intelligent, always preferring the most down-to-earth approach, but with the capacity to resolve problems using sound initiative and a degree of creativity.
- Proficient at making quick and effective decisions in stressful situations.
- Key skills and experience gained at a major industrial site where responsible for the supervision, safety and performance of a large number of staff of varying skills, background and expertise, as well as being accountable for the continued productive capacity of millions of pounds' worth of machinery and equipment.

Professional Experience
PierPoint Steel   _1984–2002_
   Supervisor
   Shift Supervisor
   Production Worker
      Supervised and directed a regular workforce of over seventy, and part-time, short-contract and agency staff numbering between ten and fifty depending on workload.
      - Liaised with senior management and consulted with them on issues concerning productivity and safe practices
      - Implemented a three-shift system for continuous production – coordinated staff cover, ensured communication between shift supervisors, maintained productivity and high work standards across all three shifts
      - Motivated and encouraged workforce while working to strict deadlines. Provided productivity measurement facilities and instigated bonus scheme to attain optimal output
      - Implemented health and safety regulations
      - Checked and monitored suitability and performance of safety equipment

Current Employment
The Watch House Project   _2002–present_
   Training Supervisor
      Trained, monitored and evaluated Community Project volunteers in basic practical skills for a variety of projects including conservation and environmental work.

Training
Completed Supervisors course which included Management, Communications and Team Building, Health and Safety and Work-Related Legislation.

Computer Skills: Windows XP – Word, Excel, Access, Outlook Express, PowerPoint

Systems and Networks Manager

James Sharpe   Page 1 of 2
123 Anystreet
Anytown AT1 0BB
Tel: 020 8123 4567
james@anyaddress.co.uk

Profile
- 15 years of management and hands-on background working in IT infrastructure.
- Experience with world-class banks and financial institutions in New York, London, Paris.
- Hold MBA in Banking and Finance.
- Chosen for the 2000 International Who's Who in Information Technology.

Areas of Expertise
network design ● systems management ● LAN administration ● strategic planning ●
team formation and leadership ● budget preparation ● project planning and management
● presentation ● business writing ● resource management ● product and design research
● vendor interface and negotiation ● systems conversion ● computer operations ● systems
implementation ● branch start-ups and automation ● disaster recovery ● system migrations
● data centre overhauls and moves ● applications support

Executive Development
Major Bank, London
Chief Executive and Manager of Network Operations   1998 to Present
Control £1 million budget and oversee five technicians in the design, implementation and
support of company's WAN and LAN infrastructure. Handle heavy resource management
and coordination with internal departments, vendors and network integration companies to
define scopes of work, technical designs, product selection, required resources, schedules
and price negotiation. Budget resources and prepare reports. Hire, schedule and review
technicians.

Projects
AT&T frame relay and Cisco router implementation, TCP/IP address conversion,
Compuserve RAS implementation, Cisco switched Ethernet 100mb/1 gb Catalyst
implementation, HP Open View and Cisco Works implementation, MS DHCP and proxy
server implementation. Managed project teams at remote sites to implement NT
servers, routers, PC hardware upgrades, and Windows 95/NT images. Co-managed
1,100-user move.

A Major Investment Bank, London   1995 to 1998
Network Manager
Managed WAN daily support, hardware installation/configurations and network changes.
Monitored/configured private frame relay voice and data network. Monitored ACC routes
and NT servers. Performed Windows NT 3.51 server and workstation installations. Configured
ACC routers, Adtran CSUs and Newbridge 3612 and 3606 multiplexors for remote site
installations.

A Large Multinational Bank, Paris   1992 to 1995
Network Operations Supervisor
Managed all network and computer operations for the international hub site, reporting directly
to the Technology Manager and supervising a team of technicians and computer operators.
Supervised three direct reports, supported traders, reviewed/upgraded operations, handled
troubleshooting, researched products and interfaced/negotiated with vendors.

James Sharpe 020 8123 4567

- Completed full office start-up in Luxembourg in three months. Implemented LAN, voice, data, and video capabilities. Hired and trained computer operator to support local users. Implemented support procedures and documentation.
- Saved company over £50,000 annually: Migrated video conferencing from leased lines to ISDN, cleaned up multiplexor maintenance contracts, discovered overpayment on WAN lines. Set up a new process to review all invoices and pre-approved all purchases and communications costs before forwarding to Technology Manager.

Technology Expertise

Hardware: Cisco 7206/4700/25XX, Cisco PIX firewall, Cabletron MMAC+/Smart Switch 6000's/MMAC8, Newbridge 46020/36XX, IDNX 20/12, CYLINK link encryptors, Paradyne CSUs, ACC routers, Northern Telecom Option 11, PictureTel 4000/M8000, VAX 4000/6310/8000, HSC50, RA60/80/82/90 disk drives, MTI disks in DSSI architecture, HP 9000 K100, Sun Ultra 10, HP Laserjet 3/4/5 and QMS laser printers, Dell/Digital/AST/IBM PC hardware, Intel/3Com NIC cards. Cabling knowledge includes category 3/5, IBM Type 1, fibre optic multimode, v.35, x.21, RS232.

Software: SWIFT Alliance v3.0, IBIS, ST400, Montran (CHIPS), Reuters, Telerate, ADP Executive Quotes, IFSL Green Bar Viewer, Euroclear, Tracs, Soar, MS Project 95, VISIO, MS Word/Excel/PowerPoint, Lotus Notes v4.6, MS Mail, Ami-Pro, Lotus 1-2-3, DOS, Chameleon v4.6, Sybase v11, COBOL, Pascal, BASIC.

Protocols/Operating Systems: Cisco IOS version 11.x, TCP/IP, IPX, frame relay, EIGRP, OSPF, RIP, PPP, ISDN, SNMP, DHCP, WINS/DNS, Netbeui, NeBIOS, DECnet, LAT, VAX/VMS v5.5-2, Pathworks v4.1/5.0, Windows NT Server 3.51 and 4.0, Netware 3.12, HP-UX v10.2, Solaris v2.6.1, OS/400 v2.3.

Education and Professional Development

MBA in Banking and Finance, London University
BSc in Interdisciplinary Studies, The Polytechnical Institute
Computer Operations Diploma, Institute for Data Systems
Additional technology courses: Network Design and Performance, Advanced Cisco Router, Configuration, Microsoft Project 95. SYBASE SQL Server Administration, SYBASE Fast Track to SQL Server, Fundamentals of the HP UNIX System, Pathworks V5 Migration Planning, RDB Database Administration, Pathworks Tuning and Troubleshooting, PC Architecture and Troubleshooting.

Teacher – English as a Foreign Language

Jane Swift
123 Anystreet
Anytown AT1 0BB
Tel: 020 8123 4567
jane@anyaddress.co.uk

CAREER OBJECTIVE
A position in a forward-thinking, Europe-oriented organization that will make excellent productive use of knowledge of European culture and first-rate language skills gained through extensive travel as well as formal study.

EXPERIENCE
Teacher of English as a Foreign Language
- Travelled extensively in Africa, Asia and Europe
- Delivered structured teaching programmes to several professional companies
- Taught Business English at all levels from students to Company Directors
- Organized leisure activities for multilingual groups of students at residential summer school
- Devised and taught mixed ability language courses on Student Development Programme
- Encouraged and motivated students

SKILLS
Languages
- Fluent written and spoken German
- Excellent Business and Conversational French

TUITION
- Teaching Business English to German and Swedish business people in on-site training programmes
- Teaching Student Development Programmes in Belgium
- Teaching student groups in Swedish summer school

OTHER
- Computer literate, including Word, Excel, Access and Outlook Express
- Experienced in meeting deadlines, dealing with clients, handling problems effectively, and planning and prioritizing

EDUCATION
- Hopegate College of Further Education
  - RSA Certificate
  - Teaching English as a Foreign Language

- University of the South
  - BA (Hons) 2.1
  - German Language and Literature

Telecommunications Analyst

James Sharpe
123 Anystreet
Anytown AT1 0BB
Tel: 020 8123 4567
james@anyaddress.co.uk

OBJECTIVE:

Challenging opportunity as Telecommunications Analyst

SUMMARY:

Eleven years' progressive experience providing network analysis, system planning, and product evaluation and selection. Comprehensive and cost-effective installation, troubleshooting, and maintenance of voice and data communications systems.

COMMUNICATIONS KNOWLEDGE:

BT System, PBX's, Modems, MUX's and Fibre Optics. Specifically, Northern Telecom SLI, NEC NEAX 2400, Dimension 200, Rolm CBS, Mitel SX200, Strombergh Carlson DBX 1200/5000, GTE PIC, PCM Fibre Optic System, Equinox Data Switch and T1. Functional understanding of Packet Switches, WAGNET and ETHERNET.

EXPERIENCE:

A MAJOR BROKERAGE/FINANCIAL CORPORATION: TELECOMMUNICATIONS ANALYST

> Project manager for the planning and implementation of a nationwide voice and data communications network. Included development of a multi-side RFP to replace fourteen phone systems. Issues RFPs to vendors, conducted evaluations according to formats and configurations. Network design and traffic engineering using ETN networks. 1991–Present.

DATACOM, SWINDON: TELECOMMUNICATIONS VOICE/DATA ANALYST

> Responsibilities included planning and implementating telecommunications for headquarters and field offices. Included long-range requirements, new products and software releases, and recommending upgrades as required. Reviewed and evaluated proposals, selected systems, assisted in system software design, and supervised implementation. 1989–1991.

EUROBANK, LONDON: TELECOMMUNICATIONS ANALYST

> Responsibilities included: Coordinated installation for international data communications networks in Europe and Africa. Reviewed company's product usage, and provided recommendations for effective use of data switches or data through PBX. Assisted in the selection and implementation of data switch (RS-232) for a CM subsidiary. 1987–1989.

EDUCATION: BSc (Hons) 2.1 (York University), 1980.

REFERENCES: Available upon request.

Telecommunications Management Professional

Jane Swift
123 Anystreet
Anytown AT1 0BB

MANAGEMENT PROFESSIONAL
Telecommunications Industry
Project Management/Project Implementation

TOP PRODUCING PROFESSIONAL with more than 15 years' experience building both regional and national technical service/support groups. Demonstrated expertise in customer support, sales, marketing and key account management. Combine strong planning, organization and consensus building qualifications with effective writing, presentation and negotiation skills. Exceptional planning, analytical and organizational skills.

Expert qualifications in identifying and capturing market opportunities to accelerate expansion, increase revenues and improve profit contributions. Excellent team building and interpersonal skills. Expert qualifications include:

- Quality & Productivity Improvement
- Training & Development
- Cost Reduction
- Customer Service & Retention
- Project Lifecycle
- New Business Development
- Milestone Tracking
- Corporate Winbacks
- Cross Functional Team Leadership
- Staffing & Recruitment

MANAGEMENT PROFILE
- Organized, take-charge professional with exceptional follow-through abilities and detail orientation; able to oversee projects from concept to successful conclusion. Able to efficiently and effectively prioritize a broad range of responsibilities to consistently meet deadlines.
- Demonstrated success in surpassing productivity and performance objectives.
- Proven ability to resolve problems swiftly and independently.
- Possess strong interpersonal skills; able to work effectively with individuals on all levels.
- Recognized for maximizing ongoing employment opportunities for others within the organization.
- Demonstrated ability to provide vision and then translate that vision into productive action.
- Possess in-depth knowledge of T-1 provisioning.

SELECTED ACHIEVEMENTS
- Recognized for 'continuously providing leadership in achieving business goals by managing herself and coaching others in delivering superior customer and client experience while minimizing costs'.
- Commended for 'bringing focus and stability to the successful completion of many large projects, business initiatives, and customer issues'.
- '… continuously demonstrates a delightful ability to lead and enable individuals and team effectiveness, meeting business goals… is supportive, effectively providing information and alignment with union partners, clients, process management, peers, and executives.
- Earned reputation for 'achieving her objective to balance workloads and enable team effectiveness; eliminating costly, unnecessary training differentials, and yielding additional cost savings'.
- Specially selected to participate in the elite Leadership Development Programme designed for high performing managers.
- Peak performer, consistently placed in top 10 percentile in comparison to peer group.

PROFESSIONAL EXPERIENCE
1985–Present, SCK Ltd, Eastgate
Fast-track promotions through a series of increasingly responsible positions transitioning from financial/accounting and administrative to results-oriented project management. Performance-based promotions reflect strong network background; both long distance and local.

GENERAL MANAGER: Business Customer Care   _December 1999–Present_
Supervise team of 380, including technical and clerical staff and 120 managers. Directly support top ten corporate customers, each billing in excess of £1 million per month. Built alignment with union partners to form new inbound, M8 WPOF team addressing issues raised by front-line staff. Serve as local leader for Single Nodal Provisioning 'Deliver It' Initiative; work with Process/Development team.
- Spearheaded ISDN implementation, keeping call centre a viable entity.
- Championed provisioning for the Advantis Migration Project. Was asked to take the lead in this high profile project as a 'direct result of strong leadership and management skills'.
- Recognized for 'empowering team to be innovative in resolving project issues with a sense of ownership and urgency, often exceeding expectations for facility designs, test, and turn up activities.
- Achieved status of company 'Role Model'. As member of National Centre Support Model Team, recommended national prototype approach, which was deployed.
- Initiated efficiency improvement measures drastically slashing number of technician overtime hours to achieve significant cost savings.

MANAGER: Business Customer Care   _October 1996–November 1999_
Directed the voice provisioning of outbound and inbound services for global and middle market stratas. Managed staff of 100+ employees. Employed and extensively trained staff in high-calibre customer service techniques.
- Consistently exceeded Customer Value Added, People Value Added and Economic Value Added target goals.
- Implemented service delivery processing for the IBM Winback, providing over £100 million in monthly revenue.
- Recognized as one of 30 to receive SCK's 'Leading Legend' team award, out of a 1400-member universe.

SUPERVISOR: Business Customer Care   _August 1992–September 1996_
Served as project manager of software defined networks for dedicated global Sprint customers. Achieved some of SCK's highest profile winbacks using strong customer interface skills.

SUPERVISOR: Network Services Division   _February 1989–August 1992_
Functioned as Facility Planner. Implemented SCK Message Network for the Eastern Region.
- Recipient of the 1989 Quality Award.

Previous administrative and accounting positions leading to consistent promotions
_1984–1989_

EDUCATION
London University
BSc (Hons) 2.1 Business Administration, May 1983

REFERENCES
References will be furnished on request.

Telecommunications/Information Systems Management

James Sharpe
123 Anystreet
Anytown AT1 0BB
Tel: 020 8123 4567
james@anyaddress.co.uk

Voice & Data Communications, Information Technology, Project/Budget Management, Strategic Planning

Expert in the design, development and delivery of cost-effective, high-performance technology and communication solutions to meet challenging business demands. Extensive qualifications in all facets of projects from initial feasibility analysis and conceptual design through implementation, training and enhancement. Excellent organizational, budget management, leadership, team building, negotiation and project management qualifications.

Professional Experience

International Systems, Stafford   *1995–Present*
   Achieved fast-track promotion through positions of increasing responsibility for multibillion pound international company with 30,000 employees worldwide.

Telecommunications Manager   *1998–Present*
   Responsible for management of £7.5 million department budget. Fully accountable for overall strategy for telecommunications technology acquisition and integration, vendor selection and negotiation, usage forecasting, workload planning, project budgeting, and administration. Plan and direct implementation of emerging telecommunications solutions at all domestic locations consisting of 125 facilities. Provide direction regarding telecommunications technology to affiliates throughout Europe. Lead cross-functional project teams; supervise technical and administrative staff with 20 direct reports. Fully accountable for department's strategic vision and leadership. Representative achievements include:

   - Directed £20 million annual MCI network conversion at 200 locations within six months, saving company £7.5 million over three years.
   - Designed and managed implementation of network using Lucent and Octel at more than 100 locations in 12 months, realizing annual cost savings of £1 million.
   - Served as technical project director for £6 million consolidation of Northern Europe headquarters with UK location.
   - Facilitated move of corporate headquarters involving 3,000 employees over a four-day weekend.
   - Implemented video conferencing technology at more than 60 sites.
   - Built a four-digit dialling network for International Systems locations within a four-month period.

Assistant Manager of Telecommunications   *1996–1998*

Management Trainee   *1995*

Education
BSc in Political Science, Northwest University
Professional Development/Continuing Education: Various Management Association workshops and courses; technical management courses.

Telemarketing Professional

James Sharpe
123 Anystreet
Anytown AT1 0BB
Tel: 020 8123 4567
james@anyaddress.co.uk

Profile
Telemarketing Specialist/Sales Manager/Team Leader with proven ability to lead sales teams in fast-paced, high-volume environments. Able to coordinate multiple projects and meet deadlines under pressure. Outstanding record in training, motivating and retaining employees. Knowledgeable in telemarketing business methods and applicable laws.

Telemarketing Experience
Telephone Sales Representative, United Telemarketing, Waterbury, 1999–Present

Management Trainer, Tech Net, Burbage, 1998–1999
Directed performance, training and recruiting for 13- to 15-person bay marketing long distance and wireless services by telephone to prospective customers across the country.
- Implemented creative sales contests and incentive programmes that increased revenues, boosted morale and minimized employee turnover.
- Trained top-performing sales teams on effective telephone sales and closing techniques.
- Supervised team performance through call splitting and statistical reporting. Maintained target levels for quality management.
- Exceeded corporate goals for team sales per hour and sales hours fulfilment. Consistently ranked in top three of 32 bays.

Team Leader, Family Features, Burbage, 1997–1998
Managed 9-person telemarketing team marketing family-friendly videos for privately owned international film production company with £30 million in annual revenues.
- Led successful teams recognized for commitment to company cause of promoting non-violent films with no sexual content or innuendo, and influencing the film industry to offer more films of this nature.

Sales Experience
Independent Sales Professional/Certified Flooring Inspector, Midgate, 1996–1997

Store Manager, S&K Carpets, Waterbury, 1994–1996
Managed sales and operations for retail flooring business. Directed sales teams, scheduling, goal setting, and motivational seminars. Purchased merchandise from mills, negotiated contracts and administered promotions and product merchandising.
- Achieved annual retail sales averaging £0.5 million with a gross profit margin of 35%.
- Hired, trained and managed goal-oriented sales teams with below average turnover.
- Conducted in-service training seminars for sales representatives teaching detailed product information and sales techniques.

Training
BA History, University of the South, 1994
Ongoing Professional Development: sales training and motivational seminars.

Tour Director

James Sharpe
123 Anystreet
Anytown AT1 0BB
Tel: 020 8123 4567
james@anyaddress.co.uk

Profile

- Highly successful Tour Director with 5+ years' experience providing the finest quality travel experiences for thousands of guests. Achieved 98% guest satisfaction rate throughout career.
- Recognized for outstanding organizational skills, creative programming, public speaking and presentation expertise, and the ability to consistently exceed guest expectation.
- Talent for conveying 'vision' of a place, inspiring excitement and enthusiasm. Able to analyse and fulfil guests' dreams and expectations for their trip.
- Willing to do whatever it takes to ensure guests' comfort and enjoyment, making guests feel like family.

Experience

Tour Director, Clipper Tours   1994–Present

- Top tour director for the number one tour company in the world. Clipper Tours specializes in upmarket tours and cruises to destinations around the world, hosting 100,000+ guests annually.
- Personally direct 10 months of tours to Italy, Hawaii, Colorado Rockies, Paris, Belgium, Lake District, Highlands and Islands, Italian Lakes. Oversee all aspects of 7–20 day tours for 40 guests including:

● Travel connections and transfers ● Hotel and meal arrangement/confirmation ● Anticipating and resolving problems ● Individual tour coordination ● Introducing new, innovative programmes ● Documentation and record keeping ● Ensuring complete guest satisfaction ●

Accomplishments:

- Personally hosted more than 100 return guests. Many more guests booked additional tours with Clipper.
- Trained and mentored 75 new tour directors, receiving praise for 'the insights and standards that he can teach and impart to others'.
- Selected by management to participate in programme development, modifications and enhancements. Successfully led many first run tours.
- Awarded excellent ratings from Product Manager for working to improve the product and level of customer service and for responsiveness to company's needs.

Education and Skills

Degree: British and European History, University of the South
Extensive and ongoing research in the history, demographics, industry, geography, geology, customs and culture of tour destination.
Skills: Internet research, e-mail, travel reservation/confirmation systems, conversational Italian.

Trainer

James Sharpe
123 Anystreet
Anytown AT1 0BB
Tel: 020 8123 4567
james@anyaddress.co.uk
Page 1 of 2

PROFILE

A skilled trainer with more than ten years' experience, proficient in training, mentoring, assessing and allied fields. Currently responsible for a wide range of consultative training initiatives in both the public and the private sector. Also currently responsible for the successful coordination of professional services within the company.

EXPERIENCE

- Designed and implemented a new monitoring and assessment system
- Devised and wrote training manuals, and worksheets and workbooks for specific training courses
- Organized trainers and facilities for on-site training projects
- Identified and developed training opportunities with existing clients
- Successfully trained and licensed a sales force of twenty-five within three months
- Coached teams to consistently achieve and exceed sales targets
- Awarded Resource Development Prize 1998 and 1999

EMPLOYMENT

InTouch Training
Training Consultant   1997–Present

- Member of a successful consultancy team providing a range of training services to major organizations
- Invited to carry out skills audits and training needs analyses for medium to large businesses
- Supervised projects from conception to completion, working within budget to meet training targets and coordinating teams of up to five trainers for major projects
- Designed and presented individually tailored training courses covering a wide range of sales and management issues.
- Devised and delivered management skills, stress management and personal development courses to executive personnel
- Presented training courses both to small, informal groups and large (50+) organized 'classes'

Westhouse Ltd
Head of Sales Training   1993–1997

- Established and developed base for new Sales Training Centre
- Devised, organized and delivered training courses
- Trained staff in Sales Techniques; Customer Care; Presentation Skills; amongst others
- Monitored performance

GH&T Willings &Co. Ltd
Sales Manager 199 – 1993
Sales Associate 1989 – 1991
- Developed two new territories
- Exceeded target performance by 15%
- Planned targeted marketing campaigns for sales promotion
- Achieved 125% increase in enquiries at peak of promotion with 25% conversion to sales

EDUCATION AND TRAINING
Diploma in Training and Development
CIPD Certificate in Training Practice
Member of the Institute of Training and Development
Ongoing update-training on a variety of courses through InTouch Training

Associate Member CIPD

REFERENCES
                                Furnished upon request

Travel Manager

Jane Swift
123 Anystreet ● Anytown AT1 0BB ● Tel: 020 8123 4567 ● jane@anyaddress.co.uk

PROFILE
An experienced **Travel Manager** with a pleasant, friendly manner, a genuine interest in people and a strong desire to provide clients with the best possible holiday experience

STRENGTHS
- Continual updating of product knowledge and personal skills
- Smart appearance, patient and tactful with good listening skills and excellent interpersonal skills both face to face, over the phone and via e-mail
- Remain calm and organized in a pressured environment
- Fast, accurate keyboard skills and good, general IT skills
- First-rate knowledge of travel geography, travel requirements, health requirements, passports, visas and other travel documents

EMPLOYMENT
Sun Service Travel
Travel Consultant   1999–Present
- Worked as part of team dealing with customer queries and bookings – package, fly-drive and specialist holidays as well as business travel
- Advised suitable destinations, routes, methods of travel and other options depending on client need and expectation
- Advised on necessary travel documents, health requirements, etc
- Checked and verified flight and accommodation availability, timings, budget requirements, car hire, trips and excursions
- Assisted business travellers with information and advice, frequently making and confirming bookings at short notice and to tight deadlines
- Handled cash and credit card transactions efficiently, including cancellations and changed bookings
- Consistently met, and regularly exceeded, company targets

EDUCATION
BTEC National Diploma in Travel and Tourism
The course covered all aspects of travel and tourism, including
- World-wide travel geography
- Airport operations
- Resort representatives
- Finance
- Travel services

Language Skills
- French
- Spanish
- Italian

Computer Skills
- Windows XP
- Standard business software
- Travel industry standard software

Vice President of Operations

Jane Swift
123 Anystreet
Anytown AT1 0BB
Tel: 020 8123 4567
jane@anyaddress.co.uk

SUMMARY OF QUALIFICATIONS

Vice President of Operations, Manufacturing, for US subsidiary. 20+ years' experience in the creative leadership of multisite manufacturing operations to improve productivity, quality and efficiency. Facilitated significant cost savings through expertise in:

- Operations Systems
- Strategic Planning
- Cost Management
- Facilities Design
- Offshore Production
- Manufacturing Process
- Quality Control
- Supplier Partnership
- Human Resources/Labour Relations
- Compliance

PROFESSIONAL EXPERIENCE

ABC Automotive Products, Houston, Texas   *1989–1999*

A national leader in the manufacturing of automotive water pumps with annual sales of £380 million and 1,500 employees.

Vice President of Operations

- Managed the company's two plants in Texas and Mexico. Directly supervised two plant managers, a materials manager, advanced manufacturing systems manager, distribution manager, manager for special projects, and training and a Quality Control Division.
- Initiated and secured ISO9002 certification in two plants on the first application.
- Reorganized preventative maintenance schedules that decreased scrap rates by 50% and virtually eliminated rework rates.
- Orchestrated teamwork and communication between marketing and production to ensure customers received precise delivery dates and improved quality.
- Guided efforts with a major supplier to turnaround its sub-quality standards. Avoided a change to the competition's vendors that could have been costly. Result: vendor achieved ISO9000 certification and is now rated top in field.

A1 Heating plc   *1979–1989*

A residential and industrial water heater manufacturing company.

Director of Operations, Leeds	1985–1989
Plant Manager, Glasgow	1981–1985
Manufacturing Manager, Leeds	1979–1981

- Instituted a quality control system that resulted in highest product quality in industry. Responded to suspicions from customers and suppliers about quality of product by arranging for decision-makers to see plant in operation.
- Reduced accident rate 200% and turnover rate (from 12% to 3% per month in four years) in Leeds by implementing unilateral training programmes (eg, skills, teamwork, supervisory).
- Negotiated commitments from vendors to ensure JIT system.
- Established a 5,000 sq. ft. distribution centre to improve service to mid-continent customers.
- Prevented theft of valuable copper shipments by working with police.
- Selected by senior management to solve problems on Glasgow site which resulted in opening on schedule.

- Improved Leeds plant operations efficiencies as a result of executing a comprehensive study. In four years increased output significantly and profits by 200% by optimizing space, decreasing product damage during production and consolidating shipments.
- Oversaw Glasgow plant closing and transfer to modern facilities. Responsibilities included identification of most economical way to equip new plant, comprehensive study on disposal of buildings, and employee transition management. Production levels remained stable and efforts led to promotion to Director of Operations.

Hillside Water Products plc, Darlington   _1974–1979_
  Manufacturing Engineer

EDUCATION
MBA, School of Management, University of the North
BSc (Hons) 2.1, Mechanical Engineering, University of the North

ONGOING PROFESSIONAL DEVELOPMENT
- Strategic Planning Seminar, South West University Executive Programme
- Leadership at the Peak, Centre for Creative Leadership
- World Class Manufacturing & Process Capability Studies
- Human Resources Seminar, The Manufacturing Association
- The Employee Team Concept, The Centre for Productivity

Visual Merchandising Specialist

Jane Swift
123 Anystreet
Anytown AT1 0BB
Tel: 020 8123 4567
jane@anyaddress.co.uk

With fifteen years' experience in Visual Merchandising Management, I have successfully:

- Coordinated all Visual Merchandising in Nairn's third-most-profitable store.
- Supervised visual aspects of a successful £1.5 million store renovation with responsibility for new fixtures and merchandising.
- Conducted seminar in Visual Merchandising for all new department managers in Nairn's Eastern region.
- Used innovative image control techniques that contributed to a new high-fashion store's becoming the volume leader for its entire chain in one year.

RECENT ACCOMPLISHMENTS

Visual Merchandising Manager of a Nairn's store with a £20 million sales volume, I coordinated fixtures, merchandising, and seasonal changes for all twelve departments, along with responsibility for overall store image.

- Analysed stock levels to determine new fixture needs, prepared requirement reports and coordinated on-time deliveries of all fixtures.
- Reporting directly to the Director of Corporate Visual Merchandising, I supervised five Visual Merchandising Managers brought in from other stores to assist in the project.
- Interfaced with construction personnel while directing movement of departments under construction.
- Guiding all Department Managers through renovation and construction, I familiarized them with new fixtures and applicable merchandising techniques.

EARLIER ACCOMPLISHMENTS

As District Display Director for Daisy Chain, a 100-store speciality women's ready-to-wear chain, I developed fashion awareness, coordinated displays, and trained staff, including new District Display Directors throughout the country. Reporting directly to the Corporate Display Director, I was:

- Given responsibility for image control at the company's new flagship store in Oxford Street, where fashion image was crucial. My innovative merchandising and display techniques contributed to this store's becoming the number-one-volume store for the entire company by its first anniversary.
- Recognized for my planning, organizing and coordinating abilities, I was involved in several new store openings throughout the UK and Europe.

As Display Coordinator/Visual Merchandising Manager with IMAGE Ltd, I progressed to having a five-store responsibility. Developing my functional skills, I was promoted to Visual Display troubleshooter for the region.

Jane Swift 020 8123 4567 page 2 of 2

EMPLOYMENT
NAIRN's 1987–Present
DAISY CHAIN 1983–1987
IMAGE 1979–1983

EDUCATION
A graduate of Harpdale College, with a speciality in Fashion Design, I have also completed intensive course work in Architectural Technology which has significantly contributed to my expertise in store renovation and floor plan know-how. Course work in photography has rounded out my background.

PERSONAL
Interests include fashion design and construction, sketching, and free-hand drawing.

Web Site Designer

Jane Swift
123 Anystreet
Anytown AT1 0BB
Tel: 020 8123 4567
jane@anyaddress.co.uk

Areas of Effectiveness

Professional Web Site Design
Marketing & Maintenance
Quality Custom Programming

Site Planning & Renovation
Business Solutions
Graphic Design

Experience

Web Site Designer, Co-Owner. R&G Software 1999–Present
Researcher, University of the West 1997–1999

Career Highlights

- Designed and implemented Web site for the UK Centre for Reiki Training (www.reikitr.co.uk)
- Created Web site for UTL Typographical Services based on client design and content specifications
- Stress user-friendly design, emphasizing ease of navigation, quick download times and appealing graphics
- Maintain clients' Web site registration with Internet search engines; include HTML meta tags to ensure high ranking
- Advise clients on effective marketing techniques to increase Web site traffic

Technical Expertise

HTML
Dreamweaver
Adobe Photoshop

Javascript
FTP protocols
Microsoft Access, Word and Excel

Macromedia Fireworks
search engine submittals

Education

University of the West, BSc (Hons) 2.1 Biology 1995, MSc Biology 1997

CVs for Special Situations

CVs for special
situations for persons
whose circumstances
don't 'fit the mould'.

These are CVs that performed above and beyond the call of duty for job seekers whose background didn't 'fit the mould'. They're invaluable guideposts in presenting your own experiences in the most flattering light.

James is leaving the navy for a Finance Executive position

James Sharpe, 123 Anystreet, Anytown AT1 0BB. Tel: 020 8123 4567, james@anyaddress.co.uk

Profile

Confident, dependable, versatile management professional with extensive and diverse experience in the areas of budget management, personnel management and customer service. Global perspective based upon assignments and travel abroad. Articulate problem solver with superior analytical and communication skills. Organized, meticulous and methodical; particularly adept in problem identification, research, analysis and resolution.

Qualifications

- An established record of progressively responsible positions of trust at the highest levels of government.
- A proven history of success in the administrative management of navy units.
- An innate ability to develop loyal and cohesive staffs dedicated to the task at hand.

Competencies

- communications skills
- top secret security clearance
- training and development
- human resources
- long- and short-range planning
- leadership and supervision
- computer systems
- customer relations
- budget analysis/management
- senior staff coordination
- project management
- organizational skills

Experience

Programme Director, Royal Naval College, Dartmouth   1998–2000

Oversaw operation of largest training complex in the Royal Navy, with an operating budget over £2.5 million and £100 million in real property listing.

- Supervised 150 navy and civilian personnel with 6 direct reports.
- Developed comprehensive 5-year development plan, resulting in £500K funding for improvements.
- Formulated, planned and implemented £1 million in capital improvements. Actively participated in contract negotiations with vendors and coordinated projects.
- Overcame £400K budget shortfall through budget analysis and cost control.
- Developed organizational vision, goals and key business drivers.

Programme Fleet Manager, Fleet Air Arm   1996–1998

Programme and budget manager for large organization with annual budget over £800 million.

- Supervised 20 personnel with 3 direct reports.
- Funded £2.5 million in out-of-cycle, high priority projects.
- Overcame 10% funding decrement, identifying shortfall and authoring letters of justification.
- Developed and presented plan to reorganize budget analysis, streamlining executing by 40–50% and resulting in annual savings of more than £200K.

Senior Budget Analyst, Oostende, Belgium   1994–1996

Budget and Funds Manager for the acquisition, operation and maintenance of communications and information systems.

- Prepared, presented, defended and managed an £11 million budget.
- Generated £1.4 million savings in 1996 budget through analysis and tracking expenditures.

Project Officer/Instructor   1990–1993

Developed students for leadership and management responsibilities.

- Served as instructor, counsellor and mentor for 12 students during a 20-week course. Led 8 groups in four years.
- Redesigned core curriculum and introduced building block type of instruction.

Education

Bachelor of Business Administration, University of London

Jane is changing careers

Jane Swift
123 Anystreet
Anytown AT1 0BB
Tel: 020 8123 4567
jane@anyaddress.co.uk

OBJECTIVE

A responsible and challenging entry-level position that will use my education and background, expand my knowledge, and offer opportunities for personal and professional growth.

SUMMARY OF KNOWLEDGE AND EXPERIENCE

- CUSTOMER SERVICE
- INTERFACE WELL WITH THE PUBLIC
- EXCELLENT COMMUNICATION SKILLS
- SET, MEET DEADLINES/GOALS
- CASHIERING
- MARKETING
- INVENTORY CONTROL
- KNOWLEDGE OF WORDPERFECT

- HIGHLY ORGANIZED
- KNOWLEDGE OF SPANISH
- DETAIL/EFFICIENCY ORIENTED
- RECORD KEEPING
- TROUBLESHOOTING
- TUTORING
- COORDINATION
- PUBLIC RELATIONS

EDUCATIONAL HISTORY

London University
Warren College

BSc – Psychology, 1985
A-levels: Biology, English, Art

ACCOMPLISHMENTS AND ACHIEVEMENTS

- Awarded Recognition Certificate for achieving 100% on Shoppers Report Evaluation for food service performance, salesmanship and hospitality at Callander Inns
- Society for Psychology – Student awards
- National Honour Society – Student award

EMPLOYMENT HISTORY

4/99–Present **WAITRESS**
Callandar Inns, Littlewell
2/97–3/99 **CASHIER/WAITRESS**
Allen's Restaurant, Northridge
9/94–12/96 **MARKET RESEARCHER**
Q&A Associates, Littlewell
9/93–6/95 **ASSISTANT TO TEACHER/ART COORDINATOR**
Temple Hill Children's Project

VOLUNTEER/COMMUNITY SERVICE

Temple Hill Children's Project – Tutoring

REFERENCES FURNISHED UPON REQUEST

James is changing careers to Human Resources

James Sharpe
123 Anystreet
Anytown AT1 0BB
Tel: 020 8123 4567
james@anyaddress.co.uk

Objective
Key member of a human resources consulting team using communication, organizational and collaborative skills in a challenging environment.

Related Skills and Career Achievements
Project Management

- Led a project team for the successful launch of the Kiev Vodka bottle series.
- Managed the Kiev licensing programme and facilitated the negotiation of a licence agreement that generated significant incremental exposure and sales.

Presentation

- Taught English to Year 10 and gave European Culture lectures to high school students in Thailand for two months.
- Provided orientations to teachers from China and Thailand upon their arrival in the UK.
- Presented regular Kiev Vodka marketing updates to staff.
- Contributed to the production of the winning Haverhill pitch at Lark & Hall Advertising.

Writing & Editing

- Launched a career services business to help clients define marketable skills and create results-oriented CVs.
- Developed three issues of a 10-page brand newsletter that promoted successful marketing concepts and international brand identity.
- Wrote legal correspondence to ensure adherence to brand licence agreements.

Computer Applications

- Extensive knowledge of Windows and Macintosh applications for word processing, desktop publishing, spreadsheets, presentation, database management and Internet navigation.
- Developed contact databases for *Your Home*'s advertising department.

Career Chronology

Career Marketing Consultant, Self-Employed	1999–2000
Contract Worker/Marketing, Thurlow Craig	1998
Kiev Brand Coordinator, Alco International	1992–1997
Freelancer, *Your Home* magazine	1991
Administrative Assistant, Lark & Hall	1990
Programme Assistant, Intercultural Programmes	Summers 1988–1990

Education
Bachelor of Arts, 1990
London University

James is an Educator in transition

James Sharpe
123 Anystreet
Anytown AT1 0BB

020 8123 4567
james@anyaddress.co.uk

SUMMARY

Skilled educator with 20+ years' experience creating curricula and delivering instruction, evaluating students, developing and implementing strategic plans, and managing projects. Seeking opportunity to transition existing instructional, organizational and human relations skills into a training or human resource position in a corporate environment.

QUALIFICATIONS

Instruction
- Qualified Teacher – BEd.
- Prepare lesson plans in Social Studies, Science, Math, and Language Arts.
- Instruct 25 students, addressing individual needs and learning styles.
- Evaluate students' performance and implement plans for improvement, as appropriate.
- Train students, parents and staff in the use of computer systems.
- Fulfil on-site 'Help Desk' role for students and staff using computers.

Planning
- Serve on numerous District Planning and Building Committees that address ongoing concerns of staff and the community, identifying problems and solutions.
- Chair Positive School Climate Committee that promotes a comfortable learning environment and workplace for students and staff, respectively.
- Participated in developing five-year technology plan.
- Wrote technology plan for School and monitored implementation.
- Implemented computers in the classroom.
- Chaired committee that pioneered school orchestra at a time when the district had none.

Additional Skills
- Wrote grant proposal that resulted in £3,000 in funding from government for purchase of capital equipment (computers).
- Proficient in Windows 95, Microsoft Office/Mac, ClarisWorks, Word Processing, Spreadsheets and the Internet.
- Coached Soccer, Ski Club Advisor.

PROFESSIONAL EXPERIENCE

1989–Present   Primary Teacher, New Green School, Lancaster
1976–1989   Primary Teacher, John Embury School, Chester

EDUCATION

1976 BEd
University of the North

PROFESSIONAL ENRICHMENT

Creative Learning Styles   Portfolio Assessment
Cooperative Learning   Gender Equity
Annual Computer Conference   Grant Writing
Essential Elements of Instruction

James is an Electrician changing to a career in sales and promotion

James Sharpe
123 Anystreet
Anytown AT1 0BB
Tel: 020 8123 4567
james@anyaddress.co.uk

CAREER OBJECTIVE
To support the growth and profitability of an organization that provides challenge, encourages advancement and rewards achievement with the opportunity to use my substantial experience, skills and proven abilities in a position involving Sales and Promotion within the Consumer Goods industry.

STRENGTHS
- Skilled in motivating and interacting with the public.
- Disciplined and well organized in work habits, with ability to function smoothly in pressure situations.
- Ability to identify problems and implement effective solutions.
- Possess a 'pro' company attitude dedicated to the growth and profitability of the company.

EMPLOYMENT HISTORY
MURREY ELECTRIC, Ferndale
Foreman Electrician – April 1997 to Present
Responsible for the installation and servicing of commercial, residential and industrial accounts. In my current position as Foreman, I supervise the activities of four to five electricians/helpers and have been responsible for as many as thirteen employees.

- Ability to read and effectively implement blueprints, along with extensive layout skills.
- Because of vast knowledge of jobs performed for the company and ability to deal effectively with people, was selected by management to train new employees.

PROMO POWER LTD, Dartshill
On-Premise Promotions – August 1999 to Present
Responsible for representing Windmill Brewing Company at promotional functions in on-premise accounts situated in the South East.

- I possessed the energy, enthusiasm and poise necessary for implementing successful brewery promotions, was selected for newly created position.
- Have acquired extensive knowledge of motivating/sales techniques, which has contributed substantially to increased sales at brewery promotions.
- Active in the development and coordination of brewery promotions.

EDUCATION
City & Guilds – Installation Certificate
Oakland Community College – Courses relating to Electronics (Attended 1989 and 1990)
Ferndale High School – June 1988 – 6 GCSEs, including Maths and English

REFERENCES FURNISHED UPON REQUEST

Jane is changing careers after a period of self-employment

Jane Swift
123 Anystreet
Anytown AT1 0BB
Tel: 020 8123 4567

jane@anyaddress.co.uk

Objective   Sales representative or showroom position in the fashion industry

Summary of Qualifications

- Five years' experience in design and manufacture of Women's Wear
- Extensive production management and operations experience
- Fifteen years' sales experience in inside sales, showrooms, and tradeshows
- Expertise in conducting tradeshows, designing booths, and managing customers
- Capable and flexible self-starter who is able to travel for trade shows

Work Experience

1994 to 2000 **Owner/Designer**
G & S Designs
Design and manufacture of Womens' Wear accessories, earrings, hair clips, necklaces and handbags. Extensive experience in buying, trade shows (UK and Europe), payroll, collections, invoicing. Hired 22 sales reps throughout the UK. Employed 12 people to make accessories.

1990 to 1994 **Outside Sales and Trainer**
West Hill Financial Services
Extensive selling experience cold-calling, canvassing, and prospecting to corporations for medical insurance plans. Organized and set up an entire department and trained department staff.

1984 to 1990 **Personnel and Collections Manager**
O H Sumerton
Interviewed potential employees for several department heads. Managed credit and collections. Trained managers on how to interview and hire the right person.

1978 to 1984 **Office Manager/Executive Recruiter**
Little & Prior Employment Agency
Interviewed prospective employees for professional and clerical positions with companies.

James has changed careers many times

James Sharpe
123 Anystreet
Anytown AT1 0BB
Tel: 020 8123 4567
james@anyaddress.co.uk

OBJECTIVE

A challenging position providing an opportunity to apply broad Management experience.

EDUCATION

University of the West
MBA programme – presently enrolled
BA Public Administration, Westlake College

QUALIFICATIONS

Progressively responsible management background in a large medical facility, with successful experience in the following areas:

Staff Supervision – presently responsible for 30 skilled, semi-skilled, unskilled and managerial employees. Hire, train, direct and evaluate the staff. Responsible for their output and the quality of their work. Maintain morale, motivation and positive employee relations. Solve problems, take corrective action, apply company policy.

Operations Management – direct staff and activities in several support departments, including maintenance, grounds and buildings, laundry, housekeeping. Manage a budget of nearly £250,000. Schedule all departments for the most effective use of staff, equipment and facilities.

Inventory Control/Purchasing – maintain an inventory control system for non-medical supplies and food.

Other – frequent involvement in customer and public relations, promoting the Home; work with other staff to prepare for licensing, compliance reviews; involved in property management – buying, renovating and maintaining rental properties.

EMPLOYMENT
1999 to present

Kennet Court Nursing Home
Supervisor – promoted from Assistant

1995 to 1999

Belsham Brewery, Bell's Hill
Production Line Worker

1993 to 1995

Afflick & Hill, Administrative Assistant

Jane is a disabled worker who wants to change careers

Jane Swift
123 Anystreet
Anytown AT1 0BB
Tel: 020 8123 4567
jane@anyaddress.co.uk

OBJECTIVE

Seeking a challenging position in Customer Service.

SUMMARY

- Possess a combined Customer Service and Financial background. Responsible for administering several aspects of pension plans. Significant customer service responsibilities as Office Manager and Claims Supervisor.

QUALIFICATION

- Present position requires accuracy and efficiency in assessing claims, maintaining cheque issue guidelines, maintaining and administering insurance certificate stocks and other similar activities.
- Effective verbal and written skills required for supervising up to five members of staff. Good communications skills are necessary for confidential inter-departmental communications.
- Experience includes Credit and Office Management. My responsibilities in credit include taking applications, securing credit approvals, ordering products and arranging for delivery. I also calculated salespeople's commissions. As Office Manager, I handled customer service duties, accepted and booked payments, maintained inventories, and performed other functions associated with keeping the office running smoothly.

EXPERIENCE
1989 to present

City and General Insurance
Claims Supervisor

J C Henley Ltd
Credit Coordinator – for major appliances

Carson and Bowler Ltd
Office Manager

National Cerebral Palsy Assoc.
(6 years, part-time)
Office Manager/Clerical

James is a Technology Expert changing to Web Development

James Sharpe
123 Anystreet
Anytown AT1 0BB

Tel: 020 8123 4567
james@anyaddress.co.uk

GOAL

To contribute to a Web development team where my strong technical and business skills and personal passion for computer technology will be of value.

PROFESSIONAL PROFILE

- 10+ years' experience working in cross-functional teams as a technical expert. Oversaw multiyear, multimillion pound development programmes. Produced proposals resulting in new work for organization totalling nearly £250,000.
- Achieved numerous official commendations during tenure for exceptional performance and special acts of service. Consistently received highly favourable customer feedback and successfully developed business relationships with the technical and academic community.
- Enhanced personal productivity and contributions to team through initiative to learn MS Project, MS Office, MS FrontPage, basic HTML, Internet-related applications, and information technology trends.

Demonstrated competencies in:

Technical Analysis
Strategic Planning & Problem Solving
Research, Writing, & Presentations

System Design & Information Architecture
Project & Budget Management
Customer Focus

CAREER HIGHLIGHTS

- Challenged to create a Web site for the MoD Joint Service Small Arms Programme Office to increase awareness of their programmes for overseas customers and to conduct management committee business. Within 3 months, learned basics of Web site design and programming, planned information architecture, and launched the site to positive reviews from customers and other external government agencies.
- Developed a business plan for Warrior Tactical Communications System that was approved by the customer without changes after a competitive selection process. Team awarded £144,000 for the first year's work with potential for another £250,000 in the second year.
- Wrote a 250-page technical report on the state of the art in laser technology that was the culmination of a 1-year independent research project. The study was approved and published in 1998 and is used in strategic planning by the MoD.
- Introduced a logical strategic planning tool that was used to overhaul several programmes in order to meet new timelines for success required by the Ministry of Defence.
- Devised an innovative method for monitoring system contractor's cost performance in 5 areas on a £15 million contract. Technical Director mandated that this method be management's standard for analysis of contractor performance in order to spot potentially dangerous trends early.
- Part of a team that developed communications system for use in UK/US Integrated Biological Defense System.
- Spearheaded review process leading to the successful type classification and on-schedule deployment of mortar weapon systems. Required intense coordination with numerous support organizations and government agencies to produce documents and presentations for material release boards.

CAREER HISTORY

Royal Corp of Signals
Special Operator in Electronics Warfare Group – 1999–Present
Engineering Technician – 1996–1999
Apprentice Telecommunications Technician – 1992–1995

EDUCATION

BSc Degree Electronic Engineering
BTEC Diploma

James is a blue-collar worker and wants a white-collar job

James Sharpe
123 Anystreet
Anytown AT1 0BB
Tel: 020 8123 4567
james@anyaddress.co.uk

OBJECTIVE   An opportunity to apply technical skills and communications ability in a Sales or Customer Service position.

SKILLS SUMMARY   Thoroughly familiar with the process of quoting and producing industrial products for a wide range of customer applications. Work with customers' specifications, ideas or blueprints to produce parts on a special or stock basis. Call on clients to assist with product development, to provide service in the event of discrepancies or quality questions. Duties require the ability to communicate effectively on technical problems, and to establish rapport.

In a retail setting, have held major responsibility for staff supervision and customer service, managing several roles with high customer and employee contact.

As a supervisor, held responsibility for training, scheduling, directing and evaluating the work of skilled machinists. Keep areas of responsibility supplied with tools, materials and equipment to ensure the most effective use of staff and machinery.

Acted as buyer of industrial products: drills, reamers, slotting saws, collects, high-speed carbide steels, ceramics, lubricants, and NC screw machine programmes, among others.

Operated and troubleshot sophisticated machine shop equipment, including Swiss screw machines, grinders, lathes, milling machines, drill presses. Able to program CNC equipment. Conversant with the full range of machine shop practices, as well as quality and production control procedures.

EXPERIENCE
1998 to present   **J & G Tools, Chellsworth**
Supervisor, Quality Control Inspector
Production Machinist

1994 to 1998   **Findley Foods, Tyneford**
Front End Manager, supervising an evening shift
Involved in cashiering, packing, credit voucher cashing.

1989 to 1994   **Eagle Moving Co., Tyneford**
Driver, Mechanic

PERSONAL   References available upon request.

Jane has had multiple jobs and needs to combine her experience

Jane Swift
123 Anystreet
Anytown AT1 0BB
Tel: 020 8123 4567
jane@anyaddress.co.uk

OBJECTIVE   A challenging Sales or Sales Management position, providing an opportunity to apply broad experience and a record of success in marketing a variety of products and services.

QUALIFICATIONS *Sales* – Thoroughly familiar with techniques for generating new business in industrial, commercial and consumer markets. Employed cold call, referral and other prospecting techniques. Skilled at assessing client needs and making effective sales presentations, often involving technical product details.

Have regularly exceeded sales quotas.

Sales Management – Responsibilities included selecting, training, motivating and supervising professionals in sales, service and other operations.

Performed market research and promotions, forecasting, the development of distribution systems and other marketing administration functions.

Developed marketing plans, arranged financing, helped establish distribution networks.

EMPLOYMENT   A & S Systems – Worcester
Commercial Sales Representative   1995 to present

Equinox Marketing – Worcester
Owner/Consultant   1993 to 1995

Mundy's Industries Ltd   1980–1990
Self-Employed Restaurateur
Nickelodeon Inns
Bickley Breweries
The Party Place

TRAINING   Studied Business Administration, Management and Marketing at The Institute of Business. Have received technical product and sales training in numerous courses and seminars throughout my career.

PERSONAL   Royal Navy – honourably discharged
References available upon request

Jane is changing careers to become a Salesperson

Jane Swift
123 Anystreet
Anytown AT1 0BB
Tel: 020 8123 4567
jane@anyaddress.co.uk

OBJECTIVE An opportunity to apply Medical Technological background in a challenging Sales or Marketing position.

QUALIFICATIONS

- Over six years' experience in Medical Technology in hospital laboratory and outpatient settings. Have worked successfully with physicians in a number of disciplines, including pathology, geriatrics, oncology, other areas; interact daily with laboratory staff (supervisory and technical), patients, and other people throughout the hospital.
- Thoroughly familiar with complex, sophisticated laboratory equipment, such as Coulter S plus IV, Coulter 550, MLA 700, Fibrometer. Provide technical training to other operators and to medical technology students. Accountable for the accurate calibration of equipment, basic troubleshooting, and maintenance.
- Maintenance of inventory, purchase of supplies, and quality control procedures in general.
- These duties require a person who is thoroughly knowledgeable about laboratory and highly technical equipment and associated procedures, is familiar with materials, and is precise in performance of duties.

EMPLOYMENT
1992 to present

Southvale Hospital – Kinverton
Special Haematology Laboratory Technician, promoted from Laboratory Technician

EDUCATION BSc (Hons) 2.1 Biology, 1992
London University

Additional training by laboratory equipment manufacturers

REFERENCES Excellent professional references are available upon request.

Jane is a recently divorced homemaker re-entering the workforce

Jane Swift
123 Anystreet
Anytown AT1 0BB
Tel: 020 8123 4567
jane@anyaddress.co.uk

OBJECTIVE	An entry position in Personnel or Human Resources Management, providing an opportunity to apply formal education in the field, and business experience.
EDUCATION	Midlands University BSc Psychology 2.1
SUMMARY OF SKILLS	Studies have included courses in Industrial Psychology, Personnel Management, Marketing, Management, Accounting, other Psychology and Humanities courses.
	Experience in *Interviewing/Communications*, gained from extensive dealings with customers, clients, students and peers in the organization. Capable of effective written and oral communication where the ability to gather precisely and act on it is critical.
	Background in *Counselling*, with both adults and students in academic and professional settings. Assisted with *Career Counselling* and other forms of personal assistance.
	Experience includes work as a *Telemarketing Representative* and as an Administrative Assistant. Have held leadership positions in volunteer organizations, including *Chairperson, Fundraiser, Advisory Board Member*, and *Counsellor*. Duties have required the ability to organize, set up and implement systems for getting tasks completed, as well as the ability to be persuasive and obtain cooperation.
EXPERIENCE	Telesales Services Telemarketing Representative. Working from research, leads and cold calls, identifying target markets and making over 500 sales calls per month. Provide quotes, and refer results of research for further action. Set up relevant sales administration systems.
1998 to 2000	Midlands University Worked part and full time while attending college. Assignments included: Secretary in the Admin Office, in the Development Office, and to the Director of the Nursing Programme.
ACTIVITIES	Chairperson, Children's Activity Committee; Member, Advisory Board; Fundraiser, Counsellor, Navy Officers' Wives Association; Fundraiser, Library Committee.
PERSONAL	Health: excellent Willing to travel/relocate

Appendix

CV Banks

CV Banks are the reverse of job banks. Instead of employers listing available jobs to be scanned by job hunters, CV banks are make up of CVs supplied by job applicants, intended to be scanned by prospective employers. In most CV banks, you either upload your CV in file or HTML form into the site, or fill out an online form, which will generate a CV-like document for employers to scan.

It used to be fashionable for job search experts to advise job hunters to take out newspaper ads announcing their abilities. I never endorsed this approach because I'd never met an employer who saw it as a viable avenue for finding quality employees. Even though CV banks are, in effect, an electronic version of these ads, they seem to be working. I think the reason is twofold. First of all, these banks are set up so that a computer, not a person, is doing the initial searching for candidates, and second, people who are active online are, *ipso facto*, computer literate, and therefore more desirable as employees.

An employer requesting a search from a CV database will describe the available job with a number of descriptive words and/or phrases, known as keywords. The computer then searches for those words and phrases in all the CVs in the database. An employer can typically search for up to 20 keywords or phrases. It isn't necessary that you match all twenty keywords – just one match is usually all it takes.

If you are going to post your CV online, you will most likely use one of the CV generators supplied by the job bank in question. If not, follow these guidelines.

- Use 14 point (size) Courier type, or a similar plain font.

- Avoid italics, script, underlining and boldface, along with two-column or other non-traditional formatting.

- Use upper/lower case to differentiate headings.

- Use plenty of white space.

- Do not include large paragraphs of text.

- You can use bulleted lists, but use a dash as your bullet 'point'.

If you are an experienced professional with qualifications for more than one job, you may want to post additional CVs under appropriate job titles, including the appropriate keywords and phrases for that job. Some people are concerned about confidentiality. If you upload your CV into a CV bank, theoretically your employer may find your CV online. Practically speaking, most active CV banks have ways to protect your confidentiality. You can try to improve your odds by replacing the name of your current employer with a generic name. For example, you could change 'The First International Bank of Last Resort' to 'A Major Bahamian Bank'; headhunters do this for their clients all the time.

CV banks are new for employers and employees alike. CV banks now often have hundreds of thousands of CVs, and some of them already exceed a million. CV banks are rapidly becoming an integral part of recruitment for all corporations and headhunters. My advice is to get used to maintaining your CV online on a permanent basis – it's better to find out about available jobs (no matter how) and have the opportunity to turn them down, rather than never having heard about them at all.

Index